Operating System Projects Using Windows NT®

Operating System Projects Using Windows NT®

GARY NUTT

UNIVERSITY OF COLORADO, BOULDER

 Addison-Wesley

**Addison-Wesley is an imprint
of Addison Wesley Longman, Inc.**

Reading, Massachusetts • Harlow, England
Menlo Park, California • Berkeley, California • Don Mills, Ontario
Sydney • Bonn • Amsterdam • Tokyo • Mexico City

Acquisitions Editor: Maité Suarez-Rivas
Assistant Editor: Molly Taylor
Production Editor: Patricia A. O. Unubun
Cover Design: Suzanne Heiser
Composition: abc Publishing
Text Design: Jean Hammond
Copyeditor: Laura Michaels

Many of the designations used by manufacturers and sellers to distinguish their products are claimed as trademarks. Where those designations appear in this book, and the publisher was aware of a trademark claim, the designations have been printed in initial caps or in all caps.

The programs and the applications presented in this book have been included for their instructional value. They have been tested with care but are not guaranteed for any particular purpose. Neither the publisher or the author offers any warranties or representations, nor do they accept any liabilities with respect to the programs or applications.

This book was typeset in QuarkXPress 3.32 on a PowerComputing 132. The fonts used are Formata, Lucida Sans, Mathematical Pi 6, and Zapf Dingbats. It was printed on Rolland Opaque.

Library of Congress Cataloging-in-Publication Data

Nutt, Gary J.
    Operating system projects using windows NT / Gary Nutt.
        p.   cm.
    Includes bibliographical references and index.
    ISBN 0-201-47708-4
    1. Operating systems (Computers)   2. Microsoft Windows NT.   I. Title
    QA76.76.O63 N895   1999
    005.4′469—dc21
                                        98-46037
                                        CIP

2 3 4 5 6 7 8 9 10–MA–02010099

To my parents, Bill and Viola Nutt

For giving me my work ethic,
my sense of humor (which does not show in my writing),
my vision,
and a drive to succeed.

Preface

To the Student

Operating system(s) (OS) software, by its nature, must be carefully written since it directly controls the hardware used by all of the processes and threads that execute on that hardware. In your study of the OS, you will be concentrating on how software is written so that it has "trusted behavior" on which all other aspects of the computer can rely. Since you are studying an existing OS, this means that it must be possible for you to inspect and experiment with the OS without jeopardizing its ability to provide correct behavior. As a result there are several practical challenges for experimenting with the OS. These include determining how you can study OS code in a hardware environment that has little or no development and debugging assistance. What assistance (beyond raw hardware) should be provided? If the lab environment provides assistance, what mechanisms prevent one student from clobbering the environment so that the next student cannot use it? Of course, some of these challenges can be met with money; for example, each student can be given a dedicated hardware platform that can be periodically downloaded from a shared server (presuming that the downloader is safe from experimental crashes). Or students could be given a hardware simulator so that the scope of their errors could be bounded to prevent their damaging the underlying system.

This lab manual is written to complement general information appearing in your course textbook. It contains a dozen exercises that encourage you to experiment with a modern OS, Microsoft Windows NT, without having to work in a raw hardware environment that offers little or no support. The exercises teach you to use components of the Windows NT application programming interface (API), those that many application programmers never use (because the parts are "too low level" for many programs). Focusing on these aspects of the OS API serves two purposes. First, you learn how to construct effective software that interacts directly with the OS, rather than with higher-level abstract machines (such as database managers, windows systems, and high-level file systems). Second, by using the OS API directly, you gain important insight into how Windows NT is designed and implemented.

Part 1 contains an overview of Windows NT. This overview is likely to talk about several things that are unknown to you, since you will be reading this at the beginning of your OS course. Work your way through Part 1 just to get a feeling for how NT is built, and then go back and browse through it periodically as you work the exercises. It gives the "big picture," but not many details.

Part 2 consists of 12 exercises. Each exercise has an introduction explaining Windows NT concepts and details relevant to the exercise. Sometimes you will find that a quick review of the relevant parts of Part 1 will help you frame the work before you dive into the details. This introduction shows how the generic concepts that you will have learned in lectures and your textbook are realized in Windows NT, while the exercise provides a link between general concepts and Windows NT details. The exercise then poses a problem on which you will work, using the detailed Windows NT-specific information that is provided to solve the problem.

Since the emphasis in this lab manual is on OSs (as opposed to Windows programming), all of the exercises use the character-oriented console, **cmd.exe**. For those of you who have used MS-DOS, this will feel a little like a return to those days. However, after an exercise or two, you will realize that the NT **cmd.exe** console is much different from the MS-DOS **command.com** shell and that NT is much different from MS-DOS. There is no question that the graphics and user interface aspects of Windows NT are important. But they can also offer substantial new material for you to learn that has little to do with OSs. By using **cmd.exe**, you can narrow your focus to OS issues without having to learn about the windows and graphics issues. You can learn more about the graphics aspects of Windows NT application programming by consulting books devoted to this topic (for example, see Rector and Newcomer (1997)).

All of the exercises are based on C programs that are compiled and linked in the Microsoft Visual C++ environment (even though none of the programs are visual and none are to be written in C++). However, this environment provides full access to all of the Microsoft header files, libraries, and other tools used to write software that interacts with the OS over the normal API. If you do not know C, you will have to learn it before you can use the Windows NT programming interface. If you have been introduced to C, the exercises will encourage you to hone your programming skills.

This manual can be purchased as part of a bundle—containing this lab manual, two CD-ROMs, and an OS textbook—or as a stand-alone lab manual without the CD-ROMs. (The CD-ROMs also contain electronic versions of some of the software used in the exercises. If you have the unbundled version of the manual, consult the web page to get this software.) Your school's laboratory probably will have already been setup as a Windows NT lab. It can be configured for general-purpose computing, yet can still be used to solve the exercises in this book. If you are using the bundled version, you can use the CD-ROMs to install the current version of NT and Visual C++ on your own computer. By buying a bundle, you have a license to use NT and Visual C++ on your own machine.

It is difficult to coordinate the exact contents of the CD-ROM with the hardcopy manual, as both are written simultaneously, so I placed the exact content and installation details of the CD-ROM on the CD-ROM itself in the README file. Good luck in your study of OSs. I hope this manual is a valuable learning tool in seeing how OS concepts appear in Windows NT.

To the Instructor

Thank you for considering this lab manual for your undergraduate OS class. I have written it in response to a market need that I feel has existed and that Addison-Wesley has observed. Those of us teaching undergraduate OS need contemporary material that will allow our students to get nontrivial, hands-on experience with Windows NT.

As I noted in the preface to my OS textbook (Nutt, 1997), undergraduate OS textbooks make a fundamental choice about whether they will focus on concepts and issues or on the details of a specific OS. The conceptual approach has an advantage in that it concentrates on ideas and technology that transcend any particular OS, while a more concrete approach helps you to teach one particular OS (or in the extreme case, one version). There are pros and cons for each approach, though the trend appears to be toward those that teach abstract concepts that apply to all OSs.

In the first edition of my textbook I chose to focus on concepts and issues, but using a strong thread of examples and exercises from Linux. In the undergraduate OS class at the University of Colorado, the teaching assistants have had their hands full addressing as many hands-on aspects of Linux as possible in the laboratory component of the class; they really needed a lab manual. At the time I wrote the textbook, Linux was the best real OS on which to build exercises; it provided a contemporary implementation of UNIX, and the source code was (and still is) publicly available on the Internet. Now (a couple of years after I wrote the OS textbook), Windows NT is rapidly emerging as an OS of significant commercial importance; it is also a much more modern OS than is Linux. These factors are the motivation for writing this laboratory manual for Windows NT rather than for Linux. My undergraduate OS class uses a subset of the exercises in this manual to replace the Linux exercises.

Of course, it is tempting to simply write the lab manual as an extension of my textbook. However, in a market in which there are several good textbooks (some more established than mine), I realize that not every instructor wants to use my textbook. I feel that a good lab manual should be able to complement any undergraduate OS textbook that addresses general concepts and issues, whether that textbook is my own or those by Silberschatz and Galvin (Fifth Edition, 1998), Deitel (1990), Stallings (1995), or others.

The exercises I have chosen for this manual focus on the Win32 API rather than the Native NT API. There are several important reasons for doing this.

- For students to experiment with the internals of an OS, they will either have to build an entire OS or use an existing OS as a base that they can modify.

    - If you choose to have them build an entire OS, the project will tend to be too difficult for most students taking a first course, or the OS will be too simple (another toy OS).

    - If you decide to use an existing OS as a base, you will ordinarily need a copy of the OS source code so that students will be able to modify it, compile it, install it, and test it. As of this writing, that is not a feasible approach with Windows NT (due to the size of the NT source code and the incorporation of Microsoft intellectual property in the source).

    - In either case, you are likely to have to commit substantial amounts of time to supporting the laboratory.

- If students are to write supervisor code for NT, there is a wealth of documentation in the Device Driver Kit (DDK), Software Development Kit (SDK), and other sources. As of April 1998, the full set of development tools were distributed on about three dozen CD-ROMs. It is simply infeasible to ask students to learn the Microsoft development environment, to learn how to develop a driver, and then to write a driver as one exercise in an OS course. Professional programmers would be given several months (working at full-time) to accomplish the same job.

- Microsoft has provided strong support for the Win32 API, and essentially does not support the Native NT API. The Win32 API is the official OS API for NT, Windows 9*x*, and Windows CE (consumer electronics) (CE actually has its own version of Win32 API). The Win32 API allows a programmer to experiment with most of the OS components without writing supervisor code.

- An interesting aspect of the preparation of the manual has been the wonderful cooperation of Microsoft, particularly of Microsoft Research (through its University Relations program). The OS researchers have universally recommended that the manual be based on the Win32 API. (However, like those of us teaching and studying OS at universities, they also see the value of ultimately having a version of the NT source code available for education at some time in the future.)

- Ultimately, my experience is that the overwhelming majority of students taking a first course in OS have never written multithreaded code before taking the class. There is tremendous value to having students learn about processes, synchronization, deadlock, security, virtual memory, file management, and so on at the conceptual level and then having them write multithreaded code to exercise those facilities in NT (or Linux) in their lab. This is the ultimate reason for building this lab manual around the Win 32 API.

Because Windows NT is such a large software product, there are a number of tools for observing its behavior. Unfortunately, the tools are not concentrated in one part of the Windows NT product but are appended to various products. I have selected a subset of all of the tools and put them on the CD-ROM set that accompanies the bundled version of this manual. These tools allow students to explore NT's behavior via the normal graphical NT interface. I have specifically chosen *not* to use a kernel debugger as part of the exercises. There are two reasons for this. First, the debugger works best with a checked build of NT (which is not a good version of NT to have on generic lab machines). Second, the debugger typically is run on one machine and the kernel to be inspected is run on another. My experience with university teaching labs is that this is simply untenable.

The lab you need in order to support the exercises in this manual can be a plain-vanilla Windows NT lab. I have developed all solutions using NT Workstation. There is no requirement for a Windows NT Server, though having one might make your life easier for distributing various kinds of information. One TCP/IP exercise suggests that the solution machine needs to be connected to other machines; however, I have written the solution on stand-alone UNIX machines and NT machines and then tested it on networks of machines.

The trick is in being sure that the solution uses Internet addresses and the socket library. If that has been done, the single machine solution moves to the network with no problem.

There is a separate instructor's manual available to teachers who adopt this book, available from your local Addison-Wesley sales representative. The instructor's manual contains some information that is inappropriate for the lab manual, but that I believe is useful for the instructor to know before assigning an exercise. In particular, the manual contains a solution to each exercise. Although this manual provides enough information to solve any exercise, you might want to provide supplementary information from the solution to simplify the exercise. There is a wealth of information available regarding general NT programming, but not so much that focuses on the OS itself. Besides the books listed in the References sections (exercise-specific references are listed at the end of each exercise, and all references are listed at the end of the manual), I maintain a World Wide Web site for this book on which I post current information:

http://www.cs.colorado.edu/~nutt/ntman.html

Send me a link to your NT OS teaching materials, and I will include it. Please feel free to check the site for recent information, as well as other Web sites that have articles and other useful materials.

A lab manual is a formalized set of homework assignments. As all instructors know, assignments sometimes contain bugs (even after they have been used several times). As you use the manual, if you would like clarification of some point, notice some errors that should be fixed, have suggestions for how to make the exercises better, or just want to chat about the manual, please send me e-mail (nutt@cs.colorado.edu).

Acknowledgments

The idea for this lab manual came from and was heavily supported by two very high-energy people: Maité Suarez-Rivas, Acquisitions Editor at Addison Wesley; and Susanne Peterson, University Relations manager at Microsoft. Maité invited me to write the manual, provided research resources, focused the book on the market, coordinated all the publication steps so that the manual could be published quickly, and provided continual encouragement. Susanne invited me to visit Microsoft, provided software and equipment, and created an environment in which I was able to completely focus on this book during the summer of 1998. I am extremely grateful to both for their energy, encouragement, and support of the project. And they are both really nice people.

There are a number of people at Microsoft who talked to me about the project and provided encouragement, feedback, and ideas for the manual. Microsoft Research, headed by Rick Rashid, was my contact organization. Rick and Dennis Adler supported the project from the outset, providing resources to help with it and allowing me to meet with various researchers, including Mike Jones, Galen Hall, and Rich Draves from the OS research group in Microsoft Research. Bruce Beachman of Microsoft also listened to the ideas for the manual and provided encouragement and insight into how to prepare it. Mike Jones also reviewed various versions of the manual. The people in the Microsoft's University Relations program (in addition to Susanne Peterson) who provided various kinds of support were Kirsten Taylor (a full spectrum of assistance), Kurt Messersmith, and David Ladd (source code licensing).

David Solomon of David Solomon Expert Seminars (**www.solsem.com**) not only wrote the best book I know of on NT internals, but also graciously talked to me about the way NT is designed, giving me a nice "jump start" to understanding the NT kernel.

Norman Ramsey (University of Virginia) provided me with a set of notes for a comprehensive course project he used in his undergraduate OS class at Purdue University in 1996. Ann Root, an undergraduate student at Purdue and a graduate student at the University of Colorado, told me about the course project. Ann provided me with her solution to Ramsey's Purdue project. The assignment and solution are the foundation of Exercises 10 and 11. Scott Morris is the local NT expert in the Computer Operations group in the Department of Computer Science at the University of Colorado. He helped in innumerable ways, from making my NT configuration work properly, to helping me understand simple (but undocumented) notions for developing Windows NT code, to reviewing this manual. Lynda McGinley, Computer Operations Manager, also encouraged the development of the manual by ensuring that we had a Windows NT teaching lab at the University of Colorado even though her organization is firmly grounded in various versions of UNIX.

This manual was written, reviewed, and published in an incredibly short amount of time. The reviewers were required to respond to the drafts in a few weeks rather than the more leisurely month or two; thanks to Vladimir Akiss (California State University — Los Angeles), Dr. Eric A. Fisch (KPMG Peat Marwick LLP), Sang-Uok Kum (University of North Carolina), Cliff Martin (Bell Labs), Martha C. McCormick (Jacksonville State University), Ravi Mukkamala (Old Dominion University), Yuan Shi (Temple University), and Dr. Gregory B. White (U.S. Air Force Academy).

The staff at Addison-Wesley is highly professional and able to respond to very high-pressure schedules to produce a quality product. Maité's assistant, Molly Taylor, did a great job of distributing materials to reviewers and obtaining quick feedback. Laura Michaels edited my draft manuscript, greatly improving it in the process. I worked with Pat Unubun, Production Editor, on my OS textbook and again with this manual. She is a master at production, able to work under incredible scheduling pressure while ensuring a high-quality product.

Gary Nutt
Professor
University of Colorado
Boulder

Contents

Operating System Projects Using Windows NT®

part 1

The Organization of NT

This part of the manual provides a general overview of the organization of Microsoft's Windows NT, or simply *NT*, to provide a link between NT and the knowledge of OS that you have acquired (or will be acquiring) using your textbook. It also provides a general framework from which you can look more closely at individual components as you solve the lab exercises. Since you are learning OS concepts at the same time you are doing these exercises, more details are provided with the exercise for which they are most appropriate.

Windows NT is a commercial OS, first released for public use in July 1993 (Solomon, 1998). Microsoft OSs, particularly Windows 95 and Windows 98 (together designated as Windows 9*x*) and Windows NT, are among the most widely used commercial systems available today; thus Windows NT is a highly practical system for studying how an OS works. Windows NT is also a modern system, with a computational model based on processes and threads (rather than just processes). It also has a pervasive underlying object model. Even so, Windows NT carries on the MS-DOS legacy, meaning it supports 16-bit application programs written for MS-DOS.

General Architecture

The product goals for Windows NT were that it should be an *extensible*, *portable*, *reliable*, and *secure* OS for contemporary computers (including symmetric multiprocessors) (Solomon 1998). These terms can mean many things, so they warrant some discussion to see how they influenced the Windows NT design.

Extensibility

There are at least two dimensions to the extensibility aspect. The first relates to OS configurations. A Windows NT machine can be configured for a workstation or a server. In either configuration, the OS uses the same fundamental source code, but different components are incorporated into each at compile time. This allows Windows NT to be optimized to perform best according to the way the machine will be used—as a workstation or as a server—without building two different OSs. The exercises in this manual can all be solved on a Windows NT Workstation configuration. (Exercise 6 uses the network, but it can be solved using two workstations or a workstation and a server.)

The second, and perhaps a more significant, aspect of extensibility is in the way the OS software is structured. Windows NT is designed using an *extensible nucleus* software model (see Nutt, 1997 Chapter 18; Silberschatz and Galvin, 1998, Chapter 3). In this approach, only the most essential OS functions are implemented in a small nucleus of code (often called a *microkernel*). Additional mechanisms are then implemented on top of the nucleus to define policy as needed. This approach has the advantage that key mechanisms (such as protection mechanisms) can be carefully designed and tested as one trusted subassembly that can then be used to implement many different policies. This is a basic approach to support the goals of good security and reliable operation. The *NT Kernel* provides these essential low-level mechanisms as a layer of abstraction from the hardware (see Figure 1). The *NT Executive* is designed as a layer of abstraction of the NT Kernel. It provides specific mechanisms (and many policies) for general object and memory management, process management, file management, and device management. Together, the NT Kernel and the NT Executive provide the essential elements of the OS, though this nucleus is extended yet again by the subsystems (as explained in the next couple of paragraphs).

Although the NT Kernel and the Windows NT Executive are designed and implemented as distinct software modules, they are combined into a single executable, **NTOSKRNL.EXE**, before they are actually executed (Solomon, 1998). **NTOSKRNL.EXE** also invokes additional dynamically linked libraries (DLLs) whenever they are needed. Thus the logical view of Windows NT—that of a modular nucleus—is quite different from the way the executable actually appears in memory. In your study of Windows NT, it is best to use the logical view for considering different aspects of the OS, since that is the model under which it is designed. However when writing programs that use Windows NT, your knowing that the OS is implemented as a monolithic executable file might sometimes influence how you use the OS.

Figure 1

NT Organization

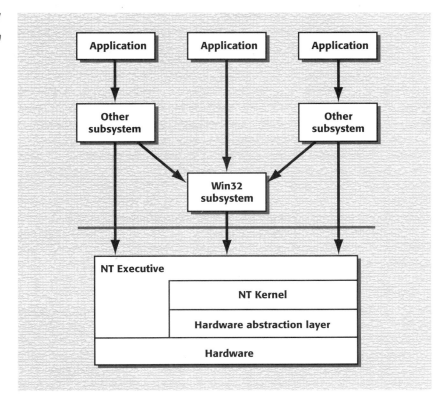

The next layer of abstraction of Windows NT is the subsystem layer. Subsystems provide application *portability* for Windows NT software. An *NT Subsystem* is a software module that uses the services (mechanisms) implemented in the Kernel and the Executive to implement more abstract "services," especially the services offered by some target OS. For example, Version 4.0 has a POSIX subsystem that executes on top of the Kernel and the Executive that makes Windows NT look like POSIX; such subsystems are called *environment subsystems*, or *personality modules*. Other subsystems implement specialized services such as the security subsystem. All subsystems (and all application programs that use the subsystems) execute when the processor is in user mode. Subsystems are the key component in allowing Microsoft to support various computational models, such as the MS-DOS and Win16 program models (personalities). Application programs written to run on MS-DOS use the MS-DOS subsystem interface. This subsystem provides the same API to the application as does MS-DOS, thereby allowing old MS-DOS programs to run on a Windows NT system.

Portability

The portability aspect of Windows NT overlaps its extensibility. Subsystems allow Windows NT to be extended to meet various application support requirements, and they are also a cornerstone of portability (since a subsystem allows application programs written for other OSs to be easily ported to Windows NT). Microsoft has built various subsystems to implement OS personalities of interest to their customers. Besides the MS-DOS subsystem, there are subsystems to support Win16 applications and POSIX programs, as well as a new Win32 subsystem. In general, it is possible for software developers to implement any subsystem to satisfy their general requirements for OS service; such a subsystem uses the Executive/Kernel interface. Even so, the Win32 subsystem takes a special role in Windows NT because it implements various extensions of the NT Executive that are needed by all other subsystems; every subsystem relies on the presence of the Win32 subsystem. While it is possible to add new environment subsystems to Windows NT, and to omit most of them, the Win32 subsystem must always be present.

Another aspect of portability that has driven the design of Windows NT is the ability to port Windows NT, itself, across different hardware platforms. Microsoft's goal was to be able to reuse the Kernel, Executive, and subsystems on new microprocessors as they became available without having to rewrite the Kernel (or Executive, and so on). The goal was for Windows NT, itself, to be written to be portable. Windows NT's designers carefully identified the things that were common across a wide set of microprocessors and the things that were different. This allowed them to create a *hardware abstraction layer* (HAL) software module to isolate the Kernel (and the rest of the OS) from hardware differences. The HAL is responsible for mapping various low-level, processor-specific operations into a fixed interface that is used by the Windows NT Kernel and Executive. The HAL also executes with the processor in supervisor mode.

The HAL, Kernel, and Executive are supervisor-mode software that collectively export an API that is used by subsystem designers (but not by application programmers). Environment subsystem designers choose a target API (such as the Win16, POSIX, or OS/2 API) and then build a subsystem to implement the API using the supervisor portion of Windows NT. Microsoft has even chosen its own preferred API—the Win32 API—which is also the API for the Win32 subsystem. Windows NT application programs are written to work on the Win32 API rather than on the interface to **NTOSKRNL.EXE**. The hardware abstraction layer (HAL) sections through the NT Subsystems section consider these components in a little more detail (starting at the HAL section and working up to the subsystem level part of the NT Subsystems section).

Reliability and Security

Both the reliability and security requirements for Windows NT are reflected in the details of how the Kernel and Executive are designed and implemented (rather than in the overall organization). Reliability is supported by separating the HAL, Kernel, Executive, and subsystem functionality from one another, thus eliminating unnecessary interactions. It is further supported through the software design techniques used in implementing Windows NT.

It is easier to identify how security has influenced Windows NT's design. Windows NT is designed to meet standard requirements for trusted OSs. According to Solomon (1998), in 1995 Windows NT was certified at the C2 level by the United States National Computer Security Center and in 1996 at the F-C2/E3 level by the United Kingdom Information Technology Security Evaluation and Certification Board. Much of the security mechanism is implemented in a Security Subsystem, that depends on the Security Reference Manager in the Executive. Note that even though the presence of these mechanisms and the existence of certification makes it possible to create very secure systems, if the application software does not use the security mechanisms, the overall system will not be especially secure.

The Hardware Abstraction Layer (HAL)

The HAL is a low-level software module that translates critical hardware behaviors into a standardized set of behaviors. The HAL functions are exported through a kernel-mode DLL, **HAL.DLL**. The OS calls functions in **HAL.DLL** when it needs to determine the way the host hardware behaves. This allows the Windows NT code to call a HAL function (rather than just use a hardwired address) everywhere a hardware-specific address is needed. For example, device interrupts usually have addresses determined by the microprocessor architecture, and they differ from one microprocessor to another. The HAL interface allows Windows NT to reference the interrupt addresses via functions rather than by using the hardware addresses directly.

The HAL implementation for any specific microprocessor provides the appropriate hardware-specific information via the corresponding function on the HAL API. This means that it is possible to use the same source code on a Digital Equipment Alpha processor as is used on an Intel Pentium processor. It also means that it is possible to create device drivers for Windows NT that will also work without change in Windows 9x.

The use of the HAL is transparent above the Executive/Kernel interface. Subsystem and application programmers are generally unconcerned with the type of processor chip in the computer. Windows NT provides a fixed set of services independent of the hardware platform type.

The NT Kernel creates the basic unit of computation and provides the foundation for multitasking support. It does so without committing to any particular policy/strategy for process management, memory management, file management, or device management. To appreciate the level of support the Kernel provides, think of the Kernel as offering a collection of building components such as wheels, pistons, lights, and so on, that could be used to build a sports car, a sedan, a sports utility vehicle, or a truck. Similarly, the Kernel's clients can combine the components to build a compound component that defines a policy for how the low-level components are used.

The Kernel provides objects and threads (computational abstractions) on top of the HAL and the hardware. Software that uses the Kernel can be defined using objects and threads as primitives, that is, these abstractions appear to Kernel client software as natural parts of the hardware. To implement objects and threads, the Kernel must manage the hardware interrupts and exceptions, perform processor scheduling, and handle multiprocessor synchronization.

Objects

The NT Kernel defines a set of built-in *object types* (usually called *classes* in object-oriented languages). Some kernel object types are instantiated by the Kernel itself to form other parts of the overall OS execution image. These objects collectively save and manipulate the Kernel's state. Other objects are instantiated and used by the Executive, subsystems, and application code as the foundation of their computational model. That is, Windows NT and all of its applications are managed at the Kernel level as objects.

Kernel objects are intended to be fast. They run in supervisor mode in a trusted context, so there is no security and only limited error checking for Kernel objects, in contrast to normal objects, which incorporate these features. However, Kernel objects cannot be manipulated directly by user-mode programs, only through function calls. Kernel objects are characterized as being either *control objects* or *dispatcher objects*.

Control Objects

Control objects implement mechanisms to control the hardware and other Kernel resources. When an application program creates a new process, it requests that the Kernel create a type of control object, a new *process object*; the OS returns a *handle* (reference pointer) to the object after it has been created. The application refers to the object—in this case, a process—by using the handle. When the application program manipulates the process, it is manipulating the underlying kernel process object. There are other control objects. The *asynchronous procedure call*

(APC) object is an object that can be used to interrupt another thread and cause it to execute a specific procedure. An *interrupt object* is an object created to match up to each interrupt source so that when a designated interrupt occurs, the corresponding object will receive a message. A *profile object* is an object that can be used to monitor the amount of time a thread spends executing different parts of the code. Other control objects exist to handle power failure when it occurs, to check to see if power has failed, to do power management, and so on. You will be introduced to various control objects in the ensuing exercises.

Dispatcher Objects

Dispatcher objects are used to implement threads along with their scheduling and synchronization operations. Each dispatcher object has built-in characteristics that are used to support user-level synchronization (see Exercise 4). A process object (a type of control object) creates a computational abstraction that can have an address space and a set of resources. However, in Windows NT the process object cannot execute. A dispatcher object called a *thread object* is the active element of the computation abstraction; it has its own stack and can execute within a process. Whenever any application program is to be executed, it must have an associated process (control) object and a thread (dispatcher) object. You will run and observe several thread objects in Exercise 1, and in Exercise 2, you will begin writing programs that use both process and thread objects. Other dispatcher objects are used primarily to implement one form or another of synchronization. While a single synchronization primitive would be sufficient (ultimately, all synchronization is based on the Kernel spinlock described shortly), the Executive will implement a set of variants to simplify the use of dispatcher objects for synchronization. Again, various object types will be introduced in exercises where you need to use them.

Threads

As mentioned in the discussion of objects, a thread is an abstraction of computation. A Windows NT process object defines an address space in which one or more threads can execute, and each *thread object* represents one execution within the process (see Figure 2). In a UNIX environment, there can be only one thread executing in each address space. Pictorially, this means there would be only one "path traversal" through the address spaces shown in Figure 2. A UNIX process does not differentiate between the address space concepts of a process object and the execution aspects of a thread object. As in other modern operation systems such as Mach, Chorus, and Amoeba, in the Windows NT environment it is common to have more than one thread—a logical path traversal through the code in an address space—executing in a process. The separation of the thread concept from the rest of the process concept has been done so that it is natural to think of several different "threads of execution" within a single ad-

Figure 2

Processes and Threads

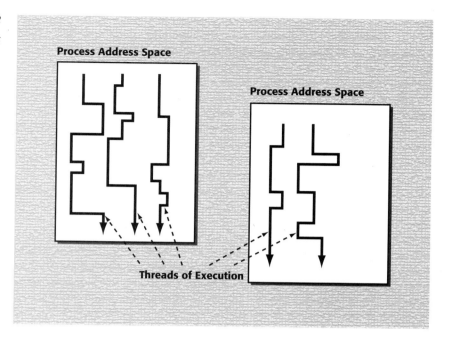

Process Address Space

Process Address Space

Threads of Execution

dress space, all sharing the same resources. Your OS textbook provides a more general discussion of threads (sometimes also called *lightweight processes*).

Traps, Interrupts, and Exceptions

In Windows NT terminology, the Kernel *trap handler* is responsible for reacting to hardware interrupts and processor exceptions (such as system service call, execution errors, and virtual memory faults). Whenever an interrupt or processor exception is recognized by the hardware, the trap handler (see Figure 3) moves into action. It is responsible for doing the following.

- Disabling interrupts
- Determining the cause of the interrupt or exception
- Saving processor state in a trap frame
- Reenabling interrupts
- Changing the processor to supervisor mode if required
- Dispatching specialized code, for example, an Interrupt Service Routine (ISR), a DLL, an exception dispatcher, or the virtual memory handler, to handle the trap

In the case of an interrupt, the trap handler will normally run an ISR for the specific interrupt. For exceptions, the trap handler might address the cause itself or invoke the appropriate OS code to react to the exception.

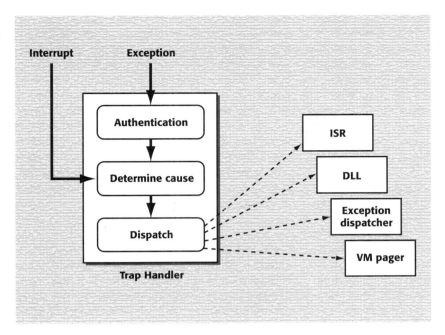

Figure 3

Trap Handler

As in all "system call interface" OS designs (see Nutt (1997), Chapter 3; Silberschatz and Galvin (1998), Chapter 2), supervisor-mode functions are invoked by an application program when it executes an instruction that causes an exception; in many hardware sets, this is the *trap* instruction. The trap handler must be used to call system functions, since the processor mode needs to be switched from user to supervisor. Before the mode can be switched, the OS must be assured that the code to be executed (while the hardware is in supervisor mode) is trusted code. Therefore user programs are not allowed to link and call these functions directly. Instead, they can be invoked only through the trap handler. In Windows NT, the trap handler uses a DLL, **NTDLL.DLL**, to authenticate the call and start the OS code; the application links **NTDLL.DLL** into its address space and then calls entry points in the DLL. These points are translated into traps (using the host hardware mechanism for raising an exception) that cause the processor mode to be switched to supervisor mode and a secure call to be made on the OS code.

Interrupts are used to allow a device to notify the OS when the device completes an operation. Windows NT's interrupt management generally follows the same design that other OSs have used for a number of years (explained in your textbook). Each device operation is initiated by the device's driver. The thread initiating the operation might wait for the I/O call to complete (said to be a *synchronous I/O call*) or continue running concurrently with the I/O operation (said to be an *asynchronous I/O call*). Traditionally (for example, in standard C programs), the API does allow the application thread to use asynchronous I/O, though asynchronous I/O is fully supported in Windows NT. The API used with Windows NT extends the normal C routines so that application programs can use asynchronous I/O operations.

In either the synchronous or asynchronous case, the processor continues to execute software concurrent with the device operation—the calling thread's code, in the asynchronous case, or another thread's code, in the synchronous case. The device will eventually signal the processor that it has completed the I/O operation by raising an interrupt. This causes the trap handler to run and to determine which device has completed and then to run an ISR that will finish the housekeeping related to completing the I/O operation. Each time the user moves the mouse or types a key or information arrives on a connected network, an interrupt is raised, the trap handler runs, and an ISR is called to manage the incoming information. In Exercise 1, you will try to determine the effect on the overall machine's performance that is related to such interrupt occurrences.

Thread Scheduling

The Windows NT thread scheduler is a timesliced, priority-based, preemptive scheduler. The basic unit of processor allocation is a time quantum computed as a multiple of the number of clock interrupts (for example, a time quantum might be three ticks of the host system's clock). On most Windows NT machines, the time quantum ranges from about 20 to 200 milliseconds (ms). Servers are configured to have time quanta that are six times longer than for a workstation with the same processor type.

The scheduler supports 32 different scheduling queues (see the discussion of multiple-level queues in your textbook). As in all multiple-level queue schedulers, as long as there are threads in the highest-priority queue, then only those threads will be allocated the processor. If there are no threads in that queue, then the scheduler will service the threads in the second highest-priority queue. If there are no threads ready to run (that is, no *runnable* threads) in the second highest-priority queue, the scheduler will service the third highest-priority queue, and so on.

There are three levels of queues:

- *Real-time level*, consisting of the 16 highest-priority queues
- *Variable-level*, consisting of the next 15 higher-priority queues
- *System-level*, consisting of the lowest-priority queue

The scheduler attempts to limit the number of threads that are entered into the real-time queues, thereby increasing the probability that there will be little competition among threads that execute at these high-priority levels. (There is a model used for real-time scheduling on the Win32 API. It requires that a thread be authorized as a real-time thread before it is placed in a real-time level queue.) However, Windows NT is not a real-time system and cannot *guarantee* that threads running at high priority will receive the processor before any fixed deadline. The highest-level queue processing continues through the variable-level queues, down to the system-level queue. The system-level queue contains a single "zero page thread" to represent an idle system. That is, when there are no runnable threads in the entire system, it executes the zero page thread until an interrupt occurs and another thread becomes runnable. The zero page thread is the single lowest-priority thread in the system, so it runs whenever there are no other runnable threads.

A thread's base priority is normally inherited from its process. The priority can also be set with various function calls, provided the caller has the authority to set the priority. The Win32 API model defines four priority classes:

- REAL TIME
- HIGH
- NORMAL
- IDLE

Each thread also has a relative thread priority within the class, any of the following:

- TIME CRITICAL
- HIGHEST
- ABOVE NORMAL
- NORMAL
- BELOW NORMAL
- LOWEST
- IDLE

Thus a thread could be in the **HIGH** class and operating at the **ABOVE NORMAL** relative priority at one moment, but then be in the **HIGH** class and operating at the **BELOW NORMAL** relative priority a little later. Base priority is defined by the thread's class and the class's **NORMAL** relative priority. If the priority class is not **REAL TIME**, then the thread's priority will be for one of the variable-level queues. In this case, Windows NT might adjust priorities of threads in the variable level according to system conditions. Windows NT does not change the priority of a thread that has been placed in the real-time levels.

The thread scheduler is also *preemptive*. This means that whenever a thread becomes ready to run, it is placed in a run queue at a level corresponding to its current priority. If there is another thread in execution at that time and that thread has a lower priority, then the lower-priority thread is interrupted (it is not allowed to finish its time quantum) and the new, higher-priority thread is assigned the processor. In a single-processor system, this would mean that a thread could cause itself to be removed from the processor by enabling a higher-priority thread. In a multiprocessor system, the situation can be more subtle. Suppose that in a two-processor system, one processor is running a thread at level 10 and the other is running a thread at level 4. If the level 10 thread performs some action that causes a previously blocked thread to suddenly become runnable at level 6, then the level 4 thread will be halted and the new level 6 thread will begin to use the processor that the level 4 thread was using.

This brief discussion of NT scheduling should give you a good intuitive feel for how the NT scheduler has been designed and why it is implemented in the Kernel rather than in a higher layer of the software. Scheduling must be very efficient and be completely guided by the interrupt and exception activity that occurs in the system. Time quanta are determined by clock interrupts, and they happen relatively frequently. The scheduler is within the same logical OS layer as the trap handler, so the interactions between the two can be designed to be trusted (limited error checking) and efficient.

Multiprocess Synchronization

Single-processor systems can support synchronization by disabling interrupts (see your textbook). However, Windows NT is designed to also support multiprocessors, so the Kernel must provide an alternative mechanism to ensure that a thread executing on one processor does not violate a critical section of a thread on another processor (Exercise 4 discusses critical sections in more detail). As is traditional in multiprocessor OSs, the Kernel employs *spinlocks*, by which a thread on one process can wait for a critical section by actively testing a Kernel lock variable to determine when it can enter the critical section. If the hardware supports the test-and-set instruction (or other machine instruction that is logically equivalent to test-and-set), spinlocks are implemented using the hardware. Spinlock synchronization is used only within the Kernel and Executive. User-mode programs use abstractions that are implemented by the Executive (see Exercise 4).

The NT Executive

The NT Executive builds on the Kernel to implement the full set of Windows NT policies and services, including process management, memory management, file management, and device management. Since Windows NT uses object-oriented technology, its modularization does not strictly follow the classic separation of

OS functionality as described in your textbook. Instead, the NT Executive is designed and implemented at the source code level as a modularized set of elements (Solomon, 1998; Nagar, 1997):

- Object Manager
- Process and Thread Manager
- Virtual Memory Manager
- Security Reference Manager
- I/O Manager
- Cache Manager
- LPC facility
- Runtime functions
- Executive support functions

Object Manager

The Executive Object Manager implements another object model on top of the Kernel Object Manager (see Figure 4). Whereas Kernel objects operate in a trusted environment, Executive objects are used by other parts of the Executive and user-mode software and must take extra measures to assure secure and reliable operation. Exercise 3 is devoted to Executive objects (more details will be provided then). The discussion in this subsection provides the general view of how the Executive Object Manager works.

Figure 4

Handles, Executive Objects, and Kernel Objects

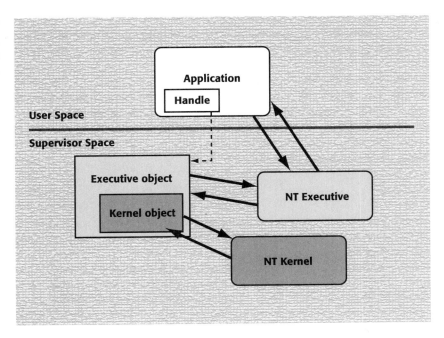

An Executive object exists in supervisor space, though it can be referenced by user threads. This is accomplished by having the Object Manager provide a *handle* for each Executive object. Whenever a thread needs a new Executive object, it calls an Object Manager function to create the object (in supervisor space), to create a handle to the object (in the process's address space), and then to return the handle to the calling thread.

Sometimes a second thread will want to use an Executive object that has already been created. When the second thread attempts to create the existing object, the Object Manager notes that the object already exists, so it creates a second handle for the second thread to use to reference the existing Executive object. The two threads share the single object. The Object Manager keeps a reference count of all handles to an Executive object (see Exercise 3). When all outstanding handles have been closed, the Executive object is deallocated. Thus it is important for each thread to close each handle it opens, preferably as soon as it no longer needs the handle.

There is a predefined set of about 15 object types for the Object Manager. When an object is created, it includes an object header (used by the Object Manager to manage the object) and a body to contain type-specific information. The header includes the following:

- Object name: Allows the object to be referenced by different processes.
- Security descriptor: Contains access permissions.
- Open handle information: Contains details of which processes are using the object
- Object type: Contains details of the object's class definition.
- Reference count: Holds the count of the number of outstanding handles that reference the object.

The information in the header is managed by the Object Manager. For example, when a new handle is created to an object, the Object Manager updates the open handle information and reference count. The object type information defines a "standard" set of methods that the object implements (by virtue of being an Executive object), such as **open**, **close**, and **delete**. Some of these methods are supplied by the Object Manager, and some must be tailored to the object type; however, the interface is determined as part of the object header.

The object body format is determined by the Executive component that uses the object. For example, if the Executive object is a file object, the body format and contents are managed by the File Manager part of the I/O Manager in the Executive.

Process and Thread Manager

The Executive Process and Thread Manager (or simply the Process Manager) serves the same purpose in Windows NT that a process manager serves in any OS. It is the part of the OS responsible for the following:

- Creating and destroying processes and threads
- Overseeing resource allocation
- Providing synchronization primitives
- Controlling process and thread state changes
- Keeping track of most of the information that the OS knows about each process and thread

In short, it manages all aspects of threads and processes that are not managed by some other specialized element (such as object-specific characteristics and the file characteristics).

The Process Manager implements the process abstraction that will be used at the subsystem and application levels. Implementing the abstraction means that the Process Manager defines a number of data structures for keeping track of the state of each process and thread (see Figure 5, where solid lines represent pointers and dashed lines represent code referencing the contents of a data structure). The base process descriptor is called an *executive process control* (or EPROCESS) *block*. The EPROCESS block contains much the same information one might expect to find in any process descriptor, including identifications, resource lists, and address space descriptions (see your textbook for details; also, Solomon (1998) lists 59 fields in an EPROCESS block). The EPROCESS block also references a Kernel-level *process control block* (PCB, or sometimes called the KPROCESS block), which contains the Kernel's view of the process. The NT Kernel manipulates its portion of the EPROCESS block, and the NT Executive is responsible for maintaining the remaining fields (except a few fields that are used by the Win32 subsystem).

There is also a close relationship between an Executive process and a thread. Just as there is an EPROCESS block, there is also an *executive thread control* (ETHREAD) *block* for each thread in a process. Since the thread exists within a process, the EPROCESS block references the list of ETHREAD blocks. Information about the thread that is managed by the Process Manager is stored in the ETHREAD block. And because the thread is built on a Kernel-level thread object, there is also a *Kernel thread control* (KTHREAD) *block* containing the information about the Kernel thread object that is managed by the Kernel-level thread management (discussed in the previous section on the NT Kernel). The EPROCESS block references a KPROCESS block, which references a set of

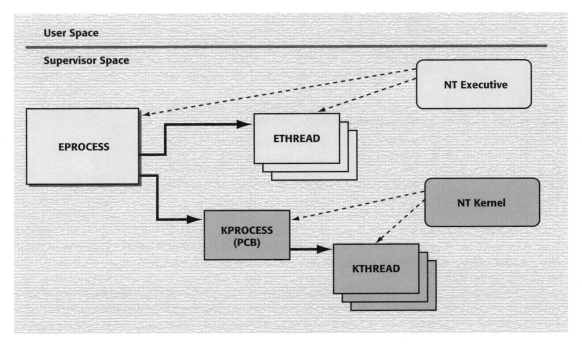

Figure 5

Process and Thread Descriptors

KTHREAD blocks. The EPROCESS block also references a set of ETHREAD blocks, each of which references the same KTHREAD blocks.

The **NTOSKRNL** function **NtCreateProcess** is called to create a process; that is, the Win32 API **CreateProcess** function calls **NtCreateProcess** (you will use **CreateProcess** in Exercise 2). When **NtCreateProcess** is called (ordinarily by **CreateProcess**), it performs the following work in setting up the process.

- Calls the Kernel to have it create a Kernel process object.
- Creates and initializes an EPROCESS block.
- Creates an address space for the process.

A process has no ability to execute code in its address space; it must have at least one thread, called the *base thread*, to execute the code. The **NtCreateThread** Executive function creates a thread that can execute within the process. (The Win32 API **CreateProcess** function calls both **NtCreateProcess** and **NtCreateThread**; the **CreateThread** function calls

NtCreateThread to create additional threads within a process.) **NtCreateThread** performs the following work.

- Calls the Kernel to have it create a Kernel thread object.
- Creates and initializes an ETHREAD block.
- Initializes the thread for execution (sets up its stack, provides it with an executable start address, and so on).
- Places the thread in a scheduling queue.

Virtual Memory Manager

Windows NT is a *paging virtual memory system*. As you will read in your text-book, a paging virtual memory system saves a process's address space contents in secondary storage, loading portions of the image from the secondary storage into the primary storage (or executable memory) on a page-by-page basis whenever it is needed.

When a process is created, it has 4 gigabytes (GB) of virtual addresses available to it, though none of the addresses are actually allocated at that time. When the process needs space, it first *reserves* as much of the address space as it needs at that moment; reserved addresses do not cause any actual space to be allocated; rather, virtual addresses are reserved for later use. When the process needs to use the virtual addresses to store information, it *commits* the address space, meaning that some system storage space is then allocated to the process to hold information. Ordinarily, a commit operation causes space on the disk (in the process's *page file*) to be allocated to the process; the information is stored on the disk until it is actually referenced by a thread.

Like all paging virtual memory mechanisms, when an executing thread references a virtual address, the Virtual Memory Manager ensures that the page containing that virtual address is read from the page file and placed at some system-defined location in the physical executable memory. The Virtual Memory Manager *maps* the virtual address referenced by the thread into the physical memory address where the information is loaded.

The Virtual Memory Manager has been designed so that a large portion of each process's address space (usually half of it, though different configurations of Windows NT use different fractions) is mapped to the information used by the system when it is in supervisor mode (see Figure 6). There are a few important implications of this decision, as follows.

- A process can directly reference (but not necessarily access) every location in the system space.

Figure 6

Virtual Memory

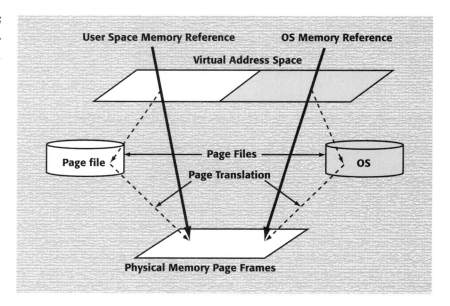

- Every process shares the same view of the system's space.
- Such a large, shared virtual address space makes memory-mapped files (see Exercise 8) feasible.

In Figure 6, when a thread references an address in the user space, the virtual memory system loads the target location into the physical memory prior to its use so that the thread can read or write the virtual memory address by referencing a physical memory address. The same mapping takes place for OS memory references, though these references are protected, and every process's OS addresses map to the the OS memory rather than to the application-specific part of the address space. The introduction to Exercise 7 provides more details on Windows NT's virtual memory, including a description of the Win32 API functions used to manipulate the virtual address space.

Security Reference Manager

The NT Kernel supports secure operation by including low-level mechanisms for authentication. The Security Reference Manager is the Executive-level mechanism to implement the critical parts of certifiable security policies. It is constructed to check object access according to any given protection policy (specified within subsystem components that manage the specific access that a process is trying to perform).

The Security Reference Monitor is a protection mechanism used by the Security Reference Manager in conjunction with a security policy module executing in user space. Windows NT includes a user space subsystem component, the *Local Security Authority (LSA) server*, to represent the desired security policy. The LSA uses its own policy database, stored in the machine's Registry, to hold the details of the particular machine's policy. (The policy for the particular machine can be changed by editing the policy database.) The authentication mechanism the LSA server uses to compare access requests with the database contents can also be provided on an installation-by-installation basis, though a default mechanism is provided with NT.

The Security Reference Manager authenticates access to Executive objects. Whenever any thread makes a system call to access an Executive object, the part of the Executive that handles the access passes a description of the attempted access to the Security Reference Monitor. The object contains a security descriptor identifying the object's owner and an *access control list (ACL)* of processes that are permitted access to the object. The Security Reference Monitor determines the thread's identity and access type and then verifies that the thread is allowed to access the object (according to the information in the ACL).

I/O Manager

The I/O Manager is responsible for handling all the input/output operations to every device in the system. Its operation can be quite complex (Solomon, 1998).

- The I/O Manager creates an abstraction of all device I/O operations on the system so that the system's clients can perform operations on a common data structure.
- The client can perform synchronous and asynchronous I/O.
- The client can invoke the Security Reference Monitor whenever security is an issue.
- The I/O Manager must accommodate device drivers written in a high-level language by third parties. Those drivers must be able to execute in supervisor mode. Installation and removal of a device driver must be dynamic.
- The I/O Manager can accommodate alternative files systems on the system's disks. This means that some files systems might use the MS-DOS format (see Exercises 10–12), others might use an industry standard CD-ROM format, and yet others might use NT's own file system (NTFS).
- I/O Manager extensions–device drivers and/or file systems–must be consistent with the memory-mapped file mechanism implemented in the Virtual Memory Manager, so extension designs are constrained by the facilities provided by the manager.

The I/O Manager is made up of the following components, as shown in Figure 7 (Nagar, 1997).

- *Device drivers* are at the lowest level. They manipulate the physical I/O devices. These drivers are described generically in your textbook.
- *Intermediate drivers* are software modules that work with a low-level device driver to provide enhanced service. For example, a low-level device driver might simply pass an error condition "upward" when it detects it, while an intermediate driver might receive the error and decide to issue a retry operation to the lower-level driver.
- *File system drivers* extend the functionality of the lower-level drivers (such as intermediate and device drivers) to implement the target file system.
- A *filter driver* can be inserted between a device driver and an intermediate driver, between an intermediate driver and a file system driver, or between

Figure 7

The I/O Manager

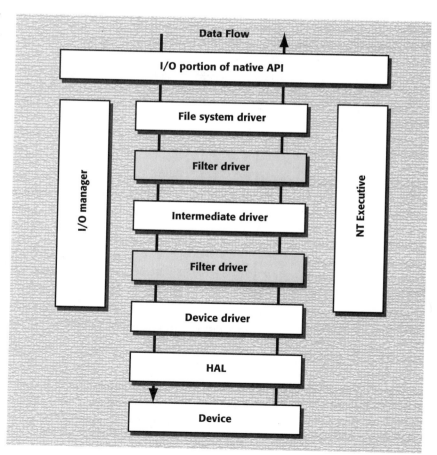

the file system driver and the I/O Manager API to perform any kind of function that might be desired. For example, a network redirector filter driver can intercept file commands intended for remote files and redirect them to remote file servers.

Drivers are the single component that can be added to the NT Executive to run in supervisor mode. The OS has not been designed to support third party software, other than drivers, that want to add supervisor mode functionality. In today's commercial computer marketplace, a consumer can buy a computer from one vendor and then buy disk drives, displays, graphic adapters, sound boards, and so on, from other vendors. The OS must be able to accommodate this spectrum of equipment built by different vendors. Therefore it is mandatory that the OS allow third parties to add software drivers for each of these hardware components that can be added to the computer.

The NT I/O Manager defines the framework in which device drivers, intermediate drivers, file system drivers, and filter drivers are dynamically added to and removed from the system and are made to work together. The basic idea of a stream of modules between the API and device was first used in the AT&T System V UNIX I/O streams (Ritchie, 1984). The dynamic stream design allows one to easily configure complex I/O systems; the System V streams were the basis of the network protocol implementations.

Also similar to System V streams, the I/O Manager directs modules by issuing *I/O request packets* (IRPs) into a stream. If the IRP is intended for a particular module, that module responds to the IRP; otherwise, it passes the IRP to the next module in the stream. Each driver in the stream has the responsibility of accepting IRPs, either reacting to the IRP if it is directed at the driver or passing it on to the next module if it is not.

All information read from or written to the device is managed as a stream of bytes, called a *virtual file*. Every driver is written to read and/or write a virtual file. Low-level device drivers transform information read from the device into a stream and transform stream information into a device-dependent format before writing it. In Exercise 12, you will have an opportunity to implement a form of virtual file for a floppy disk drive.

As a result of the design of the I/O system architecture, the API to the I/O subsystem is not as complex as one might expect. Russinovich (1998) lists 28 function calls in the Version 4.0 interface, and Nagar (1997) lists 19 essential functions. For example, subsystems can use **NtCreateFile** or **NtOpen** to create a handle to an Executive file object, **NtReadFile** and **NtWriteFile** to read and write an open file, and **NtLock** and **NtUnlock** to lock a portion of a file.

Cache Manager

A classic bottleneck to an application's performance is the time the application must wait for a physical device to process an I/O command. As processors become faster, that fraction of the total runtime spent waiting for devices to complete their I/O operations increasingly dominates the total runtime. The classic solution to the problem is to devise ways for the thread to execute concurrently with its own device I/O operations. This means that the thread is able to predict information that it will need before it actually needs it and issue an I/O request in anticipation of using data, while concurrently processing data it has already read.

The Cache Manager is designed to work with the Virtual Memory Manager and the I/O Manager to perform read-ahead and write-behind on virtual files. The idea is a classic OS idea. That is, since files are usually accessed sequentially, whenever a thread reads byte i, it is likely to read byte $i + 1$ soon thereafter. Therefore, on a read-ahead strategy, when the thread requests that byte i be read from the device, the Cache Manager asks the Virtual Memory Manager to prepare a buffer to hold $K + 1$ bytes of information from the virtual file and instructs the I/O Manager to read byte i and the next K bytes into the buffer. Then when the thread requests byte $i + 1, i + 2, \ldots, i + K$, those bytes will have already been read, so the thread need not wait for a device operation to complete. The write-behind strategy works similarly.

Most of the Cache Manager's operation is transparent above the **NTOSKRNL** API. The Win32 API has only four attributes that it can set when **CreateFile** is called to influence the Cache Manager's operation (see Exercise 9). These attributes are essentially information to assure the Cache Manager that the thread will access the information in the file sequentially. The main clients for the Cache Manager are drivers that are added to the I/O Manager. It is these modules that customize the file system and use the file-caching facilities provided by this manager.

The Native API

While the Executive and Kernel are designed and programmed as separate modules, they are combined into the **NTOSKRNL.EXE** executable when NT is built. The combined Executive and Kernel module (with the underlying HAL) implements the full NT OS. In Version 5.0, **NTOSKRNL** exports about 240 functions (Russinovich, 1998), most of which are *undocumented*, meaning that only subsystem developers should base their software on the functions.[1] Developers call this interface the *NT Native API* (Russinovich, 1998; Nagar, 1997) or the *Executive API* (Solomon, 1998). In this book, it is called the Native API. Microsoft provides Windows NT with a set of complementary subsystems, some of which provide more abstract APIs that application programmers are expected to use.

NT Subsystems

Software systems are often constructed as a layered architecture. Layer *i* is constructed using the services provided by layer *i* − 1 ("at the layer *i* − 1 interface"), creating its own services and exporting them through its own (layer *i*) interface. There are several reasons for the popularity of layered architectures.

- It is a simple strategy for dividing and conquering a large problem.
- Each layer implements a well-defined subset of the total system functionality.
- The functionality at layer *i* can be designed and tested (or proven correct) as a manageable unit.
- Layer *i* + 1 services can simplify the way work is done using layer *i* or lower.
- Layer *i* + 1 services can be ported across different implementations of layer *i*.

In the Windows NT architecture, *subsystems* provide a layer of service above the Native API. There can be many different subsystems, some related, but others independent of one another, as functionality is added to the computer system. For example, a typical Windows NT system includes

- the Win32 subsystem,
- the WinLogon service (to authenticate users, using the LSA server and Security Reference Monitor described in the NT Executive section, when they begin to use the system),

---

[1] Note that even though *application* programmers are generally discouraged from using the undocumented Executive/Kernel functions, various development kits for creating new device drivers or otherwise extending the kernel functionality *rely* on this API. You do not have to work for Microsoft to use the API, but you do need considerable extra knowledge to do so. More important, your code might have to be changed with each new version of Windows NT or other Microsoft OS.

- a remote procedure call service, and
- perhaps a Win16 subsystem.

If the Windows NT machine were required to support POSIX application programs, a POSIX subsystem could be added as a component in the subsystem layer.

Each subsystem uses the Native API to provide the services it implements. The *environment subsystems* behave as a traditional interior layer. In the layered architecture approach, they use the Native API, add functionality and services, and then export their own API. In the Microsoft strategy, subsystem APIs are *documented* APIs, meaning that a programmer can write new software at the next higher-level layer and be assured that the API will be unchanged when implementations at a lower-level layer in the architecture are changed.

Figure 8 shows how this layering works in NT. The *Win32 Subsystem* exports a documented interface, the *Win32 API*, as a set of about 1,000 functions $\{f_0, f_1, \ldots, fn\}$. The Win32 API is a documented interface. An application programmer can write software above the Win32 subsystem that calls the functions, $\{f_0, f_1, \ldots, fn\}$ to accomplish an application-specific task.

The Win32 Subsystem also provides one other type of service: It implements a user interface management system, since the Executive/Kernel does not have one of these. This is primarily a matter of practicality—when the system begins to run, *some* part of the system software needs to read the keyboard and mouse and manage the display. Rather than have each environment subsystem provide its own user interface, the Win32 Subsystem implements the common window manager for all subsystems. This means that there is a single human-computer interaction model implemented in a single subsystem, but used by all other subsystems.

A subsystem's design can be simple or complex. In the simplest case, each function or service that the subsystem exports is implemented wholly within the

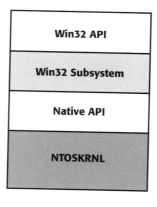

Figure 8

The Win32 API

subsystem itself. For example, the subsystem might keep a data structure filled with information it extracts from information obtained through the Native API. When a program queries the subsystem, it simply reads the data structure and returns a result without ever interacting with the OS.

A slightly more complex case occurs when a subsystem function requires that the subsystem implementation interact with the OS via the Native API. For example, the Win32 API function **CreateProcess** causes the Win32 subsystem to call the Native API functions **NtCreateProcess** and **NtCreateThread**.

The most complex design requires that the interaction between the subsystem and the OS be more complicated than a function call or two. The Executive provides a special interprocess communication facility called the *Local Procedure Call* (LPC) facility. The LPC facility allows one process to call a function that is implemented in another process. This requires special OS activity, since the target procedure is not known to the compiler and link editor and is not determined until the processes are running. When the calling process starts an LPC, the OS takes the call request, finds the procedure in the target process's address space, and calls the target procedure. Two processes can communicate with one another by making LPCs back and forth. The most complex subsystem designs use LPCs to invoke Executive functions (see Exercise 5 for additional discussion).

Win32 API: The Programmer's View of NT

The Win32 API is the "official OS interface" to all Microsoft OSs: Windows NT, Windows 95, Windows 98, and Windows CE. The rationale for having a single OS API relates to portability. That is, if all Microsoft OSs can export the same API, then an application writer can produce application software that will work on all OS versions. (This is the same strategy that UNIX implementers have used for many years; different kernel implementations provide a standard system call interface for all UNIX applications. The Berkeley Software Distribution (BSD) UNIX and POSIX system call APIs have many different implementations.) Further, enhancements to any of the OS products still provide the same services (presumably of a better quality) via the same, fixed interface. The cost of adopting this strategy is the need for a subsystem between the OS's native API and the API used by the application programmers.

MS-DOS created a set of fundamental OS services on which application programmers came to depend. Unfortunately, the original MS-DOS API is very old (MS-DOS first came out in about 1980). As a result, it had many built-in dependencies on 16-bit address spaces, single thread of execution, and so on. The MS-DOS API was upgraded to a Windows interface, now generally regarded as the Win16 API (implemented by the Win16 subsystem). Yet that still was not adequate to allow programmers to use the full power of Windows NT, Windows 9x, and CE. As shown in Figure 9, all of Microsoft's current OS family implement some variant of the Win32 API. Whenever an application programmer writes code for a Microsoft OS, the only documented interfaces available are the Win32 API versions for each OS. There are few differences between the Windows 9x and Windows NT implementations of Win32 API. Since CE is aimed at such hardware as palmtop computers and television set-top boxes, its variant of the Win32 API is distinctly different from the "mainstream" API. Those differences will be apparent when you use the API documentation in solving the exercises.

The Win32 API has about 1,000 function calls (remember that the Native API has about 240 functions). The Win32 API uses most of the same abstractions that appear at the Native API, including processes, threads, objects, handles, and files. Specific parts of the Win32 API are introduced with each exercise as needed. As you gain experience using Win32 API, you will quickly learn to use the remaining parts on your own.

One reason the Win32 API is so much larger than the Native API is that the Win32 API also includes the interface to all of the graphics and user interfaces components, code that is not part of NT.[2] In this lab manual, the graphics and user interface portions of the Win32 API are ignored. Interested programmers should consult one of the many books on Windows programming (such as Rector and Newcomer, 1997) to learn about this topic.

The Lab Environment

The Executive and Kernel have been designed to provide OS functions independent of whether there is a graphics window user interface; all of the windows functionality is implemented in the Win32 subsystem and the supervisor mode DLLs, **USER32.DLL** and **GDI32.DLL**. It is entirely possible to study Windows NT design and implementation with only a minimum of attention to the windows and graphics functions. All exercises in this book are written so that you execute your solutions using a simple ASCII shell, the NT console (**cmd.exe**). The **cmd.exe** interface has the appearance of the MS-DOS com-

---

[2] Technically, one might argue with this statement. In Version 3.x NT, much of the graphics and user interface code was implemented in the Win32 subsystem as user-mode code, but in Version 4.0, considerable portions of this code were moved into system space. Since the Win32 API is the documented interface, application programmers continue to use the same interface to obtain services, but the Version 4.0 implementation can provide substantially higher performance because of the supervisor-mode implementation of these functions.

Figure 9

Microsoft OS Family

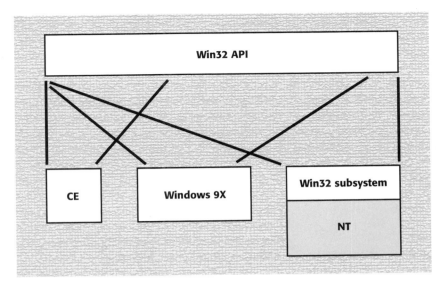

mand.com shell, but it has supplementary functionality that can be implemented only in a multitasking environment such as Windows NT. Programmers familiar with the MS-DOS shell will find the Windows NT shell intuitive to use but substantially more powerful.

Even though your solutions will be run from **cmd.exe**, it is convenient for you to develop your software in the full Windows environment. Your lab machine should be configured as a normal NT Workstation. The CD-ROMs that accompany the bundled version of this book include a copy of NT that you can install on your own PC.

The solutions to the exercises have been prepared using Microsoft Visual C++ Version 5.0. This software package is designed to develop software for the Win32 API environment; it provides all of the libraries and compiling tools for using the OS. The CD-ROM also includes a copy of Visual C++.

Some of the exercises use tools to inspect the state of Windows NT as it executes. The manual does not presume the existence of all tools available, as some of them are delivered only with specialized products. The tools that are needed are introduced in the exercise where they are first used.

Your instructor might have already installed the environment on your laboratory computers, so you should be able to start with the exercises immediately. If you have the CD-ROMs, you can also install them on your own PC.

You can learn more about the details of Windows NT by reading reference materials devoted to NT internals.

- Solomon (1998) provides the most current and comprehensive discussion of Windows NT internals, and much of the explanation in this manual of NT's internal behavior is derived from his book (and from discussions with David Solomon).

- Nagar (1997) provides a detailed discussion of how the I/O Manager can be extended to meet specialized needs. This book has much more programming information than does Solomon's book. Since the file system is the part of the supervisory-mode software that is intended to be extended, this book focuses on that aspect of the OS.

- Richter (1997) and Hart (1997) are devoted to the low-level details of programming the Win32 API. Also, Richter (1997) provides the most detailed examples and explanations of how to use Windows NT via the Win32 API, and it is highly recommended if you want to learn more about Win32 API programming. There are many examples in Richter that are similar to the examples in this lab manual, though all of those examples use the full graphics interface rather than the **cmd.exe** interface used in this manual.

- Rector and Newcomer (1997) provide a higher-level view of the interface (including more comprehensive information about programming the graphical part of the interface).

- Davis (1996) provides a comprehensive description of the network APIs used when programming Windows NT.

Because of the commercial importance of Windows NT, there are many other excellent sources of information. Some of it is accessible over the Web. Start at the main Microsoft site **www.microsoft.com**. Also, the site, **www.sys-internals.com**, is maintained by an organization that is independent of Microsoft, yet which has incredibly detailed information. While solving the exercises in this manual, you will almost certainly benefit from a visit to these sites.

part 2

The Lab Exercises

The exercises in this book are intended to complement the materials you learn in your undergraduate OS course. In the lecture part of your course, you are focusing on concepts and issues, with side discussions on Linux, UNIX, and/or NT. In this manual, the goal is for you to put those theories into practice via a series of hands-on exercises for Windows NT.

The dozen exercises in this manual use the Win32 API. By the time you have completed them, you will have studied and experimented with considerable OS software and should have gained a deep insight into how Windows NT and other modern OSs are designed.

The exercises address almost all the aspects of the OS. Following is a summary of each exercise.

- **Exercise 1**: Introduces the computational model that application programmers use. The intent of this exercise is to introduce you to the way processes, threads, and objects are organized.
- **Exercise 2**: The first programming assignment. You will learn to write software to create processes and threads.
- **Exercise 3**: Focuses on the characteristics of Executive objects. Here, you will learn how the Executive exports objects to user space and what mechanisms are used to manipulate Kernel objects.
- **Exercise 4**: Concentrates on using Executive synchronization objects. You will learn how the Windows NT synchronization model is built and how different types of objects can be used to achieve different kinds of synchronization.

- **Exercise 5**: Introduces Windows NT's interprocess communication mechanisms. The file I/O model is used as the interface for these mechanisms, so it is also explained in this exercise.

- **Exercise 6**: Extends the interprocess communication tools to those that work over a network. You will learn how to use Windows NT's TCP/IP tools while you gain insight as to how they are designed.

- **Exercise 7**: Introduces the virtual memory model and teaches you how to control its behavior.

- **Exercise 8**: Describes the memory-mapped file mechanism, the OS mechanism that supports most of NT's cross-address space communication tools.

- **Exercise 9**: Looks at efficient file operations, specifically file buffering (caching) and asynchronous file I/O.

- **Exercise 10**: Introduces you to several of the issues involved in disk device I/O without your having to write a kernel-level Windows NT device driver.

- **Exercise 11**: Focuses on the part of the I/O manager that administers files (copying files, listing directories, erasing files, and so on).

- **Exercise 12**: Extends Exercise 11 by having you build file read and write routines. Besides reading and writing the data, you will learn about file caching (also called buffering) and asynchronous procedure calls.

The Lab Exercises

one

Managing Multiple Tasks

In this exercise, you are to observe the behavior of Windows NT processes and threads. Every Windows NT installation has many different processes and threads in execution at one time. In this exercise, you will use various tools to observe the status and activity of these processes, threads, and various other objects. You will learn about:

▶ Processes and threads

▶ The Task Manager

▶ The Process Viewer

▶ The Performance Monitor

INTRODUCTION

Almost all contemporary computers use the von Neumann architecture. A von Neumann computer is built on the idea that computation can be accomplished by storing a program in the executable memory and then having the control unit fetch and decode instructions from the memory. The control unit then directs other hardware components to execute the instruction. At this level of computing, there is no notion of user, process, or sharing. There is just the idea that the control unit executes one instruction after another from the memory.

A multiprogramming OS creates an abstraction in which multiple programs can be stored in the machine's memory at the same time and the control unit periodically switches from executing instructions in one of the programs to executing instructions in a different one. At the hardware level, it is irrelevant that some instructions are from one program and others are from another one.

From the control unit perspective, such a shift is nothing more than a branch instruction. However, from the perspective of the different program users, this means that the computer executes one program for a while and then switches to another one—the processor is being shared by means of time multiplexing. The OS can perpetuate this multiprogramming perspective by creating ways to enable programmers to load programs into memory, cause them to be executed, cause one program to temporarily suspend the execution of another, and so on. Building this kind of software environment results in defining strategies called software abstractions. Part 1 showed that the NT Kernel creates abstractions of threads and objects on top of the von Neumann hardware. The NT Executive uses the Kernel abstractions to create the model of a process in which a thread can execute. The thread is prevented from executing programs that are not in the memory allocated to the process—its address space—and threads in other processes are prevented from executing the program in its address space. This exercise gives you some experience in observing NT processes and threads and related concepts.

The Windows NT computational model uses the traditional OS notion of a program in execution and the idea that the executing program can use the system's resources. Files and other resources can be requested and used by these executing programs just as they are in other contemporary OSs. However, unlike older systems, the Windows NT computational environment refines the process model into one that separates processes and threads. The traditional notion of a process is replaced by the contemporary idea that a process defines a logical environment in which computation can take place—an address space with a set of system resources—and one or more threads that perform work within the process's address space.

The simplest instance of the Windows NT process-thread idea is for a single thread to execute within a process. This corresponds exactly to the idea of a process in a classic OS such as UNIX and is also the result when you write code to create a process (see Exercise 2). However, the NT Process Manager also allows programmers to write programs that create other threads in a process, all executing the process's program. As in other OSs, concurrent operation means that the multiple threads logically execute at the same time, though in a uniprocessor system they will execute sequentially in some arbitrary serial order.

When you start your Windows NT workstation, perhaps 15–20 processes are created with over 100 threads. What are all of these processes and threads doing? There are several different tools you can use to find out which processes are running at any given time. (Whenever you start one of these tools, you will be creating another process for that tool. As you peruse the list of processes using a tool, you will "see yourself" in the list.) Two such tools that you will use throughout these exercises are the Task Manager and the Process Viewer.

Task Manager (TASKMGR.EXE)

The Task Manager can be started in a number of ways, for example by pressing Ctrl-Shift-Esc or by pressing Ctrl-Alt-Del and then selecting the Task Manager option from the dialog box that is displayed. The Task Manager reads system status from the Executive and dynamically displays that status in a window. There are three displays.

1. A display of the *applications* that are currently running. An application program is an executable image. One or more processes might be using it concurrently.
2. A display of the *processes* that are currently running. Each process is listed, along with its internal process identification, the fraction of the total processor (CPU) time it has recently used, the CPU time the process has used since it was created, and the process's current memory utilization. You will probably be surprised to see that most of the time has been used by the "System Idle Process."
3. A display of the processor and memory *performance*. The graphics displays are plots of the CPU and memory utilization, with a "digital speedometer" to the left of the time plot. The speedometer shows the instantaneous CPU/Memory utilization, and the plot shows the recent history of instantaneous utilizations. This display also shows the total number of handles (to Executive objects) that have been allocated, the total number of threads that are currently executing, and the total number of processes that exist. The memory information is discussed further in Exercise 7.

Process Viewer (PVIEW.EXE)

The Process Viewer is actually part of the Visual C++ environment. You can run it from **cmd.exe** by typing the full pathname of the location of **PVIEW.EXE** on your disk or invoke it from the "Start/Programs/Visual C++" menu. Process Viewer is another graphics window application that provides considerable information about the OS status. First, it tells you the official name of your computer. Next, it presents a scrollable window that describes the set of processes that are currently active; this should have the same processes in it as the Task Manager displays in the Processes display. One new piece of information in the process display is the ratio of time the process has spent in supervisor ("Privileged") mode versus the time it has spent executing in user mode. The first line in the Process Viewer window is "_Total," meaning the sum of times for the other lines.

Part 1, Section C includes a discussion of thread scheduling. The Process Viewer shows the key information used by a thread for scheduling. The "Priority" field shows the process's priority class, and the "Thread Priority" field shows the Win32 thread priority settings used by all of the threads. There is a scrollable window to list all threads that execute in the process currently highlighted in the "Process" scrollable window. If you select one of the threads in the "Thread(s)" window, the Process Viewer will tell you detailed information about that thread (its User PC value, Start Address, the number of Context Switches it has incurred, and its current dynamic priority).

Process Viewer takes a snapshot of the system status when it is started and whenever you tell it to take a new snapshot by selecting the "Refresh" button. Note that it is easy to be fooled by studying an old snapshot while the system has moved on to another state.

Some System Processes

Windows NT has many different processes in execution on every machine. The following list offers a taste of some of those you should see when using the inspection tools. You should also be able to pick out others that reflect work you are currently doing on your workstation.

System Idle Process. The System Idle Process (or "idle" or zero page thread process) is created to run whenever nothing else is running. It has only a single thread and is present on every NT system.

System. The System is a process that hosts threads that will run only in supervisor mode to perform various OS functions. This process is used by various parts of **NTOSKRNL** or drivers. You can expect to see many threads running in this process if you inspect it using the Process Viewer.

Session Manager (SMSS.EXE). The Session Manager serves two purposes. First, it initializes various parts of the Executive and the Win32 subsystem. Second, after the system has completed the startup sequence, it provides a bridge between applications and the debugger.

Win32 Subsystem (CSRSS.EXE). The Win32 Subsystem is the part of the subsystem that manages the display and keyboard, as well as other work to support the Win32 API.

Windows Logon (WINLOGIN.EXE). When a user intends to start using Windows NT, or quits using NT, Windows Logon manages the procedure. As a result of a successful user logon, this process will create a **USERINIT.EXE**

process that will launch another process (**EXPLORER.EXE**) to handle the human-computer interaction. **USERINIT.EXE** will then terminate.

Local Security Authority Server (**LSASS.EXE**). During user authentication, the **WINLOGIN** process will interact with the LSA server (mentioned in Part 1, Section D), or **LSASS** process. It implements the user space part of the authentication procedure for accessing objects, interacting with the Executive Security Reference Monitor mechanism.

Services (**SERVICES.EXE**). NT provides a number of "services" that might be a driver or some system process. Examples of services are the part of the OS that manages print spooling and various network tasks. **SERVICES** will create miscellaneous other processes, depending on how the system is configured and what the user/administrator has asked it to do.

Process and Thread Descriptors

The background information in Part 1 (Sections C and D) combined with the previous information should have enabled you to develop an intuitive view of processes and threads. The Process Manager must keep track of all of this information in a set of data structures (recall the description of the EPROCESS, KPROCESS, ETHREAD, and KTHREAD blocks in Part 1).

When a process is created, a Kernel process object is created to hold the Kernel's information about the process. Next, an Executive process object is created (the Kernel process object is saved inside the Executive process object; see Figure 4). The thread that created the process is given a handle to the Executive process object that it uses to reference the object in all future interactions with it. The Executive process object contains the following information (Solomon, 1998).

- Kernel process object (the part of the descriptor managed by the Kernel), including
  - pointer to the page directory,
  - kernel time,
  - user time,
  - process's spinlock,
  - process base priority,
  - process state, and
  - list of the Kernel thread descriptors that are using this process
- Parent identification: A way to uniquely identify which process created this one

- Exit status
- Creation and termination times
- Information about the memory being used by the process
- Security information
- A description of the executable image being used by the process (including a pointer to a user-space Process Environment Block)
- Process priority class used by the thread scheduler
- A list of handles used by this process (the list of resources used by the process)
- A pointer to a block of Win32-specific information associated with this process

You can see that the Task Manager and Process Viewer are obtaining information from the Kernel process object.

PROBLEM STATEMENT

This exercise introduces you to the Windows NT multithreaded application environment by having you experiment with multiple processes, each having multiple threads. There is a worksheet (MS Word 97 document) on the CD-ROM (also available from the manual's web page) that you can copy and open to complete the homework. Close all other windows on your desktop, retrieve the worksheet for Exercise 1 (**worksheet1.doc**) from the course materials, open the document, and follow the instructions. There is also a copy of the worksheet at the end of this exercise.

LAB ENVIRONMENT

All tools used in this exercise are packaged in the software on the CD-ROMs that accompanies this book. They are also available with the standard NT and Visual C++ product packages.

Tools: Task Manager, Performance Monitor, Process Viewer, and **winmsd.exe** (a program provided with NT's administrative tools)

ATTACKING THE PROBLEM

In the worksheet, you are asked to perform some activity to change the status of the processes being inspected. The simplest activity you can perform to cause the system to do work is to move the mouse. This causes the mouse device to start producing a sequence of information about its current location and sending it to the computer, which causes I/O interrupts. The Windows system must ultimately get the mouse input and change what it shows on the display (another I/O instruction). You can provide more work for the system by moving an entire window around the display (instead of just the cursor). You can also introduce work by running different commands in the **cmd.exe** window.

You will find the **cmd.exe** command **start** to be quite useful. It works as follows. Type to **cmd.exe**:

```
start <an_NT_command>
```

This command will create a new console (**cmd.exe**) window and run the command in that window.

You will also use two "synthetic" programs (from the CD-ROMs or the web page). You can run them from **cmd.exe** with

```
cpuload <number_of_threads> <run_time>
```

and

```
diskload <number_of_threads> <run_time>
```

Both commands take two command line parameters, the numbers shown in angular braces. The first, **number_of_threads**, is used by the synthetic program to create as many threads to run in the process as you request. The second parameter, **run_time**, is the number of seconds that the synthetic program should execute before it terminates. You can start a multithreaded process running one of these programs and inspect its behavior using the Process Viewer. You should notice a strong correlation between **number_of_threads** and the number of threads that Process Viewer reports. Finally, the **diskload** program depends on the presence of a text file named "**dummyin2.txt**" on which the program performs file operations. If your environment does not include such a file, create one with random text characters using the NT notepad application.

These programs are designed to make demands on the computer's hardware resources following a specific pattern. Such a program is called a *synthetic workload generator*. That is, a synthetic workload generator is an actual program that uses the machine's resources (it creates a real workload on the machine), but it does not accomplish any useful work. Each synthetic workload generator begins as a process and a thread that immediately creates several other threads to execute in the process's address space. These threads will sporadically use large amounts of different system resources. You will use various tools to inspect their effect on the system and then report your findings on the worksheet.

Windows NT is built with a number of performance counters to measure its own performance. The Performance Monitor is a Windows tool to display a trace of the value of any of those performance counters over time. It is easy to use. Start the Performance Monitor either by typing, from **cmd.exe**, the **perfmon** command or by selecting it from the "Start/Administrative Tools" menu. This will create a relatively large window with nothing in it. You can trace/plot any counter by selecting "Add to Chart . . . " from the Performance Monitor's "Edit" menu. The default set of counters returned are those that relate to the "Processor" performance ("Processor" appears in the "Object:" field of the dialog box). You can select any counters for the processor or scroll through the object list to find another class of counters in which you are interested. This should be enough information to get you started using the Performance Monitor. Experiment with it.

Finally, there is a program delivered with the Visual C++ package called **pstat.exe** (located in the Visual C++ **bin\winnt** folder). Run it from **cmd.exe**. After doing this once, you will want to run it through a screen-by-screen viewer, such as

pstat.exe | more

or pipe its output to a file

pstat.exe >temp.txt

so that you can browse through the **temp.txt** file using the notepad application.

REFERENCES

Solomon, David A., *Inside Windows NT,* Second Edition, Microsoft Press, Redmond, Wash., 1998.

Worksheet for Exercise 1

1. Be sure that all windows are closed except the one in which you are reading and editing this document. Start a window running **cmd.exe** (select "Start/Programs/Command prompt").
2. Type the **hostname** command to find the name of the computer you are using.
3. Type **winmsd.exe** to determine the following.
   a. Which version of Windows NT are you using?
   b. What is the type and speed of the CPU in your machine?

c. How much space is formatted into your C: drive?

d. How much space is used on your C: drive?

e. How much physical memory is configured into your machine?

f. How much of the memory is used by the Kernel?

g. How many services are running?

4. Terminate **winmsd.exe**, and start **perfmon.exe** ("Performance Monitor"). Select "Edit" from the "Add to Chart" menu. Add counters for interrupts/second, privileged time, processor time, and user time (all from the "Object: Processor" counter set). (Leave this tool running until you have finished answering question 6.)

a. What do each of these plots represent?

b. What operations can you perform using **cmd.exe**, the mouse, and/or the keyboard to make the number of interrupts/second be as large as possible?

c. What operations can you perform using **cmd.exe**, the mouse, and/or the keyboard to make the amount of privileged time be as large as possible?

d. What operations can you perform using **cmd.exe**, the mouse, and/or the keyboard to make the amount of processor time be as large as possible?

5. The VC++ package contains a program named **pview.exe** ("Process Viewer"), stored in a path similar to (but perhaps slightly different from)

C:\Program Files\DevStudio\VC\bin\winnt\pview.exe

Notice that this is a static display of information, meaning that when the tool starts, it determines the data it will show and then the display does not change. You can update the display to show newer data by using the "Refresh" button. (Leave this tool running until you have finished answering question 6.)

a. How many processes are running?

b. What is the idle process?

c. What fraction of the total time does the idle process spend in Privileged time and User time?

d. What is the base priority class of the idle process?

e. What is the priority class of the thread running in the idle process?

f. What is the dynamic priority of the idle thread in the idle process?

g. What is the **pview** process?

h. What is the base priority class of the **pview** process?

i. How many threads are running in the **pview** process?

j. What is the priority class of the thread running in the **pview** process?

k. What is the dynamic priority of each of the threads in the **pview** process?

l. Does any process have more than two threads running? (If so, which ones?)

6. Start the Task Manager by pressing Ctrl-Shift-Esc.

a. What applications are currently running?

b. Look at the "Processes" display. The "PID" field is the process's internal identifier; what is the correlation between a process's PID and the parenthesized hexadecimal number in the Process Viewer (**pview**) display?

c. Look at the "Performance" display. Which plot on the Performance Monitor is the same as the "CPU Usage History" curve in the Task Manager?

d. Is there any plot on the Performance Monitor that provides the same information as the "Memory Usage History" plot in the Task Manager?

e. How many handles are currently open in the entire system?

f. How is this correlated to the number of Executive objects in the system?

g. How many threads exist in the system?

h. How many processes exist in the system?

7. Close the Task Manager, Performance Monitor, and Process Viewer. Run the program in

...\Exercise 1\Programs\CPULOAD.EXE <N> <RUN_TIME>

This is a synthetic program that creates a process with N threads that will run for **RUN_TIME** seconds and then halt. Run the program with $N = 3$ for any runtime you choose (perhaps a couple of minutes).

a. How many threads are running in the process? If it is not the same as N, why not?

b. What is the effect of the threads on the CPU usage?

c. Is the CPU load primarily privileged or user computing?

d. What is the range of dynamic priorities under which the **CPULOAD** threads run?

8. Run the program in

...\Exercise 1\Programs\DISKLOAD.EXE <N> <RUN_TIME>

This is a synthetic program that creates a process with N threads that will run for **RUN_TIME** seconds and then halt. Run the program with $N = 3$ for any runtime you choose (perhaps a couple of minutes).

a. What resources are this process and its threads using most heavily?

b. What tools can you use to quantify their use of the resources?

c. What measure of usage can you supply?

two

Writing Multithreaded Software

In this exercise, you will write software that creates and uses multiple processes and multiple threads. It contains a lot of detailed information, so it has been partitioned into two parts. In Part A, you write code to create multiple processes, and in Part B, you create multiple threads within a process. You will learn about:

▶ Invoking Windows NT services

▶ Using object handles

▶ Determining the system time

▶ Using the online documentation

▶ The details of the CreateProcess, CreateThread, and _beginthreadex functions

INTRODUCTION

This exercise introduces you to the methodology for constructing concurrent software (the discussion continues through the next three exercises). Writing concurrent software is useful for two reasons. First, modern application software is written as units that execute concurrently. Second, since application software uses the concurrent model, modern OSs such as Windows NT must provide many different tools for programmers to manage concurrent applications. This exercise considers concurrency at both the process and thread levels. The programs you wrote in your introductory programming course, data structures course, and even in a programming languages course all probably assumed that when the code was compiled and executed, a single process with a single thread of execution would run your algorithm. You have been trained to think in terms of sequential execution of an algorithm.

The next generation of software attempts to take advantage of the multiple processors in your computer or of other processors available over the network. This means that traditional sequential models of computation are rapidly being replaced by concurrent models with multiple processes and threads. Part 1 and Exercise 1 have provided the conceptual information about processes and threads in Windows NT. Now you are ready to start looking at the details for creating processes and threads using the Win32 API.

Creating a Process

One process can create another process by calling the Win32 API **CreateProcess** function (which, in turn, calls the Native API functions **NtCreateProcess** and **NtCreateThread**). Whenever a process is created, the calling process is directing the Executive to perform a large amount of work: to set up a new address space and allocate resources to the process and to create a new base thread. Once the new process has been created, the old process will continue using its old address space while the new one operates in a new address space with a new base thread. This means that there can be many different options for creating the process, so the **CreateProcess** function has many parameters, some of which can be quite complex.[1] After the Executive has created the new process, it will return a handle for the child process and a handle for the base thread in the process.

Following is a copy of the function prototype for **CreateProcess** (taken verbatim from the Win32 API reference manual). The first thing you should notice is that the function prototype does not use any standard C types. Instead, it uses a set of types defined in the **windows.h** file (see the "Simple Types" entry in the online Visual C++ documentation), many of which are implemented as standard C types. This level of indirection in name types creates an abstract interface that Windows NT implementers can use as they wish.

---

[1] Contrast this with the simple **fork ( )** call used in UNIX, in which there are *no* parameters; the child's behavior is completely defined by the parent's profile and default behavior. If you are already familiar with the UNIX system call interface, the difference between **fork** and **CreateProcess** will give you a good idea of the kinds of differences you will see between the Win32 API or Native API and the UNIX system call interface.

```
BOOL CreateProcess(
        LPCTSTR lpApplicationName,
            // pointer to name of executable module
        LPTSTR lpCommandLine,
            // pointer to command line string
        LPSECURITY_ATTRIBUTES lpProcessAttributes,
            // pointer to process security attributes
        LPSECURITY_ATTRIBUTES lpThreadAttributes,
            // pointer to thread security attributes
        BOOL bInheritHandles,       // handle inheritance flag
        DWORD dwCreationFlags,      // creation flags
        LPVOID lpEnvironment,
            // pointer to new environment block
        LPCTSTR lpCurrentDirectory,
            // pointer to current directory name
        LPSTARTUPINFO lpStartupInfo,
            // pointer to STARTUPINFO
        LPPROCESS_INFORMATION lpProcessInformation
            // pointer to PROCESS_INFORMATION
);
```

The ten parameters in **CreateProcess** provide great flexibility to the programmer, but for the simple case, a default value can be used for many of them. In this exercise, you will use a relatively simple set of parameters and address the details of the other parameters in subsequent exercises.

lpApplicationName **and** lpCommandLine

The first two parameters, **lpApplicationName** and **lpCommandLine**, provide two different ways to define the name of the file that is to be executed by the process's base thread.[2] **lpApplicationName** is a string representation of the *name* of the file to be executed, and **lpCommandLine** is a string representation of the C-style *command line* to run the process from **cmd.exe**. A set of rules explains the conditions under which each name should be used. That is, if you pass a **NULL** for **lpApplicationName** and a command line string for **lpCommandLine**, your code will be consistent with most C environments (including UNIX environments). This is the recommended approach. Be sure to

---

[2] The reasons for providing both ways are related to compatibility with multiple subsystems. This is an example of how the pressures of commercial products cause software to have compromises in its design.

consult the online Win32 API reference manual (see the Appendix for more on how to use the Microsoft Developers Network—MSDN—online documentation for NT, Visual C++, and other Microsoft products) to understand the details for these parameters, such as how pathnames are handled.

For example, suppose you want to create a process and have it run the **notepad.exe** program on a file named "**temp.txt**". You set **lpCommandLine** to point at the string with the filename[3] for notepad.

```
#include   <string.h>
...
strcpy(lpCommandLine,
    "C:\\WINNT\\SYSTEM32\\NOTEPAD.EXE temp.txt");
CreateProcess(NULL, lpCommandLine, ...);
```

LpProcessAttributes, lpThreadAttributes, **and** bInheritHandles

The two security attribute parameters, **lpProcessAttributes** and **lpThread-Attributes**, and the **bInheritHandles** parameter can all be set to their default values: **NULL** for the security attributes and **FALSE** for the inheritance. The use of the security attributes and the inheritance flag is explained in Exercise 3. The previous **CreateProcess** call can now be refined to

```
CreateProcess(NULL, lpCommandLine, NULL, NULL, FALSE, ...);
```

dwCreationFlags

The **dwCreationFlags** parameter is used to control the priority and other aspects of the new process.

The child process can be created with any of the four priority classes by passing the **HIGH_PRIORITY_CLASS**, **IDLE_PRIORITY_CLASS**, **NORMAL_PRIOR-ITY_CLASS**, or **REALTIME_PRIORITY_CLASS** as a value. The default value is **NORMAL_PRIORITY_CLASS**, unless the parent has **IDLE_PRIORITY_CLASS** (in which case the child also has **IDLE_PRIORITY_CLASS**).

A process with **HIGH_PRIORITY_CLASS** has threads that will preempt the threads of processes with an **IDLE_PRIORITY_CLASS** or **NORMAL_PRIOR-ITY_CLASS**. **HIGH_PRIORITY_CLASS** threads are usually time-critical

---

[3] The pathname shown in the code is the one on my system. The **notepad.exe** file may be located in a different location on your machine, depending on how it was set up.

processes. **IDLE_PRIORITY_CLASS** threads run only when there are no other threads to run.

REALTIME_PRIORITY_CLASS threads preempt all other threads of all other classes.

Other flags can be passed using the **dwCreationFlags** parameter (by logically ORing their values together). See the MSDN documentation for all of the possible values. One flag that you will find useful for this exercise is the **CREATE_NEW_CONSOLE** flag, which causes the new process to be created with its own console (**cmd.exe**) window.

If the goal was to create a new child process with a high-priority class and its own console window, the **CreateProcess** call would be refined as follows.

```
CreateProcess(NULL, lpCommandLine, NULL, NULL, FALSE,
        HIGH_PRIORITY_CLASS | CREATE_NEW_CONSOLE, ...);
```

lpEnvironment

The **lpEnvironment** parameter is used to pass a new block of environment variables to the child. If the parameter is **NULL**, the child uses the same environment variables as the parent. If it is not **NULL**, it must point to a **NULL**-terminated block of **NULL**-terminated strings, each of the form

name=value

If you use a non-**NULL** value for this parameter, be careful to distinguish between ordinary 8-bit ASCII and 16-bit Unicode characters. If you use **NULL** for this parameter, the example call becomes the following.

```
CreateProcess(NULL, lpCommandLine, NULL, NULL, FALSE,
        HIGH_PRIORITY_CLASS | CREATE_NEW_CONSOLE,
        NULL, ...);
```

lpCurrentDirectory

The **lpCurrentDirectory** string specifies the current drive and full pathname of the current directory in which the child should execute. The drive is prefixed to the full pathname using conventional MS-DOS notation. A **NULL** value causes the child to execute using the same current drive and directory as the parent. Using a **NULL** for the current drive and directory refines the sample **CreateProcess** call to the following.

```
CreateProcess(NULL, lpCommandLine, NULL, NULL, FALSE,
       HIGH_PRIORITY_CLASS | CREATE_NEW_CONSOLE,
       NULL, NULL, ...);
```

lpStartupInfo

The startup information is a C **struct** used to pass a set of miscellaneous parameters regarding window characteristics and redirection information for the console and keyboard. The information is stored in a structure of the following type.

```
typedef struct _STARTUPINFO { // si
       DWORD cb;
       LPTSTR lpReserved;
       LPTSTR lpDesktop;
       LPTSTR lpTitle;
       DWORD dwX;
       DWORD dwY;
       DWORD dwXSize;
       DWORD dwYSize;
       DWORD dwXCountChars;
       DWORD dwYCountChars;
       DWORD dwFillAttribute;
       DWORD dwFlags;
       WORD wShowWindow;
       WORD cbReserved2;
       LPBYTE lpReserved2;
       HANDLE hStdInput;
       HANDLE hStdOutput;
       HANDLE hStdError;
} STARTUPINFO, *LPSTARTUPINFO;
```

An instance of this data structure must be created in the calling program. Then its address must be passed as a parameter in **CreateProcess**. Consult the MSDN reference manual to see what all of the parameters mean. In this manual, you will use only the last three fields, and that will be in Exercise 5.

Warning: CreateProcess does not presume to know the length of the structure whose address is passed as the **lpStartupInfo** parameter. *Be sure to initialize the size field in the* **STARTUPINFO** *structure before passing it to* **CreateProcess**.

The example call can now be refined to the following.

```
STARTUPINFO startupInfo;
...
ZeroMemory(&startupInfo, sizeof(STARTUPINFO));
startInfo.cb = sizeof(startupInfo);
CreateProcess(NULL, lpCommandLine, NULL, NULL, FALSE,
       HIGH_PRIORITY_CLASS | CREATE_NEW_CONSOLE,
       NULL, NULL, &startupInfo, ...);
```

lpProcessInformation

The last parameter is the **lpProcessInformation** parameter, which points to another Win32 structure that must be supplied by the calling program, as follows.

```
typedef struct _PROCESS_INFORMATION {
       HANDLE hProcess;
       HANDLE hThread;
       DWORD dwProcessId;
       DWORD dwThreadId;
} PROCESS_INFORMATION;
```

There is no length field in this structure, so the calling process simply needs to allocate an instance of **PROCESS_INFORMATION** and pass a pointer to the instance into **CreateProcess**. When the function returns, the four parameters will have been filled in to reflect

- the handle of the newly created process (the **hProcess** field),
- the handle of the base thread (**hThread**),
- a global process identifier (**dwProcessId**) that can be used by another process to locate the newly created process, and
- a global thread identifier (**dwThreadId**).

CreateProcess allocates a handle to the process and the thread when it creates them; they are returned in the **PROCESS_INFORMATION** data structure. To avoid the possibility of creating a "handle leak" (whereby the handle is implicitly allocated to the parent process), you must explicitly deallocate each handle, for example by calling **CloseHandle**. Of course, when a process terminates, all of its handles (kept in a list in the process's descriptor) will be automatically released. Even so, since a handle is a system resource, you should make it a practice to always explicitly close handles as soon as you are through using them.

Notice that **CreateProcess** returns zero if it fails and nonzero otherwise. Win32 provides an integer error number for the last error that occurred. It is good practice to check for an error on a Win32 API call and then to check the last error if the call failed.

Here is the code for a full call to create a process.

```
#include     <windows.h>
#include     <stdio.h>
#include     <string.h>
...
STARTUPINFO startInfo;
PROCESS_INFORMATION processInfo;
...
strcpy(lpCommandLine,
        "C:\\WINNT\\SYSTEM32\\NOTEPAD.EXE temp.txt");
ZeroMemory(&startInfo, sizeof(startInfo));
startInfo.cb = sizeof(startInfo);
if(!CreateProcess(NULL, lpCommandLine, NULL, NULL, FALSE,
        HIGH_PRIORITY_CLASS | CREATE_NEW_CONSOLE,
        NULL, NULL, &startInfo, &processInfo)) {
    fprintf(stderr, "CreateProcess failed on error %d\n",
                GetLastError());
    ExitProcess(1);
};
...
CloseHandle(&processInfo.hThread);
CloseHandle(&processInfo.hProcess);
```

Creating a Thread

You can also create additional threads in the current process using the **CreateThread** Win32 API function (which uses the **NtCreateThread** Native API call). Since each thread represents an independent computation of a shared program on shared data, all within the context of an existing process address space, creating a thread requires that the programmer supply information relating to the execution environment for this thread while presuming all of the process-specific information.

The best way to discuss the procedure for creating a thread is to first look at the function prototype.

```
HANDLE CreateThread(
    LPSECURITY_ATTRIBUTES lpThreadAttributes,
            // pointer to thread security attributes
    DWORD dwStackSize,
            // initial thread stack size, in bytes
    LPTHREAD_START_ROUTINE lpStartAddress,
            // pointer to thread function
    LPVOID lpParameter,    // argument for new thread
    DWORD dwCreationFlags, // creation flags
    LPDWORD lpThreadId
            // pointer to returned thread identifier
);
```

This prototype uses six parameters to describe the characteristics of the new thread. In this case, the function will create only one handle (the one for the thread) and return it as the result of the call. Again, this means that a system resource is implicitly allocated on a successful call to **CreateThread**, so the programmer is obliged to explicitly close the handle when it is no longer being used.

To see an example of how **CreateThread** is called, a running example is used to create a new thread to run in the current process.

LpThreadAttributes

This is the same as the security attribute parameter used in **CreateProcess**, except of course there is a value only for the thread. For the simple case, it should be set to **NULL**. As mentioned earlier in this exercise, the use of the security attributes is explained in Exercise 3. The example **CreateThread** call looks like this:

CreateThread(NULL, ...);

dwStackSize

Since each thread executes independently of the other threads in the process, each has its own stack. This parameter gives the programmer a chance to set the size of the stack, though usually one would just use the default, signified by setting the value of the parameter to zero.

CreateThread(NULL, 0, ...);

LpStartAddress **and** lpParameter

With a process, it was necessary to provide the name of an executable file. However, for a thread, it is only necessary to provide the OS with an address in the current address space where the new thread should begin to execute. The **lpStartAddress** parameter is such an address. In conventional programming languages (such as C), it is generally not possible for a computation to simply start off in the middle of some procedure. A branch to a new logical context is handled by bundling the new code in a procedure and then calling the procedure at its entry point. The **lpStartAddress** is the address of an entry point for a function that has a prototype of the form

DWORD WINAPI ThreadFunc(LPVOID);

That is, in a language that checks the type of a called entry point compared to the function call (as is done in C++ and ANSI C), there must be a function prototype before an entry point address can be used as a parameter. Of course, this means that there must also be a function to implement the prototype, the function that the new thread will begin executing after it is created.

One other complication in this scenario relates to passing parameters to the function that will be executed by the new thread. Since there is a function call and prototype, if a parameter is to be passed, then either its type must be known and declared or a **void** * type must be used (to tell the compiler that the type of the parameter to the thread's function is unknown at compile time). **CreateThread** uses the latter approach; this is why the function prototype uses **LPVOID** (which is defined as a **void** *). The **lpParameter** value will be passed to the function when the new thread starts to execute it.

For the example call, assume that there is a function with the prototype

DWORD WINAPI myFunc(LPVOID);

that the new thread is to begin executing. Further, assume that the "parent thread" intends to pass an integer argument to the new "child thread." Now the example call will take the following form.

int theArg;
...
CreateThread(NULL, 0, myFunc, &theArg, ...);

dwCreationFlags

The **dwCreationFlags** parameter is used to control the way the new thread is created. Currently, there is only one possible flag value that can be passed for this parameter: **CREATE_SUSPENDED**. This value will cause the new thread to be created but to be suspended until another thread executes

ResumeThread(targetThreadHandle);

on the new thread. (**targetThreadHandle** is the handle of the new thread.) The default value is zero, which causes the thread to be active when it is created. Adding this parameter, the example call becomes

CreateThread(NULL, 0, myFunc, &theArg, 0, ...);

LpThreadId

The last parameter is a pointer to a system-wide thread identification **DWORD**. (This is analogous to the **dwThreadID** field in the **PROCESS_INFORMATION** record returned by **CreateProcess**.)

DWORD targetThreadID;

...

CreateThread(NULL, 0, myFunc, &theArg, 0, &targetThreadID);

A Complication in Using CreateThread

The previous section explained how to create a thread, *unless you happen to be using the C runtime library* (which you are, for these exercises). The C runtime library was derived in a UNIX context, in which there is no distinction between processes and threads. In the Windows NT context, many threads can be executing in a single address space. All threads have access to all of the information in the address space—after all, that is the very meaning of "executing in an address space." On the positive side, this means that it is easy for threads to share information with one another by writing into the process's variables (those that are not allocated in some thread's stack). On the negative side, this means that every variable that is not in a stack can be read or written by every thread, even if the variable might have information that is relevant only to one of the threads.

Richter (1997) provides an excellent example of such a variable, **errno**. If you have never used **errno**, think of it as a global variable that is set by a runtime function if there happened to be an error on the call; this is analogous to the value returned by **GetLastError** ( ) in Win32 API. In the UNIX context, there is no function call to get the last error; the process thread simply reads **errno**.

As long as there is only one thread executing the process—this is the only way UNIX processes can be defined—this works fine. But in Windows NT, a *race condition* can arise, as follows. Suppose there are two threads, R and S, executing in a process, and both decide to call C runtime functions concurrently. This means that on a uniprocessor system, either R or S, say R, will call the function and return. For this example, suppose that R's call resulted in an error and that **errno** got set to reflect the nature of the error (that is, R should check **errno** as soon as it has detected that its call failed). Now suppose that the thread scheduler interrupts R just after it returns but before it checks **errno**. The scheduler then dispatches S, and S calls its runtime routine. The call S made also fails, so the runtime package sets **errno** to let S know the nature of the error, *overwriting the previous value that R would have read had it not been interrupted*. S detects the call error and reads **errno** without a problem. Eventually R is given the processor and resumes execution. The first thing it does is check **errno**, and *it will see the result from S's call rather than from its own call.*

This situation will happen only under certain situations, so the error it produces will be sporadic and extremely difficult to find. How can this problem be avoided? Microsoft has provided an alternative function to **CreateThread**, called **_beginthreadex**, to be used with programs that use multiple threads at the same time they use the C runtime library. The problem occurs with any globally accessible variable used by this library (there are several of them). The Microsoft solution is to have the NT C runtime library provide a *copy* of each of these variables for each thread. Then, when a thread interacts with the runtime library, variables are shared only between the runtime code and the thread, not among all threads. The **_beginthreadex** function creates the copy for a thread in conjunction with an embedded call to **CreateThread**.

The details of **_beginthreadex** follow, beginning with its function prototype.

```
unsigned long _beginthreadex(
     void *security,
     unsigned stack_size,
     unsigned ( __stdcall *start_address )( void * ),
     void *arglist,
     unsigned initflag,
     unsigned *thrdaddr
);
```

Despite the apparent differences between the types of the parameters to **_beginthreadex** and those for **CreateThread**, you can declare the parameters described for **CreateThread** and pass them to **_beginthreadex**. This means we can translate the example **CreateThread** call described previously and program it as follows.

```
DWORD WINAPI myFunc(LPVOID);
...
```

```
LPSECURITY_ATTRIBUTES lpThreadAttributes = NULL;
DWORD stackSize = 0;
int theArg;
DWORD dwCreationFlags = 0,
DWORD targetThreadID;
...
_beginthreadex(
        (void *) lpThreadAttributes,
        (unsigned) stackSize,
        (unsigned (_stdcall *)(void *)) myFunc,
        (void *) &theArg,
        (unsigned) dwCreationFlags,
        (unsigned *) &targetThreadID
);
```

This is ugly, but it works. You can make it look better with judicious use of macros. Before you code this up and try to compile it, be sure to see additional related remarks in the Lab Environment section of this exercise.

PROBLEM STATEMENT

A command line interpreter (such as NT's **cmd.exe**, DOS's **command.com**, or UNIX's Bourne shell or C shell) is a program that provides a text-based interface for a user to direct the OS. A user runs a program from a command line interpreter by typing the name of a file that contains an executable program, followed by a set of parameters used by the program. This is the same information provided as the **lpCommandLine** parameter that is passed to **CreateProcess**. The command line interpreter parses the line to get the name of the file and then causes another thread or process to execute the command. In a UNIX-style shell, the command line process actually creates a new process that will load and execute the program from the file. The command line interpreter waits for the command to be executed and its host thread to terminate before returning a command line prompt to the user. In Part A of this exercise, you will write a program that creates a new process and executes a command in that new process; this is a fundamental part of the work done by **cmd.exe**. Part B concentrates on multiple threads. There, you will write a program to start many threads executing within a process.

Part A

Write a C program that can create a collection of processes (each with its base thread) when a user runs your program. Using the standard **cmd.exe** features, you can "launch" a process just by typing its name. If you want to start a process in its own console window, you can use the **start** command (see Exercise 1). For example, if you type a command line such as

start cmd.exe

to **cmd.exe**, then **cmd.exe** creates a new window and starts a new process with its own copy of the **cmd.exe** program. Try it now if you have not used it before.

Since the goal of the exercise is for you to experiment with creating multiple processes, you need some way to provide multiple command lines to your program. Use a text editor (such as notepad) to prepare a file with command lines (made up of ASCII characters) such as you might type to **cmd.exe**. Each line should be an exact replica of a command that you would type to **cmd.exe**. Store the series of command lines in a file, say, one named **launchset.txt**. This example uses a text file with the following lines (among others) to test my solution to this exercise.

C:\WINNT\SYSTEM32\NOTEPAD.EXE jnk.txt
C:\WINNT\SYSTEM32\CALC.EXE
C:\WINNT\SYSTEM32\CHARMAP.EXE

Next, create your program and name the resulting executable **launch.exe**. Your program will create a new process to execute each command line in the file. So if the launch set file has 20 command lines, your program will "launch" 20 processes to execute the 20 command lines. Your program must also read the name of the launch set file from its own command line. Then, if a user types

launch launchset.txt

your program will execute on the **launchset.txt** file. That is, "**launchset.txt**" is a character string parameter (the name of a file in this case) that is passed to the thread executing **launch.exe**. Your **launch** program must open the **launchset.txt** file, read each command line from the file, and launch a process to execute the command.

Part B

The launch program is a multiprocess program. The second part of the exercise is for you to write a single process, multithreaded program, one that will create multiple threads to execute within a single process. Your program, call it **mthread.exe**, will take a single integer parameter to specify the number of supplementary threads to be created and executed in the process's address space. Thus the command line to run your program is

mthread N

where **N** is an unsigned integer parameter that tells **mthread.exe** to create and execute **N** additional threads. It is acceptable to add other parameters to the command line, for example, to provide some input parameters to control the execution of each thread. The **cpuload** and **diskload** programs from Exercise 1 are examples of the **mthread** program. Use the tools you learned about in Exercise 1 to verify the existence of your threads while you are debugging your solution.

LAB ENVIRONMENT

There are three things in the lab environment that you might need to know about before preparing your solution. The first is a simple matter of ensuring that the compiler and link editor know that you are writing code to be executed from the **cmd.exe** command line, not to operate in the graphics window environment. The second is related to passing parameters to a program via the command line (in ANSI C programs); you probably have already learned about this in some earlier programming class. The last is related to the compiler and link editor environment for using the C runtime library with a multithreaded program.

Win32 Console Applications

When your code is compiled, the compiler needs to know if it should generate code that makes your program use the Windows graphics facilities or if it should treat your program like an "ordinary old C program." Because the focus of this manual is on OS issues, all of the exercises are ordinary old C programs that use **cmd.exe**. None of them have the extra features that allow them to run as full Windows graphics programs.

The first difference between a Windows graphics program and a conventional C program is the prototype for the main program. A standard prototype has the form

int main(int argc, char *argv[]);

A Windows graphics program has a prototype of the following form.

```
int WINAPI WinMain(
        HINSTANCE hInstance,         // handle to current instance
        HINSTANCE hPrevInstance,     // handle to previous instance
        LPSTR lpCmdLine,             // pointer to command line
        Int nCmdShow                 // show state of window
);
```

You must use the standard prototype for your solution.

If you are using Visual C++ to create your software, you will be preparing your software in a robust environment that has workspaces and projects (see the Appendix). When you open the Visual C++ environment, it might try to use a workspace and/or project that was used earlier. Close that workspace, and open a new project using the "File" menu. Visual C++ will want you to tell it where the new project should be placed in your directory hierarchy and the type of project. You *must* select the new project option that says "Win32 Console Application" so that the compiler and link editor will be working with the right libraries and header files. See the Appendix for additional notes on using the Visual C++ environment.

Main Program Parameters

The tradition for passing parameters to a C program came from the UNIX environment, but it became a part of standardized C (that is what is meant by the phrase "ANSI C"), so it is supported by Visual C++ and NT. With the standard C header, your main program prototype has the form

```
int main(int argc, char *argv[]);
```

Notice first that when the compiler translates this code, it will expect, somewhere in the code, a statement of the form

```
return 0;
```

You can either live with the compiler warning or place a **return** statement wherever your main program is intended to terminate. To be compliant with NT, this **return** statement should be **ExitProcess(int)**, though using this instead of the **return** will cause a compiler warning.

Now, about the command line parameters. Parameters are passed to a main program as an array of **NULL**-terminated ASCII strings in the **argv** array. (**NULL** is the character value '\0'.) The strings in the array are the blocks of nonwhite characters that appear on the command line. For example, if a user types foobar framis

to a command line interpreter, the interpreter will run a program named **foobar.exe** and pass it an **argv** array with **argv[0]** pointing at the string "foobar" and **argv[1]** pointing at the string "framis". The **argc** parameter would be set to 2 to indicate that there are two "words" on the command line and hence two elements in the **argv** array.

2

When the **foobar.exe** program starts, it reads **argc** and **argv** to retrieve the strings (and treat them however it likes: as filenames as in Part A or an integer as in Part B). Most C programming manuals explain how to use **argc** and **argv**, so if you need more information, look in the textbook you used to learn C.

Multithreaded Programs Using the C Runtime Library

In the Introduction to this exercise is a discussion that explains why _beginthreadex must be used in a multithreaded program that uses the C runtime library (instead of the **CreateThread** function). Whenever **_beginthreadex** is used, the compile/link environment must also be adjusted.

First, in the Visual C++ "Project/Settings" dialog, there is a tab for setting C/C++ parameters. The default command line has a setting of "/MLd" that must be changed to "/MTd" to tell the compiler that the code is multithreaded.

Second, in the "Link" tab, the list of libraries must include "/libcmt.lib" or "/libcmtd.lib". (The first version is for production-level linking, and the second is compatible with the debugger, so it is used if you are compiling and linking a debug version—which you should be doing for these exercises.) Add "/libcmtd.lib" to the list of libraries to be used by the link editor.

You might have to add a flag, **/nodefaultlib:library**, to the command line used by the link editor. This is done by adding it to the command line prototype in the "Project Options:" box at the bottom of the "Link" settings.

ATTACKING THE PROBLEM

Part A

Part A requires that you write a program to perform the following steps.

1. Read the command line parameters.
2. Open a file that contains a set of commands.

3. For every command:

   a. Read a command from the file.

   b. Create a new process to execute each command.

4. Terminate after all commands have finished.

Here is a code skeleton, based on these steps, that you can use to start working on Part A.

```c
#include   <windows.h>
#include   <stdio.h>

int main(int argc, char *argv[]) {

// Local variables
    FILE *fid;
    char cmdLine[...];
// Read the command line parameters
// argc should be 2 and argv[1] should be the filename
// Open a file that contains a set of commands
    fid = fopen(argv[1], "r");
// For every command:
    while (fgets(cmdLine, MAX_LINE_LEN, fid) != NULL) {
    // Read a command from the file
    // Create a new process to execute each command
    }
// Terminate after all commands have finished
}
```

One aspect of this program that might be difficult to solve is how to determine when all of the processes have finished. Unfortunately, you have not yet learned enough about the OS to know how to do this! However, each of the child processes can be started in its own console window (or detached using the **DETACHED_PROCESS** flag for the **dwCreationFlags** parameter to **CreateProcess**) and then left to terminate on its own, that is, the parent process launches each of the children and then terminates. This is normally considered to be questionable style, but it is the best you can do with the tools currently at your disposal.

Part B

In Part B, you have similar work, but you will use threads to accomplish concurrent work instead of process-thread combinations. The basic steps in a solution might be as follows.

Writing Multithreaded Software

1. Read the command line argument, **N**.
2. For 1 to **N**:
   a. Create a new thread to execute simulated work.
3. Terminate after all threads have finished.

Here is a skeleton for Part B.

```c
#include   <windows.h>
#include   <math.h>
#include   <stdio.h>
#include   <stdlib.h>

static int runFlag = TRUE;

void main(int argc, char *argv[]) {
    unsigned int runTime;

    SYSTEMTIME now;
    WORD stopTimeMinute, stopTimeSecond;

// Get command line argument, N
// Get the time the threads should run, runtime
// Calculate time to halt (learn better ways to do this later)
    GetSystemTime(&now);
    printf("mthread: Suite starting at system time %d:%d:%d\n",
            now.wHour, now.wMinute, now.wSecond);
    stopTimeSecond = (now.wSecond + (WORD) runTime) % 60;
    stopTimeMinute = now.wMinute + (now.wSecond +
                    (WORD) runTime) / 60;

// For 1 to N
    for (i = 0; i < N; i++) {
// Create a new thread to execute simulated work
            Sleep(100);   // Let newly created thread run
    }

// Cycle while children work ...
    while (runFlag) {
        GetSystemTime(&now);
        if ((now.wMinute >= stopTimeMinute)
            &&
```

```
                    (now.wSecond >= stopTimeSecond)
            )
                runFlag = FALSE;
            Sleep(1000);
    }
        Sleep(5000);
    }
```

There are some new features in this code skeleton, ones that have not been in-troduced earlier. First, notice the **Sleep(K)** call. This is a Win32 API function that causes the current thread to yield the processor and block itself until *K* ms have elapsed. The thread will wake up and enter its appropriate scheduling queue. This call is placed just after the call that creates a new thread so that the creat-ing thread will block for 100 ms (0.1 seconds), thereby giving the newly cre-ated thread a chance to run. It is a standard technique in multithread programming.

A second new feature in this code skeleton is the use of system time. This code reads the amount of time the process and thread community should exist, figures out the current time, and computes the time at which the commu-nity should halt. After the worker threads have been created to do the simu-lated work, the coordinator thread checks the current time to see if it is time to halt. If it is not time to halt, the coordinator thread goes to sleep for 1,000 ms (1 second) and then awakes and checks the time again. When enough time has elapsed, the coordinator thread sets a global flag, **runFlag**, to **FALSE**, waits for 5 seconds, and terminates. Before you can really understand this strange protocol, take a look at the code skeleton used by the worker threads, as fol-lows.

```
// The code executed by each worker thread (simulated work)
DWORD WINAPI threadWork(LPVOID threadNo) {
//    Local variables
      double y;
      const double x = 3.14159;
      const double e = 2.7183;
      int i;
      const int napTime = 1000;      // in milliseconds
      const int busyTime = 40000;
      DWORD result = 0;
//    Create load
      while(runFlag) {
```

```
        // Parameterized CPU burst phase
            for(i = 0; i < busyTime; i++)
                y = pow(x, e);
        // Parameterized sleep phase
            Sleep(napTime);
        // Write message to stdout
    }
// Terminating
    return result;
}
```

Each worker thread goes through phases of using as many processor cycles as it can get to compute a power function. Then it goes to sleep for a while. Each worker does this until it sees the **runFlag** go **FALSE** and then it terminates. Notice that this solution relies on the use of a shared variable within the thread community to decide when to quit—an approach that was impossible in a community of processes! Think carefully about why threads can do this but processes cannot.

REFERENCES

Hart, Johnson M., *Win32 System Programming,* Addison-Wesley, Reading, Mass., 1997.

Microsoft, *Win32 API Reference Manual*, MSDN online documentation.

Richter, Jeffrey, *Advanced Windows*, Third Edition, Microsoft Press, Redmond, Wash., 1997.

three

Manipulating Kernel Objects

This exercise focuses on kernel objects, including those used to synchronize multiple processes. You used kernel objects in Exercise 2, but in this exercise you will look more closely at various facets of the objects. You will learn about:

▶ Kernel objects and handles

▶ The model for managing objects

▶ How to use Waitable timers

Windows NT makes broad use of objects in its implementation and through the services it provides. However, the Win32 API is not an object-oriented interface (that is, to invoke a system service, application programs call system functions rather than sending messages to the system objects). Despite the Win32 API being a C interface rather than a C++ interface, when an application obtains a resource from the OS, the resource is always regarded as some form of object. This exercise considers various facets of objects.

Windows NT documentation often uses the term "kernel object" (no capitalization) to refer to an object managed by the Executive Object Manager; it is more appropriately called an "Executive object." Part 1 noted that there are very low-level objects managed by the NT Kernel called "Kernel objects" (note the capitalization) and that a Kernel object is part of an Executive object. In the remainder of this manual, the terms kernel object and Executive object refer to the same thing, but Kernel object refers to the (sub)object type that is managed by the NT Kernel. This exercise focuses on Executive objects, especially how they are represented in the Win32 API.

The Executive generally creates a kernel object whenever it allocates a resource to a process. As part of the resource allocation, the kernel object is allocated in supervisor (also called kernel) space memory and the state of the object is set to reflect the details of the resource allocation. Since the details are implemented within an object, other software cannot generally access the object's member data except through the object's public interface. Furthermore, since the kernel object is allocated in kernel space, user-mode programs cannot even directly access the memory in which the kernel object is allocated. These two levels of protection are the foundation of secure objects in Windows NT.

The Executive supports a fixed set of classes (object types). Solomon (1998) lists the main kernel objects as follows.

Object directory. An object that can contain a collection of other objects. The Executive uses this type for various organized sets of objects.

Symbolic link. It is possible to reference another object as a symbolic name. This type is used to support that capability.

Process. An object that represents a process, specifically the process descriptor (Exercises 1 and 2).

Thread. An object that represents a thread, specifically the thread descriptor (Exercises 1 and 2).

Section. An object used in implementing shared memory among process address spaces (see Exercise 7).

File Port. An object type to represent a file descriptor when a file is opened for use (see Exercise 5).

Access Token. The object type used by the Secure Reference Monitor, the LSA server to implement user authentication, and by various other parts of the system as a basic mechanism in the protection system (see Part 1 of this manual).

Event. A class for objects that can capture the occurrence of action in the system (an *event*) so that other parts of the system can perform activities when they are assured that the action has occurred. An event object is the basis of many synchronization operations (see Exercise 4).

Semaphore. A class that implements the behavior of Dijkstra's general semaphore (see your textbook and Exercise 4).

Mutex. A class for synchronization mechanisms used to perform mutual exclusion for critical sections (see Exercise 4).

Manipulating Kernel Objects

Timer. An object type for objects that can be used to notify a thread that a given amount of time has elapsed (see the **Sleep** function call and **WaitableTimers** discussion later in this exercise).

Queue. A class to define objects that cause a thread to wait for I/O completions.

Key. A class used to access and manipulate information in the system Registry (a system-wide location where the computer's configuration information is kept).

Profile. An object type for objects that are used to measure the time to execute code segments in a process. Used by the measurement and program profiling tools.

This manual has exercises to deal with only a subset of these objects. More details of each object type that are covered appear in the exercise in which that object type is used.

Every Executive object has type-dependent member data and a standard wrapper with information that the Object Manager uses to administer the object. The wrapper contains a header that includes fields for the object's name, a description of the references to the object, and security attributes. (There are other fields in the header to implement the object model, but they are ignored in this discussion.)

Referencing an Object

Recall from Exercise 2 that when a thread uses **CreateProcess** and **CreateThread** to create another process or thread, it passes a *name* to the Object Manager. Both a *handle* and a system-wide *identification* are returned. In the **CreateProcess** case, the **PROCESS_INFORMATION** data structure is set so that there are **HANDLE**s to the new process and the new thread and **DWORD** identifications for the new process and new thread. **CreateThread** returns a **HANDLE** to the new thread and the thread identification as a **LPDWORD** (pointer to a **DWORD**) parameter. Once a user thread has obtained a **HANDLE**, it can pass the handle to the Executive as a parameter for other requests. For example, after a thread creates another thread, it passes the **HANDLE** back to the Executive when it closes the thread handle.

```
ChildThreadHandle = CreateThread(...);
...
CloseHandle(childThreadHandle);
```

When the Object Manager processes the first call that references a particular object, it

- adds the object name to a set of known object names,
- creates an Executive object with a header and body,
- initializes the fields in the header, and
- provides the object to other Executive-level components to fill in the object's type-specific body.

An Executive call might find that the desired object already exists, perhaps because a different process (or different thread) already caused the object to be created. In this case, an open handle count in the object's header is incremented to indicate that there are now two handles that reference the object. Subsequent opens on the object will continue to increment the handle count, while close operations will decrement it. If a close operation results in the handle count reaching zero (meaning there are no more user space handles referencing the object), the Object Manager removes the name from the name space. (If any subsequent references to the object occur, the name will have to be reintroduced to the name space.)

There is one more level of complexity concerning object references. Executive components may also reference an Executive object, but they will not necessarily use a handle to do it (that is, they use the object's address directly, since they run in kernel space). The object's header also includes a reference count for keeping track of the number of *all* references to the object. User space and kernel space open operations cause the reference count to be incremented, and close operations decrement it. The reference count going to zero indicates the object is not being used by any software component—either in user space or kernel space—and can therefore be deallocated (Solomon, 1998).

What is the relationship between the kernel object, a **HANDLE** to the object, and a **DWORD** identification for the object? As shown in Figure 4 (and noted previously), a kernel object is created by the Executive and Kernel and stored in kernel memory space, so it is not directly accessible by any user-mode thread. Whenever a thread has an object created in its behalf—or it otherwise begins to use a kernel object—some provision must be made by which the user-mode thread can ask the Executive to perform operations on that kernel object. A **HANDLE** is a 32-bit, user-space, process-specific reference to the object (see Figure 10). It is implemented as an offset into a process-specific handle table (Solomon, 1998; Richter, 1997). When the Executive provides a handle to a thread in a process, it searches the process's handle table (it knows how to find the process's handle table by referring to the process's descriptor; see Exercise

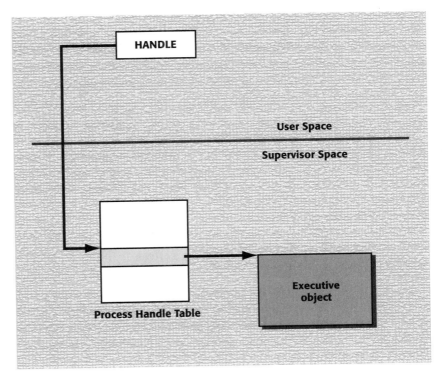

Figure 10

Handles and Handle Descriptors

HANDLE

User Space

Supervisor Space

Process Handle Table

Executive object

1). When an empty entry is found, the Executive fills in the Executive object's kernel space address in the first field, access information in the second field, and miscellaneous other information in other fields. Note that the handle table is an extension of the process descriptor and is stored in kernel space. The **HANDLE** that is returned to the user thread is the *index into the kernel space handle table* for this process. Thus the handle that a thread uses is accessible only to threads that exist in the same process address space. Even if a thread passed the **HANDLE** value to a thread in another process, that value would be meaningless.[1]

The **DWORD** system-wide identification spans address spaces. When an object's identity must be passed among address spaces, the identity is used rather than the **HANDLE**.

---

[1] UNIX file descriptors are handles of exactly the same type. The kernel keeps an open file table for each process, and the file handle is simply an offset into the table. Traditionally, **stdin** is the first offset, **stdout** the second, and **stderr** the third, thus their values of 0, 1, and 2, respectively.

Security Attributes

Function calls of the form **Create<Class>** or **Open<Class>** are used to request a system resource and hence to have a kernel object allocated and a handle returned to the calling thread. The NT Object Manager protection mechanism requires that the caller also indicate its desired access rights to the object. There are a set of generic rights that apply to every object (such as read and write); there may also be type-specific rights (such as the suspend access to a newly created process). During the **Create<Class>** operation, the Object Manager checks the caller's rights by passing a security descriptor (of type **SECURITY_DESCRIPTOR**) to the Security Reference Monitor to represent the desired access rights.

The security mechanisms depend on being able to authenticate the user that is running the software. Therefore it depends on the **WINLOGIN** process to authenticate users at the time they begin using the system. When the Object Manager creates an object, it creates a security descriptor that includes the owner's identification, a *discretionary ACL*, and a *system ACL*. Like traditional ACLs, the discretionary ACL is a list of the processes and their rights to the object. The system ACL is a list of processes and rights that should be recorded in the security audit log whenever they are used.

If access is permitted, the Security Reference Monitor returns the explicit set of access rights that the calling process has been granted and the Object Manager saves those rights as part of the process's handle descriptor in the handle table. Then, when a thread in the original process uses the handle, its access rights to the given object are compared with the granted access before the kernel code uses the handle descriptor to reference the object.

In Exercise 2, **CreateProcess** was used to create a new process. The part of the function prototype related to security is reproduced here.

```
BOOL CreateProcess(
    ...
    LPSECURITY_ATTRIBUTES lpProcessAttributes,
        // pointer to process security attributes
    LPSECURITY_ATTRIBUTES lpThreadAttributes,
        // pointer to thread security attributes
    ...
);
```

The **lpProcessAttributes** and **lpThreadAttributes** parameters are pointers to a **SECURITY_ATTRIBUTE** data structure (shown next).

```
typedef struct _SECURITY_ATTRIBUTES { // sa
    DWORD nLength;
    LPVOID lpSecurityDescriptor;
    BOOL bInheritHandle;
} SECURITY_ATTRIBUTES;
```

The **lpSecurityDescriptor** is a pointer to the **SECURITY_DESCRIPTOR** data structure, whose details are not documented, since its fields are only to be read and set using Win32 API functions (see the online MSDN documentation entry for **SECURITY_DESCRIPTOR**). It is the means by which the calling thread specifies the desired access rights that will be assigned to a new object or used to authenticate access to an existing object. For example, the Win32 API functions **GetSecurityDescriptorControl**, **SetSecurityDescriptorDacl**, and others provide tools for setting the fields in the **SECURITY_DESCRIPTOR**.

The default value for the security attributes parameters (in the **CreateProcess** call) is **NULL**, meaning there is no **SECURITY_ATTRIBUTE** data structure passed on the call. The Process Manager (and the Object Manager) interprets the **NULL** argument to mean that the child process (or thread, if this is a security attribute for a thread) uses either the existing **SECURITY_DESCRIPTOR** for an existing object or the system default if it must create a new object.

If you wish to restrict the child's access to its own process object, you must create a **SECURITY_ATTRIBUTE** and then perform Executive calls so that the underlying ACL prevents the child from referencing the object. While it would be unusual for you to restrict the child from its own process object, the same security attributes mechanism is used for every Executive object—files, memory sections, and so on.

Handle Inheritance

The entry in a process's handle table is a *capability* (see your textbook) to an object. If a thread has a handle, it can reference an entry in the handle table and hence the corresponding object in Kernel space. If N different threads in a process execute a code segment that obtains a handle to a particular object, then the process will have N distinct handle descriptors to the object in the process table. It behooves the programmer to be very careful about how many handles are obtained with any code segment that multiple threads might execute.[2]

When a new process is created, should it be able to reference the same objects as its parent? In some cases, this capability is invaluable, for example to allow a child process to be able to read a shared memory segment that the parent has already opened. In other cases, providing a reference to the parent's open objects is exactly the wrong thing to do, for example if the parent has resources open that the child is not to use. In the **CreateProcess** function call, the handle inheritance flag parameter, **bInheritHandles**, is used to specify if the child process should be able to reference the objects for which its parent has handles.

BOOL CreateProcess(

...

BOOL bInheritHandles,   // handle inheritance flag

...

);

If **bInheritHandles** is TRUE, the new process will be given its own handles to the objects that the creating process can reference. That is, the new process will have a new handle created for its use, and each new handle will have a new handle descriptor in the new process's handle table. The handle counts to the referenced objects will be increased accordingly.

If the thread that creates an object wishes, it can explicitly mark a handle as *uninheritable*. Then even if the **bInheritHandles** flag is TRUE, the new process will not get a handle to the uninheritable object. If the flag is FALSE, the new process is created without any handles to the objects that the creating process contained. While you have seen only the **CreateProcess** function use the inheritance flag, many other calls that create new objects incorporate an inheritance flag. This can be set to TRUE to mark the handle as inheritable, or FALSE otherwise. An object is created as uninheritable if the **bInheritHandles** field in the SECURITY_ATTRIBUTES data structure is set to FALSE. Thus, even if you do not want to change the security access for an object from its default behavior, but you want to mark the object as being uninheritable, you will have to in-

---

[2] A common scenario is for a child thread to obtain a handle through some common code segment, to determine that the handle is superfluous, and to close the handle, thereby removing the redundant handle descriptor.

clude a security attributes data structure in the object creation call. To mark a new thread object as not being inheritable at the time a process is created, you could write a code segment such as the following.

```
#include      <windows.h>
#include      <stdio.h>
...
SECURITY_ATTRIBUTES threadSA;
...
// Set lpCommandLine, startInfo, and threadInfo parameters
threadSA.nLength = sizeof(SECURITY_ATTRIBUTES);
threadSA.lpSecurityDescriptor = NULL;
threadSA.bInheritHandles = FALSE;
if(!CreateProcess(NULL, lpCommandLine, NULL, &threadSA, FALSE,
            HIGH_PRIORITY_CLASS | CREATE_NEW_CONSOLE,
            NULL, NULL, &startInfo, &processInfo)) {
    fprintf(stderr, "CreateProcess failed on error %d\n",
                    GetLastError());
    ExitProcess(1);
};
```

Passing Handles to Other Processes

When a thread obtains a handle, a handle descriptor is created in that process's handle table. Suppose the thread wants to provide access to the designated object to a thread in a different process. Clearly, the handle, itself, would be of no use to a thread in another process, since it is merely an offset into the first process's handle table. If there is a parent-child relationship between the two processes, handle inheritance can be used to share access. If there is no relationship, then either named objects will have to be used or the **DuplicateHandles** function can be used to create a new handle in the receiving process's address space.

The previous discussion on referencing an object suggested how named objects can be referenced by different processes. Some process creates the object with a name from a global system name space (these names are like filenames). Another process can get a handle to the object by using an open command with the right name. If the security attributes permit access, the second process will have its own handle descriptor inserted into its own handle table, and the thread will be given a **HANDLE**.

The **DuplicateHandle** function is used to explicitly create a handle in another process.

```
BOOL DuplicateHandle(
     HANDLE hSourceProcessHandle,
       // handle to process with handle to duplicate
     HANDLE hSourceHandle,      // handle to duplicate
     HANDLE hTargetProcessHandle,
       // handle to process to duplicate to
     LPHANDLE lpTargetHandle,  // pointer to duplicate handle
     DWORD dwDesiredAccess,    // access for duplicate handle
     BOOL bInheritHandle,       // handle inheritance flag
     DWORD dwOptions            // optional actions
);
```

In the discussion of these parameters, call the process that contains a handle to be replicated the "source" process and the process that is to receive the new handle, the "target" process. The **hSourceProcessHandle** is a handle in the calling process to another process that has a handle that this process needs (the target's handle to the source process must have PROCESS_DUP_HANDLE permission). The **hSourceHandle** parameter is the offset in the source process's handle table, that is, it is a handle that has meaning only in the source process. This suggests that before a target process can replicate a handle into its own address space, it must have some other way of communicating with the source so that it can obtain the **hSourceHandle** value. The **hTargetProcessHandle** is a handle in the calling process, and **lpTargetHandle** is a pointer to a variable that will be set to the offset in the target process's handle table where the replicated handle will be placed. The **hTargetProcessHandle** must also have PROCESS_DUP_HAN-DLE permission.

Waitable Timer Objects

In this exercise, you use a timer object to control your thread behavior. In Exercise 2, you used **GetSystemTime** and a shared **runFlag** variable to control when a set of threads should be halted. This method lacks fine control because it depends on one thread reading the current system time to determine if it is time to halt and, if it is not, blocking itself for some time period. We could have been more clever by computing the halt time, putting the clock reader thread to sleep for that amount of time, and then having it wake up to poll the system clock. However, there is still a better method to handle the problem, one that does not require polling and that will be useable across address spaces. That method is to use a *waitable timer*, a new kernel object type introduced in Windows NT Version 4.0 (this Win32 API function is not implemented by any of the other Microsoft OSs). A waitable timer not only provides you with a new tool for controlling execution based on asynchronous events. It also lets you create and work with another object type besides processes and threads.

A waitable timer periodically signals your process that a given amount of time has elapsed. The granularity of the request is 100 nanoseconds (10^{-9} seconds, abbreviated "ns"). Not every computer can really update its clock once every 100 ns, so this is just an expression using the best clock granularity possible with contemporary computers. The waitable timer will do the best job it can to measure time in 100-ns clock ticks.

Following is the function prototype to create a waitable timer.

```
HANDLE CreateWaitableTimer (
      LPSECURITY_ATTRIBUTES lpTimerAttributes,
              // pointer to security attributes
      BOOL bManualReset,    // flag for manual reset state
      LPCTSTR lpTimerName // pointer to Timer object name
);
```

The **lpTimerAttributes** is a security attribute parameter and is used just as it would be with **CreateProcess** or **CreateThread** (see earlier in the exercise). The **lpTimerName** parameter is provided to assign a name to the timer if it is being created or to open an existing named timer (in which case **GetLastError ( )** will return **ERROR_ALREADY_EXISTS**). The **bManualReset** parameter controls the number of threads that will be signaled when the waitable timer sends a signal. If it is set to **TRUE**, all threads that are waiting on the timer will receive a notification; otherwise, only one thread will receive notification. The function returns a **HANDLE** to the waitable timer.

A thread can obtain a handle to an existing waitable timer using **OpenWaitableTimer**.

```
HANDLE OpenWaitableTimer (
      DWORD dwDesiredAccess,    // access flag
      BOOL bInheritFlag,        // inherit flag
      LPCTSTR lpTimerName       // pointer to Timer object name
);
```

The values to **dwDesiredAccess** describe the way the process wants to use the waitable timer with this handle. You use this function if you just want a thread to be notified when the timer sends a signal, to be able to set the time period for the timer, or to have full access to all of the timer's functions (see the online MSDN documentation).

Once a waitable timer has been created, it must be set before it will produce signals. The **SetWaitableTimer** function can be used to do this.

```
BOOL SetWaitableTimer (
        HANDLE htimer,    // handle to a Timer object
        Const LARGE_INTEGER *pDueTime,
                          // when timer will become signaled
        LONG lPeriod,     // periodic timer interval
        PTIMERAPCROUTINE pfnCompletionRoutine,
                          // pointer to the completion routine
        LPVOID lpArgToCompletionRoutine,
                          // data passed to completion routine
        BOOL fResume      // flag for resume state
);
```

The **hTimer** field is the handle returned by the create or open function. The **pDueTime** is a number in the 64-bit **FILETIME** format (see the MSDN reference manual).

```
typedef struct _FILETIME { // ft
        DWORD dwLowDateTime;
        DWORD dwHighDateTime;
} FILETIME;
```

Here, the **dwLowDateTime** is the low-order 32 bits of the time in the file system format and **dwHighDateTime** is the high-order 32 bits. You can specify the **pDueTime** as a relative time or an absolute time; you distinguish relative times from absolute times by setting the 64-bit time to be the negative of the relative value (see "Attacking the Problem"). The **lPeriod** parameter specifies the time in milliseconds (10^{-3} seconds) between notifications. If it is zero, the waitable timer will produce only one notification.

Waitable timers open a new set of possibilities for getting two threads to work together. They are the first example of a Windows mechanism to coordinate the behavior of threads. Exercise 4 focuses on a spectrum of thread synchronization techniques. (An aspect of Windows NT that distinguishes it from many older OSs is its support of very general mechanisms for asynchronous coordination.) The next two parameters in **SetWaitableTimer**, **pfnCompletionRoutine**, and lpArgToCompletionRoutine are used to implement a general form of asynchronous coordination between the waitable timer and APC user threads. Exercise 12 provides the details in the context of interacting with file objects.

The **fResume** flag is a little obscure, though it is necessary for a particular usage mode for the computer. If a waitable timer is running on a computer that is in suspended mode, then if **fResume** is TRUE, the time notification will restart the computer. This means that you can write code that will restart a suspended computer and perform some action (using the APC routine).

3

The APC parameters can be used to field a timer notification, but a simpler technique is to use another Executive facility, **WaitForSingleObject**. When a thread calls this function, it is blocked until a notification is issued to this thread by the specified object. A thread can create a waitable timer, set it, and then wait for it to respond with a call to **WaitForSingleObject**. Here is the function prototype.

```
DWORD WaitForSingleObject(
        HANDLE hHandle;        // handle of object to wait for
        DWORD dwMilliseconds;  // time-out interval in
                               // milliseconds
);
```

The **hHandle** parameter is the handle for the waitable timer. The **dwMilliseconds** parameter specifies a maximum amount of time (in milliseconds) that the thread is willing to wait for the timer to expire. You can use **GetLastError** to see if the function returned because either a notification was sent by the waitable timer (**WAIT_OBJECT_O**) or the maximum amount of time expired (**WAIT_TIMEOUT**). You can also use a value of **INFINITE** for **dwMilliseconds**, meaning that the calling thread will block until it receives a notification from the waitable timer and never time out.

Here is a code skeleton that uses a waitable timer.

```
HANDLE wTimer;
LARGE_INTEGER quitTime;
...
wTimer = CreateWaitableTimer(NULL, FALSE, NULL);
// define quitTime
SetWaitableTimer(wTimer, &quitTime, 0, NULL, NULL, FALSE);
...
WaitForSingleObject(wTimer, INFINITE);
...
```

In this exercise, you create a set of cyclic processes with different handle inheritance attributes, use a waitable timer to control when the main program decides that the entire community of processes should terminate, and then terminate all of the processes.

Step I

Write a program that uses a waitable timer to stop itself K seconds after it is started, where K is a command line parameter.

Step II

Modify the program from Step I so that it creates N background processes, each running a program that terminates at a random time. Let N be a command line parameter. Each process should give all of its own handles (through handle inheritance), except the thread handles, to child processes it creates. There is a skeleton for such a child process program in the following "Attacking the Problem."

Step III

Modify the controlling program again so that when K seconds have elapsed, it will destroy the processes that have not terminated on their own. If all background processes terminate on their own, the controlling process can run for the full K seconds.

LAB ENVIRONMENT

Since waitable timers are not implemented in versions of NT earlier than 4.0 and they are not in Windows 9x or CE, you must pass a flag to the compiler to let it know you are working on Version 4.0 of Windows NT. Add /D _WIN32_WINNT=0x400 as a compiler flag using the "Project/Settings" menu in Visual C++.

ATTACKING THE PROBLEM

The organization of the controlling program is relatively straightforward. The problems you will encounter with this program will be in getting the details right.

One problem will be in handling the 64-bit file time values. Richter (1997) uses a code segment similar to the following one to create a parameter suitable for use with **SetWaitableTimer**.

```
_int64 endTime;
LARGE_INTEGER quitTime;
...
// Put the run time, K in endTime
// (the units will have to be 100 ns)
quitTime.LowPart = (DWORD) (endTime & 0xFFFFFFFF);
quitTime.HighPart = (LONG) (endTime >> 32);
```

There is also a useful example using system time in Chapter 8 of Hart (1997).

Sample Background Program

Following is an example of a program that you can use in solving Part II of the exercise. The idea is to create a process that might or might not halt on its own so that your modification to the controlling process (in Step III) must terminate the process.

```
#include   <windows.h>
#include   <stdio.h>

int main (int argc, char *argv[]) {

// Get a value for the number of this client from argv[1]
   printf("Client %s beginning to run\n", argv[1]);
   while(TRUE) {
           printf("Client[%s]: Quit (y or any other character): ",
                   argv[1]);
           if(getc(stdin) == 'y') break;
           getc(stdin);   // throw away NEWLINE
      }
      return(0);
}
```

Terminating a Process

There is a Win32 API call that allows one process to terminate another one, provided the process that intends to terminate the other has

PROCESS_TERMINATE permission on the specified handle. Following is the function prototype.

```
BOOL TerminateProcess (
    HANDLE hProcess,      // handle to the process
    UINT uExitCode        // exit code for the process
);
```

If **TerminateProcess** is called with a process handle, **hProcess**, and an unsigned integer exit code, **uExitCode**, the Process Manager will terminate the target process. Although this call can be used for this exercise, it is normally used only in extreme circumstances. The problem with the function is that it might not work with processes that are using DLLs. A DLL can be loaded separately from the **.EXE** file that a process uses for its main program execution; the **TerminateProcess** function will halt the process from executing the **.EXE** file, but the interaction with the DLL might not work. Your background process is very simple—and it does not include any DLLs—so **TerminateProcess** will work just fine.

REFERENCES

Hart, Johnson M., *Win32 System Programming,* Addison-Wesley, Reading, Mass., 1997.

Microsoft, *Win32 API Reference Manual*, MSDN online documentation.

Richter, Jeffrey, *Advanced Windows*, Third Edition, Microsoft Press, Redmond, Wash., 1997.

Solomon, David A., *Inside Windows NT*, Second Edition, Microsoft Press, Redmond, Wash., 1998.

Thread Synchronization

four

Multithreaded operation—within or across process address spaces—depends on the ability of a constituent thread to coordinate its activity with the activity of another constituent thread. This exercise concentrates on general thread synchronization within a single process address space (later you will see how to synchronize *across* address spaces). You will learn about:

▶ Windows NT synchronization principles
▶ Critical sections
▶ Synchronization mechanisms

INTRODUCTION

Multithreading is a very powerful concept because it allows different parts of an application to work on different parts of a single problem concurrently. When one part of the computation is waiting for its environment to change, its thread is blocked. However, other parts of the computation implemented by other threads can still use the processor to proceed with the other work. The multiprogramming and multithreading features discussed so far have allowed you to experiment with these aspects of Windows NT. This exercise focuses on techniques for coordinating the threads' work.

The threads in a process all operate in the same address space using the same resources to solve a common problem. That is, the threads all act in harmony to perform the desired overall computation. A *synchronization mechanism* is required to allow the multiple, independent threads to coordinate their work. Over the years, two kinds of synchronization, pictorially depicted in Figure 11, have emerged as common problems (see your textbook for a more leisurely description of these problems).

Suppose two threads, X and Y, are executing in a single process.

- In the synchronous scenario (Figure 11a), thread X performs part of the work, then thread Y performs a second phase of the work that depends on the completion of the first part, and then thread X performs the third phase of the work, which depends on the completion of the second phase. This scenario requires that the threads be able to explicitly *coordinate* the execution of certain parts of their work.
- In the asynchronous scenario (Figure 11b), threads X and Y work on the three parts of the work: Thread X completes the first part of the work, and then thread Y completes the second part concurrently with thread X, which is completing the third phase.

Recall that "concurrent execution" means that either the second part is done before the third, the third part is done before the second, or the two parts are done at the same time if there is more than one processor in the system. The first aspect of coordination is for the system to realize it can run the second and third parts concurrently. Threads X and Y are presumed to execute concurrently in the same address space. This means that there is a possibility of a race condition of the type encountered with shared variables in the C runtime library (see Exercise 2). In the case of the C runtime library variables, **_beginthreadex** is used to make a copy of each shared variable for each thread. All variables declared in the process's program are shared (except automatic variables that are declared in each thread's stack). Specifically, the variables in the data segment—the static variables in a C program—are shared among the threads in a process. Blocks of code that read or write such shared variables are said to be executing in a *critical section* of code. If two or more threads access shared variables while executing their critical sections (and at least one of them is writing the variable), the same race condition that could happen with C runtime variables can happen with ordinary program variables. The common solution to the problem is to provide an OS mechanism to enforce *mutual exclusion*, whereby if one thread is in its critical section, then other threads are excluded from entering their critical sections as long as the first remains in its critical section. Your textbook spends considerable time explaining this problem and showing you how to solve it by using synchronization primitives.

Figure 11

*Synchronous
versus Asynchronous
Operation*

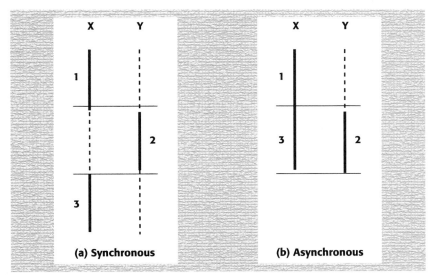

(a) Synchronous   **(b) Asynchronous**

In Windows NT, thread synchronization for coordination and mutual exclusion is implemented using Executive kernel objects. There are four types of kernel objects explicitly intended to perform different forms of synchronization:

- Events
- Mutexes
- Semaphores
- Timers (the waitable timer introduced in Exercise 3 uses the timer object)

The behavior of each of these synchronization objects is inspired by Dijkstra's semaphores (explained more fully in your textbook). Briefly, a Dijkstra semaphore behaves like an abstract data type. It is made up of a private integer variable, s, that can be manipulated only by using the abstract data type's P and V member functions. P and V behave as follows.

P(s): [while(s == 0) wait(); s--;]
V(s): [s++;]

The square braces around the P and V code are meant to emphasize that P and V are *atomic* operations, meaning that once they start they cannot be interrupted until they have completed. The **wait** operation in the P selectively breaks this uninterruptible assumption by allowing other threads to execute while s is equal to zero.

Each NT Executive object that is built using a Kernel dispatcher object (see Part 1) contains a state variable that allows the object to be in either a *signaled* or *nonsignaled* state. For example, when a process or thread terminates, its dispatcher object component transitions to a signaled state. Various operations cause the object state to transition. Then other software can test the state of the object using one of the Win32 API *wait functions* (including the **WaitForSingleObject** function you used in Exercise 3 and **WaitForMultipleObjects**, described shortly). The wait functions use a handle to access an object and to test its state. If the target object is in the signaled state, the wait function returns to the caller. If the target object is in the nonsignaled state, the wait function blocks the calling thread until one of a set of conditions is met (for example, the object transitions to the signaled state or the time-out interval for the call expires). On return from the function call, the thread is once again made runnable, meaning that it is prepared to compete for the processor. Thus the synchronization mechanism interacts with the scheduling mechanism to determine when a thread is schedulable.

What causes an object to transition from one state to the other? In some cases, the transition is a side effect of other activity by the object, while sometimes the transition is accomplished through explicit actions. Objects whose primary purpose is something other than synchronization (for example process, thread, and file objects) have implicit state transitions. Objects intended explicitly for synchronization have a spectrum of ways to cause state changes (which is why Windows NT provides more than one type of synchronization object).

Process and thread objects are created in the nonsignaled state and stay in that state throughout their lifetime. When a process or thread terminates using **ExitProcess** or **ExitThread**, then its state changes from nonsignaled to signaled. Relating this to your experience with creating processes and threads, you can now understand exactly why a controlling thread always has a schema such as the following.

```
thrdHandle = CreateThread(...);
...
WaitForSingleObject(thrdHandle, INFINITE);
CloseHandle(thrdHandle);
```

The thread is created (by the controlling process) and begins existence in a nonsignaled state. When the thread terminates, it changes its state to signaled. Meanwhile the controlling process blocks itself (without an infinite timeout) at the **WaitForSingleObject** call until the child thread terminates.

The code schema for using a waitable timer is the same. The waitable timer is created in a nonsignaled state. Then the thread that wants to wait for the timer to expire simply uses **WaitForSingleObject** on the timer's handle until it changes to the signaled state.

Can multiple threads wait on the same timer object? Can multiple threads (in multiple processes) wait on the same timer object? The answer to both questions is yes. In the first case, each thread can use its own handle to the object and then execute a **WaitForSingleObject** whenever it is ready to begin waiting for the timer to expire. The second case relates to multiple process access to the same timer object. The timer object must have been created with a name, and the name must be known to all processes that will use the timer object. If both conditions are true, a thread in the second process can use the **OpenWaitableTimer** function with the previously specified name to reference the timer object created by the first process.

If multiple threads (in the same or a different process) wait on a single timer object, when should it change from the signaled to nonsignaled state? If it "automatically" changes back to the nonsignaled state whenever any process has detected that it was in the signaled state, how will multiple threads detect the timer's notification? The answer to this lies in the **bManualReset** parameter for **CreateWaitableTimer**, a parameter that was set to **FALSE** in Exercise 3. Some synchronization objects use the auto-reset strategy for managing the state transition, while some use the manual-reset strategy. Still others allow the programmer to specify which of the strategies should be used for the particular object instance. Timer objects support either manual-reset or auto-reset, depending on the value of **bManualReset** in the creation call. If the timer object uses the manual-reset, the timer remains in a signaled state until it is manually reset to be in the nonsignaled state using the **SetWaitableTimer** function. That is, each call to **SetWaitableTimer** (re)initializes the state to nonsignaled. However, if the auto-reset strategy is used, then each time a wait function recognizes that the object transitioned to a signaled state, the state is automatically transitioned back to nonsignaled.

Wait Functions

The wait functions are used with any synchronization object to implement a variant of the Dijkstra P operation. You used **WaitForSingleObject** in Exercise 3 to receive a notification from a waitable timer. **WaitForSingleObject** can also be used with event, mutex, and semaphore objects. (**WaitForSingleObject** can infer from the object handle the type of object for which it is waiting.)

The **WaitForMultipleObjects** function call allows a thread to block while waiting for one or all of a set of objects to transition to the signaled state.

```
DWORD WaitForMultipleObjects(
      DWORD nCount,
            // number of handles in the object handle array
      CONST HANDLE *lpHandles,
            // point to the object-handle array
      BOOL bWaitAll,           // wait flag
      DWORD dwMilliseconds   // time-out interval in milliseconds
);
```

The first parameter, **nCount**, specifies the number of handles in the set of handles on which the function will block. The **lpHandles** parameter points to an array of the handles that are in the set. The third parameter specifies whether the function should wait for all objects in the set to send a notification (**bWaitAll** = TRUE) or just one to send a notification (**bWaitAll** = FALSE). The **dwMilliseconds** parameter is the time-out value to allow the function to return in a bounded amount of time if desired (as in **WaitForSingleObject**). It can have a value of **INFINITE** if no timeout is to be used. **WaitForMultipleObjects** and arrays of handles can be used in the manner illustrated by the following code segment.

```
#define N ...
...
HANDLE thrdHandle[N];
...
for(i = 0; i < N; i++) {
      thrdHandle[I] = CreateThread(...);
}
...
WaitForMultipleObjects(N, thrdHandle, TRUE, INFINITE);
```

What will happen if the **dwMilliseconds** parameter is set to zero on a call to **WaitForSingleObject** or **WaitForMultipleObjects**? The synchronous behavior of the primitives is changed so that they act like polling primitives, since the time-out immediately expires at the time of the call. On return, the calling process can check the return value to determine the state of the queried objects.

Event Objects

An *event object* is an object used to announce the occurrence of something in one thread that needs to be known in other threads, that is, it announces the occurrence of an event. There is no other "side effect" associated with an event object. An event object can use either the auto-reset or manual-reset strategy. Recall that the auto-reset strategy allows only one thread to perceive that the event object transitioned to signaled; then the object immediately transitions back to nonsignaled. The manual-reset strategy allows many threads to perceive the event occurrence, but event objects must be explicitly reset with the **SetEvent** function call. An event is created with the following.

4

```
HANDLE CreateEvent(
        LPSECURITY_ATTRIBUTES lpEventAttributes,
                                // pointer to security attributes
        BOOL bManualReset,    // flag for manual-reset event
        BOOL bInitialState,   // flag for initial state
        LPCTSTR lpName        // pointer to event-object name
);
```

The only argument requiring explanation here is **bInitialState**. Since the only purpose of an event object is synchronization, the creating thread is given the option of setting the object state to signaled (**bInitialState = TRUE**) or nonsignaled (**bInitialState = FALSE**). **OpenEvent** is used to obtain a handle to a preexisting event object that has a name. The other two relevant functions are

```
BOOL SetEvent(
        HANDLE hEvent    // flag for manual-reset event
);
```

which manually sets the state of **hEvent** to signaled, and

```
BOOL ReetEvent(
        HANDLE hEvent    // flag for manual-reset event
);
```

which manually sets the state of **hEvent** to nonsignaled.

Events are useful for handling a synchronization scenario such as the one shown in Figure 11(a), as follows.

```
int main(...) {
// This is thread X

    ...
    evntHandle[PART2] = CreateEvent(NULL, TRUE, FALSE, NULL);
    evntHandle[PART3] = CreateEvent(NULL, TRUE, FALSE, NULL);
    ... CreateThread(..., threadY,  ...) ...;  // Create thread Y
// Do part 1
    ...
    SetEvent(evntHandle[PART2]);
    WaitForSingleObject(evntHandle[PART3])
    ResetEvent(evntHandle[PART3]);
    // Do part 3
    ...
}


DWORD WINAPI threadY(LPVOID) {
    ...
    WaitForSingleObject(evntHandle[PART2]);
    ResetEvent(evntHandle[PART2]);
// Do part 2
    ...
    SetEvent(evntHandle[Part3]);
    ...
}
```

Mutex Objects

A *mutex object* also exists solely for synchronization purposes, though it is specially built to handle the critical section problem. Mutexes differ from events in the way they handle state management.

A mutex object can have an owner thread, or it can be unowned. Having ownership of the object means that the thread is "holding the mutex," that is, the mutex object is in a nonsignaled state and the holding thread is in the critical section protected by the object. A thread can become the owner of a mutex object when the object is created, when a handle to it is opened, or via a wait function. It can release the mutex object (set the mutex object state back to the signaled state) using the **ReleaseMutex** function. To understand the details, consider the function prototypes.

```
HANDLE CreateMutex(
    LPSECURITY_ATTRIBUTES lpMutexAttributes,
                          // pointer to security attributes
    BOOL bInitialOwner,   // flag for initial ownership
    LPCTSTR lpName        // pointer to mutex-object name
);
```

The **bInitialOwner** attribute determines whether the calling thread will be the owner of the mutex object. If **bInitialOwner** is set to **TRUE** (and the function call succeeds), the mutex object will be created in the nonsignaled state and the calling thread will be the owner. Like most of the other object creation functions, **CreateMutex** can fail if it selects a name that is already in use—**GetLastError** will return the value ERROR_ALREADY_EXISTS.

Once the mutex object is created, any thread in the calling thread's process can use it. If threads in other processes intend to use the mutex object, then they must know the name of the mutex object and use **OpenMutex** with the correct name. The normal rules regarding desired access and inheritance apply (see Exercise 3).

If a thread is not the owner of a mutex object but desires to become the owner, it uses a wait function to request ownership. Like wait function calls on other object types, a wait call on a mutex object will return if the object is in the signaled state. A successful wait on a mutex object (you must check the return code if you allow a timeout return) causes the calling thread to become the owner and the object's state to be changed to nonsignaled. The **ReleaseMutex(HANDLE)** function call releases ownership and changes the mutex object's state back to signaled.

Mutex objects can be used to solve the critical section problem. Suppose that threads X and Y share resource R; both threads perform some computation, access R, and then perform more computation. Since R is a shared resource, the access is a critical section. Here is a Windows NT code skeleton to handle the problem using mutex objects.

```
int main(...) {

// This is a controlling thread
    ...
// Open resource R
    ...
```

```
        // Create the Mutex objects with no owner (signaled)
        mutexR = CreateMutex(NULL, FALSE, NULL);
        ... CreateThread(..., workerThrd,  ...) ...;  // Create thread X
        ... CreateThread(..., workerThrd,  ...) ...;  // Create thread Y
        ...
}

DWORD WINAPI workerThrd(LPVOID) {
    ...
    while(...) {
    // Perform work

        ...
    // Obtain mutex
        while(WaitForSingleObject(mutexR) != WAIT_OBJECT_0);
    // Access the resource R
        ReleaseMutex(mutexR;)
    }
    ...
}
```

Semaphores

Semaphore objects implement the model with the Dijkstra semaphore semantics, that is, semaphore objects are able to maintain a count to represent integer values (rather than the implicit binary values of events and mutexes). A semaphore object is created with a call to the following.

```
HANDLE CreateSemaphore(
        LPSECURITY_ATTRIBUTES lpSemaphoreAttributes,
                                    // pointer to security attributes
            LONG lInitialCount,      // initial count
            LONG lMaximumCount,    // maximum count
            LPCTSTR lpName          // pointer to semaphore-object name
    );
```

A semaphore object keeps an internal variable with a value between zero and **lMaximumCount** (which must be greater than zero). When the object is created, the initial value of the internal variable can be set to any value in the allowable range and is specified by the **lInitialCount** argument. The state of the semaphore object is determined by the value of the internal variable. If it is set to zero, the object state is signaled, but if it has a value in the range [1:lMaximumCount], the state is nonsignaled.

The internal values of the semaphore object are manipulated indirectly using functions. A wait function decreases the value of the internal variable whenever it unblocks a thread. The **ReleaseSemaphore** function increases the internal variable count.

```
BOOL ReleaseSemaphore(
    HANDLE hSemaphore,      // handle of the Semaphore object
    LONG lReleaseCount,     // amount to add to the current count
    LPLONG lPreviousCount   // address of previous count
);
```

The **lReleaseCount** parameter specifies the amount to add to the semaphore (thereby potentially causing a state change in the object). The **lPrevious-Count** is a pointer to a variable that will be set to show the value of the count before **ReleaseSemaphore** was called (and may be set to **NULL** if you do not care about the previous value).

Semaphore objects are used when you need the synchronization mechanism count values (the problem in this exercise is Dijkstra's classic example of this case). Suppose that threads X and Y are both using units of resource R; either may request K units, use them for some period of time, and then return them. Here is an NT code skeleton to handle the problem using semaphore objects.

```
#define N ...
int main(...) {
// This is a controlling thread
    ...
// Create the Semaphore object
    semaphoreR = CreateSemaphore(NULL, 0, N, NULL);
    ... CreateThread(..., workerThrd, ...) ...;  // Create thread X
    ... CreateThread(..., workerThrd, ...) ...;  // Create thread Y
    ...
    }
DWORD WINAPI workerThrd(LPVOID) {
    While(...) {
    // Perform some work
```

4

```
        ...
        // Acquire K units of the resource
        for(i = 0; i < K; i++)
            while(WaitForSingleObject(mutexR) != WAIT_OBJECT_0);
            ...
    // Release the K units
            ReleaseSemaphore(semaphoreR, K, NULL);
        ...
        }
    }
```

PROBLEM STATEMENT

The producer-consumer problem is a classic synchronization introduced by Dijkstra to illustrate two different ways to use his semaphores. In this exercise, you design two threads to execute in a single address space. A producer thread creates "widgets," then places each widget in an empty buffer for consumption by the consumer thread. The consumer retrieves the widget from the buffer and then releases the buffer to an empty buffer pool. If there are no full buffers, the consumer is blocked until new widgets are produced. If there are no empty buffers available when the producer creates a widget, the producer must wait until the consumer releases an empty buffer.

This problem is to design and implement a process with a producer thread and a consumer thread using N different buffers (use a fixed size for N of 25). Base your solution on the solution to the producer-consumer problem shown in the following "Attacking the Problem." You will need

- a mutual exclusion semaphore to prevent the producer and the consumer from manipulating the list of buffers at the same time,
- a semaphore the producer can use to signal the consumer to start processing when it creates a full buffer, and
- another semaphore for the consumer to use to signal the producer when it creates an empty buffer.

This problem can be solved without resorting to using the synchronization objects (since your solution is posed as a thread problem rather than a process-based problem). However, you are to use one or more of mutexes, semaphores, and events in your solution.

This assignment uses the same tools and environment as for Exercise 3. If you use the waitable timer, you will need to include the /D _WIN32_WINNT=0x400 flag.

ATTACKING THE PROBLEM

Your textbook is likely to have the pseudo code solution to this problem. Here is the solution that appears in Chapter 8 of Nutt (1997).

4

```
#define    N ...
// Shared variables, including semaphores
semaphore mutex = 1;
semaphore full = 0;
semaphore empty = N;
buf_type buffer[N];

int main(...) {
    ...
// Create the producer and consumer
    ... CreateThread(..., Producer, ...);
    ... CreateThread(..., Consumer, ...);
    ...
}

Producer() {
    buf_type *next, *here;
    while(TRUE) {
        produce_item(next);
// Claim an empty buffer
        P(empty);
        // Manipulate the pool
          P(mutex);
              here = obtain(empty);
          V(mutex);
          copy_buffer(next, here);
        // Manipulate the pool
```

```
            P(mutex);
                release(here, fullPool);
            V(mutex);
      // Signal a full buffer
         V(full);
      }
   }

   Consumer() {
      buf_type *next, *here;
      while(TRUE) {
         produce_item(next);
      // Claim a full buffer
         P(full);
         // Manipulate the pool
         P(mutex);
            here = obtain(full);
         V(mutex);
         copy_buffer(here, next);
      // Manipulate the pool
         P(mutex);
            release(here, emptyPool);
         V(mutex);
   // Signal an empty buffer
         V(empty);
      }
   }
```

This pseudo code gives you an idea of how to organize your solution, but it is independent of the Windows NT synchronization primitives. There are many acceptable solutions to the problem, so you should study the different primitives before choosing the ones to use in your solution.

Critical Sections

A critical section is a Win32 subsystem synchronization primitive rather than an NT Executive primitive. It is built using the Executive objects described earlier in this exercise. Your instructor might want you to get some experience with this mechanism as well as the Executive mechanisms.

Critical sections are designed to work only within a single address space, so they can be used only for thread synchronization within a process, not across processes. You create a critical section by declaring a data structure of type **CRITICAL_SECTION** (that is, there is no call to a **CreateXXX** function); call it **critSection**. Then, before it can be used, you must initialize it by calling **InitializeCriticalSection(&critSection)**. Thereafter, any thread in the process can use **EnterCriticalSection(&critSection)** to enter the critical section and **LeaveCriticalSection(&critSection)** to leave it. The enter function is a blocking function, so the calling thread will be blocked until it is able to obtain the critical section. See the Win32 API documentation for details.

4

REFERENCES

Hart, Johnson M., *Win32 System Programming,* Addison-Wesley, Reading, Mass., 1997.

Microsoft, *Win32 API Reference Manual*, MSDN online documentation.

Richter, Jeffrey, *Advanced Windows*, Third Edition, Microsoft Press, Redmond, Wash., 1997.

Interprocess Communication

In this exercise, you explore Windows NT's facilities to support communication among threads that are implemented within different processes. Classically, this is called *interprocess communication* (IPC). Since the Windows NT file model is used as the basis of most IPC mechanisms, you will also learn more about this model. In this exercise, you will learn about:

- ▶ General Windows NT mechanisms that support IPC
- ▶ Different IPC mechanism at different system levels
- ▶ The high-level File I/O Model
- ▶ More about using pipes
- ▶ More about using the CreateFile, ReadFile, and WriteFile functions

INTRODUCTION

Threads operating in the same process use the same address space, so it is easy for them to share information among themselves. As noted in Exercise 4, kernel objects can be used for a thread in one process to signal a thread in another process. However, when two threads in different processes wish to exchange data, a completely new set of mechanisms must be used. This exercise looks at NT's mechanisms to support data transfer across process address spaces. (One other important mechanism, the memory-mapped file, is discussed in Exercise 8.)

IPC is the mechanism for allowing one (thread in a) process to share information with (another thread in) a different process. In multiprogrammed computers, IPC can be implemented by providing a shared-memory mechanism or a mechanism by which the units of computation exchange messages that are transferred over some shared medium (such as kernel space memory). Message-based IPC became very important when networks became cost-effective in the 1980s. Also, in the late 1980s and 1990s, OS researchers pushed hard to create abstract shared memory that could be implemented on top of a message-based mechanism.

NT supports a shared-memory model within a computer and a few message-based mechanisms within a computer and across a network. This exercise looks at the message-based mechanisms that are used within a computer. Exercise 6 focuses on IPC mechanisms that use a network for message delivery, and Exercise 8 describes the memory-mapped file, shared-memory mechanism.

Kernel Local Procedure Calls

A specialized IPC mechanism is used within the Executive (and is not available through the Win32 API). Called the *Local Procedure Call (LPC) mechanism*, it is built on top of Kernel port objects and used for high-speed message-passing by client and server processes within the Executive and the subsystems. For example, LPCs are used for IPC between the LSA server and the Secure Reference Monitor.

There is not much information published about LPCs, though Solomon (1998) reports that LPC is a connection-based IPC mechanism in which processes that wish to use the LPC must create a port object to manage the communication. A client process makes a connection request to a server connection port. If the request is accepted, a server communication port and a client communication port are created and logically connected with each other. This port pair is then used as the high-speed link between the two processes.

The LPC facility provides a fast way for two threads in different address spaces to exchange information at a very high rate. The logical connection can be used to transfer a block of information from one address space to another. The "procedure call" aspect of the mechanism is that a transfer occurs using "procedure call semantics," meaning that a sender initiates the data transfer and waits until the transfer finishes. The analogy is that when a procedure is called, the caller initiates the call and then waits until it returns. This is also the model used in network-based remote procedure calls. You will see in Exercise 6 a similar mechanism for creating communication connections between clients and servers over a network.

Windows Messages

The Win32 subsystem provides another IPC mechanism especially tailored for graphics Windows-based applications but independent of the NT Executive (Richter, 1997). A normal NT Executive thread is created without facilities to use the Windows messaging system. However, when the thread calls a User or GDI function, the system presumes that the application will operate in the full graphics Windows environment, so it adds the data structures required to support Windows messaging. (In particular, this means that the threads that operate as console operations—such as the applications you are writing in this lab manual—cannot use the Windows messaging system.)

The added data structures (called **THREADINFO** structures) include the following queues, as well as other flags and state variables:

- Posted-message
- Send-message
- Reply-message

Messages are directed at a window, rather than to a specific thread in the window (the thread that created the window will receive the message). When a message is received, it is appended to one of the four queues.

Which queue the message is appended to depends on the Win32 functions that sent the message.

- The **PostMessage** and **PostThreadMessage** function adds a message to the *posted-message queue*. When a thread posts a message, it returns immediately after the message has been appended to the queue.
- **SendMessage** is a fully synchronous message. When a sender calls **SendMessage**, the function appends the message to the *send-message queue* but does not return until the window thread retrieves the message.
- A **ReplyMessage** function places a message in the *reply-message queue*. This facility is used when a sender requests service that is time-consuming; the receiver may issue a **ReplyMessage** to tell the sender that it is currently processing the request.

PostMessage is used to send a message and continue processing asynchronously, that is, without waiting for the message to be processed by the receiver. **SendMessage** synchronizes the activity of the sender and receiver, since the sender will not continue executing until the receiver processes the message. (**SendMessageTimeout** also specifies a maximum amount of time the sender is willing to wait for the receiver to act on the message.)

Introduction   99

The Windows messaging system has a very sophisticated receipt mechanism that uses an event-driven programming model. All messages have registered types, many of which are recognized and handled by code in the Windows system. When a message arrives in one of the queues, it is likely to be delivered to, and processed by, the thread that created the window without the application programmer's having to write any particular code to do this. This is a powerful application-oriented IPC mechanism, but one that is built entirely in the Win32 subsystem and is logically independent of the underlying OS mechanisms in Windows NT.

The File I/O Model

You have seen how objects are the OS mechanism to represent processes, threads, timers, synchronization primitives, and kernel IPC ports. In the case of processes and threads, the object serves two purposes: to be a descriptor for the behavior of the process or thread and to provide a simple signaling model for programmers to use to manipulate the descriptors. The object is more than a container for the resource descriptions. A programmer can use a wait function to determine when the object ceases to exist. Processes and threads represent one pier supporting the computational model, and files and other resources represent two more piers. Like processes and threads, an Executive file object serves the purpose of holding the Executive's information about a particular open file. The object has the usual object properties for security, inheritance, and signaling. Creating a file will cause a file object to be created and a handle descriptor to be placed in the creating process's handle table.

File objects are used to represent various other system resources, particularly devices, including some that are simply abstractions of hardware or of OS resources. The rationale for this design decision is that the I/O model for all of these devices and abstractions is intended to look as much like ordinary file I/O as possible. The essential elements of this abstraction are that a "file" is a named byte stream of characters that can be accessed by sequentially accessing bytes one after the other. A 64-bit *file pointer* is associated with each instance of an open file. When a file is opened, the file pointer is set to zero. When an I/O operation reads or writes K bytes, then the file pointer is advanced by K. File objects (and the **CreateFile** function call) are used with files, directories (see Exercise 11), disk drives (see Exercise 10), serial and parallel ports, pipes (see later in this exercise), sockets (see Exercise 6), and the console.

The file pointer can also be manually moved with the **SetFilePointer** operation, as follows.

```
DWORD SetFilePointer(
        HANDLE hfile,            // handle of file
        LONG lDistanceToMove,
            // number of bytes to move file pointer
        PLONG lpDistanceToMoveHigh,
            // address of high-order word of distance to move
        DWORD dwMoveMethod   // how to move
);
```

The use of a 64-bit file pointer causes somes difficulties in the programming model. The **lDistanceToMove** parameter is a signed 32-bit quantity that can move the file pointer 2^{31} forward or backward from the position specified in the **dwMoveMethod** parameter (which indicates, from the beginning of the file, the current position in the file, or the end of the file). The **lpDistanceToMoveHigh** parameter is the high-order part of a 64-bit distance to move on the call and the high-order part of the 64-bit final file pointer position on return. The low-order 32 bits of the final file pointer position are returned as the value of the function call.

Notice that operations such as **SetFilePointer** manipulate the file pointer value in the file handle (not the file object) and that all of the threads that change the file position using the same file handle share the file pointer. Thus if one thread calls **SetFilePointer** and then performs a **ReadFile**, there is no assurance that another thread might not perform another **SetFilePointer** between the first such operation and the read operation, thus possibly producing a race condition. (This race condition can be a major barrier to implementing file caching as done in Exercise 12.)

Consider the following file creation function.

```
HANDLE CreateFile(
        LPCTSTR lpFileName,        // pointer to name of the file
        DWORD dwDesiredAccess,   // access (read-write) mode
        DWORD dwShareMode,        // share mode
        LPSECURITY_ATTRIBUTES lpSecurityAttributes,
            // pointer to security attributes
```

```
    DWORD dwCreationDisposition,   // how to create
    DWORD dwFlagsAndAttributes,    // file attributes
    HANDLE hTemplateFile
        // handle to file with attributes to copy
);
```

The **lpFileName** specifies the name of the file to be created or opened. The **dwDesiredAccess** parameter behaves as discussed in Exercise 3. It has only three possible values: 0, GENERIC_READ, and GENERIC_WRITE. A zero means no access is desired, so it is used only when **CreateFile** is querying the file object to determine its current state. GENERIC_READ and GENERIC_WRITE can be combined by ORing the values (GENERIC_READ | GENERIC_WRITE) if the file is to be read and written.

The **dwShareMode** parameter can have any of the following values:

- **zero** (no sharing)
- **FILE_SHARE_DELETE** (subsequent open operations will succeed only if they request delete access)
- **FILE_SHARE_READ** (future open operations must be for reading)
- **FILE_SHARE_WRITE** (subsequent open operations must be for writing)

These flags, too, can be combined with a logical OR operation.

The **lpSecurityAttributes** parameter is treated the same as for other objects (see Exercise 3). The **dwCreationDisposition** parameter describes what the function should do if the file already exists at the time the create function is called. It has values

- **CREATE_NEW** to indicate that the call should fail if the file exists,
- **CREATE_ALWAYS** to overwrite an existing file, and
- **OPEN_EXISTING** to just open the existing file.

The **dwFlagsAndAttributes** parameter is used to pass various file-specific options to the File Manager, with **FILE_ATTRIBUTE_NORMAL** being the simplest form of open. (You will explore other options in subsequent exercises.)

The **hTemplateFile** parameter can be used to pass a handle to a different file that contains extended file attributes (this is not covered in this lab manual).

In earlier exercises, you used the C runtime functions to read and write files. There are also Win32 API functions to perform file I/O.

```
BOOL ReadFile(
    HANDLE hFile,  // handle of file to read
    LPVOID lpBuffer,
                // address of buffer that receives data
    DWORD nNumberOfBytesToRead,   // number of bytes to read
    LPDWORD lpNumberOfBytesRead,
                // address of number of bytes read
    LPOVERLAPPED lpOverlapped
                // address of structure for data
);
```

The **hFile parameter** is a handle to the file object. The **lpBuffer** is a pointer to a block (of type **VOID**) of bytes where the result of the read can be stored (this is analogous to the buffer parameter in the C runtime **fread** operation). Also similar to the C routine, **nNumberOfBytesToRead** is the number of bytes that should be read on the function call. The **lpNumberOfBytesRead** parameter is filled in when the function returns to reflect the number of bytes that were actually placed in **lpBuffer** by the call. If **ReadFile** succeeds, it returns a nonzero value. If the function returns nonzero and the **nNumberOfBytesToRead** is zero, this indicates that the file pointer was beyond the current end of the file at the time of the call. **lpOverlapped** is discussed in Exercise 9.

```
BOOL WriteFile(
    HANDLE hFile,  // handle of file to write to
    LPCVOID lpBuffer,
                // pointer to data to write to file
    DWORD nNumberOfBytesToWrite,  // number of bytes to write
    LPDWORD lpNumberOfBytesWritten,
                // address of number of bytes written
    LPOVERLAPPED lpOverlapped
                // pointer to structure needed for overlapped I/O
);
```

The parameters for **WriteFile** are analogous to those for **ReadFile**. The function returns a nonzero value on success and a zero value on failure.

Using the File I/O Model: Pipes

A *pipe* is an IPC abstraction for passing information from one process's address space to another process. Pipes were popularized in UNIX as the primary mechanism for performing IPC in the early versions of that OS. Undoubtedly, the popularity of pipes led to their inclusion as an IPC mechanism in Windows NT. Pipes are an Executive mechanism, but they are implemented using the memory-mapped file facility (see Exercise 8).

NT supports two varieties of pipes: *anonymous* (patterned closely after UNIX unnamed pipes) and *named*. An *anonymous pipe* is a half-duplex (one-way communication), character-based IPC mechanism. A *named pipe* is a full-duplex (two-way communication), character-based IPC mechanism that can be used over a network (see Exercise 8).

A pipe has a read end and a write end, each having its own handle. Once a pipe has been created, **ReadFile** and **WriteFile** can be used to read and write the two ends of the pipe.

You can create a pipe with the following.

```
BOOL CreatePipe(
    PHANDLE hReadPipe,    // address of variable for read handle
    PHANDLE hWritePipe,
                         // address of variable for write handle
    LPSECURITY_ATTRIBUTES lpPipeAttributes,
                         // pointer to security attributes
    DWORD nSize          // number of bytes reserved for pipe
);
```

You must allocate space for the read and write handles (**hReadPipe** and **hWritePipe**). Then you pass the resulting pointers, provide the security attributes, and provide a suggested number of bytes, **nSize**, to use to implement the pipe. (The OS will use the value of **nSize** as a parameter in determining how much memory to use to implement the pipe.) It is acceptable to pass zero for **nSize**, meaning that NT will use a default pipe size.

If you attempt to read an empty pipe, the **ReadFile** call will block the calling thread until there is data in the pipe.[1] If you attempt to write to a full pipe, the **WriteFile** call will block until there is space for the characters to be written to the pipe. Since a pipe is essentially a memory buffer (as opposed to a real file), Windows NT does not support the seek operation on a pipe.

The challenge in using pipes is in getting them set up so that multiple processes can use them. A problem is that an anonymous pipe is created by

---

[1] Though overlapped I/O has not yet been discussed, it is worth noting here that Windows NT does not support overlapped I/O on anonymous pipes.

one process, with read and write handles in that process's address space. How can another process get the file handles from the creating process? The standard techniques for passing a handle from one process to another are to use a global name (anonymous pipes do not have names), handle inheritance, and handle duplication. The classic UNIX solution to the problem is a variant of handle inheritance.

Here is a technique used in Hart (1997). It takes advantage of the fact that the processes that use the pipe are siblings—a common parent creates the pipe and passes the handles as redirected **stdin** and **stdout** to the children.

```
int main(int argc, char *argv[]) {
    HANDLE readPipe, writePipe;
    SECURITY_ATTRIBUTES pipeSA;
    STARTUPINFO srcStartInfo, sinkStartInfo;
...
// Create the pipe
        pipeSA.nLength = sizeof(SECURITY_ATTRIBUTES);
        pipeSA.lpSecurityDescriptor = NULL;
        pipeSA.bInheritHandle = TRUE;
        if(!CreatePipe(&readPipe, &writePipe,
                &pipeSA, 0)) {
            fprintf(stderr, "...", GetLastError());
            ExitProcess(1);
        }


// Create process to write the process
// Make handles inheritable
        printf("Main: Creating producer process\n");
        ZeroMemory(&pStartInfo, sizeof(STARTUPINFO));
        srcStartInfo.cb = sizeof(STARTUPINFO);
        srcStartInfo.hStdInput = GetStdHandle(
                STD_INPUT_HANDLE);
        srcStartInfo.hStdOutput = pfWritePipe;
        srcStartInfo.hStdError = GetStdHandle(
                STD_ERROR_HANDLE);
        srcStartInfo.dwFlags = STARTF_USESTDHANDLES;
        if(!CreateProcess(..., &srcStartInfo, ...)){
            fprintf(stderr, "...", GetLastError());
            ExitProcess(1);
```

```
        }
// Create process to read the pipe
// Make handles inheritable
        ZeroMemory(&cStartInfo, sizeof(STARTUPINFO));
        sinkStartInfo.cb = sizeof(STARTUPINFO);
        sinkStartInfo.hStdInput = fcReadPipe;
        sinkStartInfo.hStdOutput = GetStdHandle(
                STD_OUTPUT_HANDLE);
        sinkStartInfo.hStdError = GetStdHandle(
                STD_ERROR_HANDLE);
        sinkStartInfo.dwFlags = STARTF_USESTDHANDLES;
        if(!CreateProcess(..., &sinkStartInfo, ...)){
            fprintf(stderr, "...", GetLastError());
            ExitProcess(1);
    }


// Close pipe handles
    CloseHandle(readPipe);
    CloseHandle(writePipe);
    ...
}
```

The created processes use any I/O functions to read and write **stdin** and **stdout**.

PROBLEM STATEMENT

You are to write a multiprocess program, with three processes, to manipulate information in a "pipeline" fashion (See Figure 12).

- The first process, called the *source* process, is a source of information. It should use NT's file interface to read information from a file and then use any mechanism you wish to write the information to a pipe.
- The second process, called the *filter* process, reads information from the source (passed via the pipe), performs a simplified filtering step (such as converting uppercase characters to lowercase ones and vice versa), and then writes the data to a second pipe. The second pipe is used for IPC between the filter and the sink (the third) process. Be sure that you write the filter so that it does not block on empty input when it has output information to transmit.

Figure 12

Source, Filter, and Sink Processes

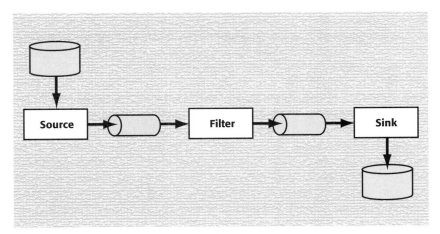

- The third process, called the *sink* process, reads the pipe from the filter and writes the information to a second file.

This exercise is interesting in part because it uses pipes as an IPC mechanism to pass data across address spaces, and because the intermediate filter must read the incoming pipe asynchronously with respect to writing results to the output pipe.

LAB ENVIRONMENT

This exercise uses the same environment as for the previous exercises.

ATTACKING THE PROBLEM

This exercise challenges your skills for organizing several processes and their components so that they work together. You can use the tools described in the exercise's Introduction or explore other Windows NT tools and use them.

It will be quite difficult for you to test the asynchronous behavior of your solution without introducing some artifact to make the various processes operate at different speeds. So you are to introduce some code to simulate processes that have a lot more work to do than the actual processes you write. The idea is that you have your processes sleep (or perform a busy loop) for random amounts of time. This will allow information to build up in the pipes.

5

Windows NT provides a facility for getting random numbers via the C runtime library. Following is a code segment that uses that facility. It should give you the guidance you need to include the simulated work in your source, filter, and sink processes.

```c
#include  <stdlib.h>    // srand() & rand()
#define P_RAND_SEED      1234
int main (int argc, char *argv[]) {
    const int delay = 500;
    ...
    srand(P_RAND_SEED);         // Set random# seed
// Main loop
    while(...) {
      ...
      simulatedWork(rand()%delayFactor);
                      // Random delay
      ...
    }
    ...
}
```

REFERENCES

Hart, Johnson M., *Win32 System Programming*, Addison-Wesley, Reading, Mass., 1997.

Microsoft, *Win32 API Reference Manual*, MSDN online documentation.

Richter, Jeffrey, *Advanced Windows*, Third Edition, Microsoft Press, Redmond, Wash., 1997.

Solomon, David A., *Inside Windows NT*, Second Edition, Microsoft Press, Redmond, Wash., 1998.

Using TCP/IP

In this exercise, you experiment with Windows NT's facilities for IPC across a network, including the Internet. You will learn about:

► Microsoft WinSock sockets
► How to use the TCP/IP network protocols
► Writing software with multiple input sources

INTRODUCTION

Modern computer systems exist in an open network environment that is compatible with the International Standards Organization Open System Interconnect (ISO OSI) architectural reference model. The ISO OSI model is a layered architecture of network protocols. A network protocol is an agreement among host machines that determines the method by which they will exchange information. At first blush, network protocols might not appear to be a technical topic worthy of extensive study. However, experience shows that the topic is nontrivial and has been the subject of intensive research and development for several years.

The ISO OSI model has seven layers of network protocols (Tanenbaum, 1989).

Physical layer. Defines the manner in which signals will be transmitted among host machines on a physical network. The network device is responsible for generating and receiving these signals. This is analogous to the RS-232 standard for communications devices.

Data link layer. Partitions a stream of bytes from the physical layer into a frame. It implements error and flow control for frame transmission and receipt.

Network layer. Uses frames to carry a higher-level abstraction called a packet. Packets can be transmitted from a host machine on one network to a host machine on a different network.

Transport layer. Implements byte streams and reliable packet delivery for its users. That is, it will fragment and regenerate a stream of bytes from a collection of packets that are transmitted over a network layer and then provide a protocol that ensures packet delivery.

Session layer. Provides additional services to the byte stream, such as high-level naming and bidirectional transmission services.

Presentation layer. Provides services to format the byte stream, for example character mapping and number conversion.

Application layer. Implements application-specific functionality.

It is traditional to group layers of the protocol together into informal clusters, since they are often implemented in these clusters.

Low-level protocols. Consists of the physical and data link layer protocols. For local area networks, these layers have generally converged onto a small number of choices: Ethernet (IEEE 802.3), Token Bus (IEEE 802.4), and Token Ring (IEEE 802.5). Cable modems and specialized telephone services are expected to provide relatively high-speed, cost-effective alternatives in the next few years. For longer distances, dedicated data transmissions systems continue to evolve. Low-level protocols are generally implemented in hardware.

Mid-level protocols. Consists of the network and transport layer protocols. Today, the dominant protocols (discussed later in the exercise) are the ARPAnet at the network layer and either TCP or UDP at the transport layer. These layers are implemented as kernel-mode software.

High-level protocols. Consists of the presentation, session, and application layers. Important examples include remote procedure call protocols (Xerox Courier and Sun RPC/XDR). They are implemented in libraries, though they sometimes require Kernel-mode support.

The mid-level protocols are implemented in the NT Executive and Kernel, so this lab manual focuses on those.

The Network Layer

The purpose of the network layer is to use the data link layer access to a single network to distribute information over a logical network of networks called an *internet*. At the data link layer, a frame can be addressed to any other host on the same network. The network layer provides added functionality and an extended address space and routing facilities so that a host on one network can send a packet to a host located on a distinct (but reachable) network. The basic technique is that each network includes one or more gateway machines connected to two different networks. A *gateway machine* has the capability to read data link layer frames on one machine, to retrieve the information from the frame, and then to forward the information in a frame on the second network. The two most significant functions in the network layer are

- a host's communication environment is expanded from a single network to a network of networks, and
- facilities are provided at the network layer to route packets among the addressable hosts.

Data link layer frames encapsulate a block of data. The network layer adds a new level of formatting on the information contained in a frame, thereby resulting in a network layer packet (the packet is wholly enclosed within a frame when it is transmitted over an individual network). Network packet addresses must specify the destination *network* and *host* addresses for the packet to be routed. Since there can be many different processes at the receiving host machine, the network layer also includes a "mailbox" address within a host machine called a *port*. While a data link layer address identifies a machine address (usually hardwired into a controller card) for delivering frames, the network layer address is a triple, <network, host, port>.

The Internet[1] is an international internet that connects networks all over the world. If you use an Internet Service Provider to access the Internet, you are probably connecting to the provider by establishing a dialup connection and then using the provider's gateway machine to enter the Internet.

As internets grow, the routing table in a gateway machine grows. Of course, any *particular* host is not likely to need to communicate with *all* other hosts on an internet. Therefore the gateway retrieves routing information as it is needed and keeps only a subset of the destination hosts that it regularly uses in its local routing tables.

As the internet grows, its overall reliability decreases. That is, if a gateway (or other host) has a reliability of, say, 90%, then the overall reliability of N machines as a collection is 0.9^N. For example, if there are four gateways, then the reliability is $0.9^4 = 0.6561$, or only about 66%. A combination of reasonably re-

---

6

[1] The *Internet* (note the capitalization) refers to a specific public internet that we have all used, if only to browse web sites.

liable machines will become unreliable if every machine must be up all of the time. When a machine is taken down (for example, it crashes or goes down for maintenance or some other reason), some of the routing tables must be changed in various gateways. Thus routing table maintenance is a critical aspect of the operation of the internet. Further, the network layer provides a functionality loophole in which packets can get lost due to momentary failures in the routing mechanism.[2]

In theory, it is possible to use the features and functions of the network layer as the basis of application programs. In practice, a network layer is not suitable as an API because it provides only the minimum of services for flexibility, error checking, and so on. These applications would view the network as *an unreliable packet (datagram) network*, a type of network that makes its "best effort" to deliver packets (but makes no guarantees). Applications that use the unreliable packet network would have to compensate for situations in which packets might be lost in a low-level protocol (for example, checksum errors or unacknowledged buffers in the data link layer). In addition, application programs must compensate for the possibility that a stream of packets could be delivered out of order (for example, sequential packets were routed through the internet on different paths).

In the UNIX world, the ARPAnet *Internet Protocol* (IP) became the popular standard as the network layer implementation (Stevens, 1994). It also became entrenched as the primary network layer in the international Internet. IP uses a 32-bit packet address, formatted to include the internet and host portions of the address; additional space is used to encode the port portion of the address. Today, there is concern that the 32-bit internet-host portion of the address is insufficient. There is a movement toward a new IP standard (called "IP Version 6") that will use 64-bit addresses.

The Transport Layer

The ISO OSI transport layer provides an API that is intended to be used by user-mode application programs. There are two primary classes of service provided at the transport layer API.

Datagrams. The datagram service is a packet-oriented service, logically similar to the packet interface exported by IP (but with error checks, flexible features, and so on). If an application uses the datagram service, the

---

[2] Transmission failures are usually much more likely in the data link layer or physical layer. The important point here is that packet communication at the network layer interface is unreliable.

transport layer guarantees that if an individual packet (the datagram) is delivered, it will be intact. However, it does not ensure that the packet will be delivered or that if a series of packets are to be sent to a host, they will arrive in the same order in which they were sent. Datagrams are a lightweight transport layer mechanism that can use IP to send individual blocks of information to any <net, host, port> in the address space.

Connections. This service provides a means for reliable, end-to-end transmission of byte streams—"files"—over the network. Whereas the datagram service uses a "telegram" model, the connection level of service is modeled after telephone service. This approach uses the notion of a *circuit* over the (inter)network for communication. A sender establishes a circuit by placing a call to the receiver; the receiver can accept or refuse the call. If the call is accepted, a circuit is established and each packet of information transmitted on the connection will automatically be sent to the designated receiver. Further, packets are abstracted into byte streams; the application can send a block of bytes over the connection, and the receiver retrieves the data by a simple byte stream, file read operation. Thus a connection-oriented service fits naturally into the Windows NT file model. The connection service is also often called a *virtual circuit* service, since it is an abstraction of physical circuits.

Today there are two dominant transport layer protocols, one for the datagram service and one for the connection service. Like IP, these protocols have been around for years (popularized in UNIX-based implementations), so they also use ARPAnet standards. The *User Datagram Protocol* (UDP) provides the datagram service, and the *Transmission Control Protocol* (TCP) provides the connection-oriented service. The WinSock package is the Windows NT implementation of TCP and UDP.

Naming

Network naming adds another level of complexity to network IPC, one that is generally ignored in this exercise, but which you will have to learn much more about to make general use of network protocols. You might have seen many of the barriers between address spaces within a machine. Those barriers are generally penetrated (to share information across address spaces) by taking advantage of the existence of the shared, protected kernel address space. A common technique in this environment is to name objects using names from a global Windows NT name space. Then when process B needs to use an object that has been named by process A, it uses the agreed-upon name to locate the object through NT's Object Manager.

For a process on one machine to use objects on another machine, there must be a similar name space, but that name space must be large enough that it incorporates the name spaces within every machine on the network. In the internet environment, a process on one machine uses the <net, host, port> address to locate another machine and then uses the normal name space within the destination machine to locate a resource. This procedure can result in very long names, and names can change as services migrate around the network. This has led to the invention of *name servers* (also sometimes called *directory services*) on the network. The basic idea is that a name service exists at a well-known <net, host, port>. An application can communicate with the name server (using the well-known internet address) to look up the internet address of a machine that provides the desired service. The name server behaves very much like a telephone directory service.

Sockets

There is logical gap between the idea of internet addresses of the form <net, host, port> and handles that exist within a process's address space for reading and writing information. The Berkeley Software Distribution (BSD) version of UNIX was a leading-edge network system. It established a handle-like data structure, called a *socket*, for dealing with network ports. In the BSD model, the sender and the receiver software is written to send information to a socket if it is to be transmitted using a transport layer protocol and to receive information from a socket if it is to be received using a transport layer protocol. Thus a socket is an "end" on which to connect a network layer protocol, either UDP or TCP.

UDP services are used by creating a socket, instructing the socket that it will be used for a datagram service, and then reading and writing datagrams over the socket (sockets are bidirectional).

TCP services require a little more work, since the connection must be established before it can be used. After both processes have created a socket, one of them must establish the virtual circuit by initializing its socket to act like a virtual circuit. The OS code on the remote end accepts (or rejects) the request to connect the virtual circuit. Then it configures a socket so that it will behave like a virtual circuit. When a pair of processes has finished with a virtual circuit, they should "tear it down," since network resources are required to keep the virtual circuit intact.

There is a complication in the socket scenario. The transmitting process can determine the internet and host names for the receiver (in either the UDP or TCP case), but how can it know the receiver's socket identification? The problem is that a socket is like a handle; it is created by a process at runtime, so a name server would be hard-pressed to manage every socket on every computer whenever some thread created a new one. Therefore the BSD socket package includes another facility by which a programmer can *map* a socket (handle) to a port number that exists in the internet name space. This procedure is called *binding* a socket to an internet address (see Figure 13).

The WinSock Package

The Microsoft WinSock package is closely modeled after the BSD UNIX Socket package (in fact it uses much of the same code). It allows the programmer to use UDP and TCP with IP, as well as other protocols. In this lab manual, the focus is on using TCP.

The **socket** WinSocket call causes a communication port to be created for the calling process. A socket can be thought of as an endpoint for network commu-

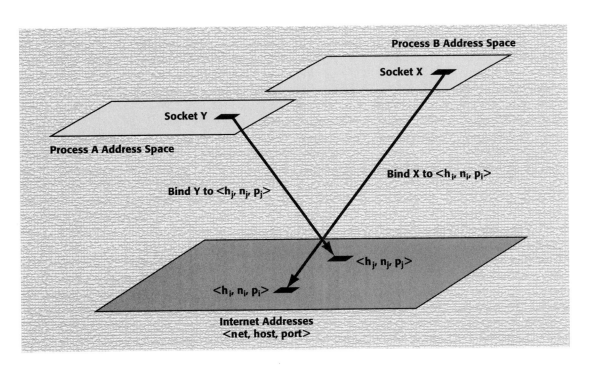

Figure 13
Binding a Socket

nication; it is reflected in the network package as an index (handle) into a table of socket descriptors. A socket call has the following form.

```
SOCKET socket(
     int af,
     int type,
     int protocol
);
```

The **af** parameter specifies the name space to be used (you will use the AF_INET domain). The **type** parameter specifies the nature of communication that will occur on the port, for example datagrams, virtual circuits, or others. You will use the SOCK_STREAM value with TCP. If you wanted to use UDP and datagrams, then you would use the SOCK_DGRAM value.

The **protocol** parameter identifies the protocol to be used with the port. There can be one or more protocols that can be used with the specified **commType**, though as a practical matter there is usually just one. The specified **protocol** must be compatible with the specified **commType**. If you use SOCK_STREAM and pass a value of zero for **protocol**, the system will use TCP; similarly, SOCK_DGRAM uses UDP. Once this call has been made, the process will have a SOCKET communication descriptor.

The socket name is introduced to the internet (or other) name space with the bind system call. The specific form of the call is as follows.

```
int bind(
     SOCKET s,
     const struct sockaddr FAR* name,
     int namelen
);
```

The **s** parameter is the SOCKET value returned by a **socket** call. The **name** parameter is a data structure describing the <net, host, port> name that should be associated with the socket. If another thread on the internet sends information to the <net, host, port> that is bound to socket **s**, then the information will be readable using **s** as a communication endpoint (handle). The **sockaddr** data type is defined as follows.

```
struct sockaddr {
     u_short sa_family;
     char sa_data[14];
};
```

sockaddr is intended to work for all address domains; sockaddr_in is used with TCP/IP.

```
struct sockaddr_in {
    short sin_family;
    u_short sin_port;
    struct in_addr sin_addr;
    char sin_zero[8];
};
```

Since bind works with different kinds of sockaddr data structures, the name-len field is the length of the sockaddr type being used. It must be provided so that bind can determine the length of the second parameter.

The connect call is used by a client thread to initiate a connection.

```
int connect(
    SOCKET s,
    const struct sockaddr FAR* name,
    int namelen
);
```

The name parameter identifies an exported name for some communication <net, host, port> in another process. The call will result in locating an internal communication port at the opposite end of the virtual circuit (provided it has been bound to some name in the name space accessible to the calling process using bind). Of course, there are many circumstances under which connect can fail, such as the name does not appear in the name space. (The WSAGetLastError( ) function returns the network error in the case of failure.) The namelen parameter again provides the length of the second parameter.

The listen call is executed by a process that intends to accept connect requests for a virtual circuit. That is, a server process would normally be prepared to accept connect requests from clients on the network.

```
int listen(
    SOCKET s,
    int backlog
);
```

The effect of the call is to specify the maximum number of pending connections, backlog, that the process is willing to support at any given time on a particular incoming socket, s. That is, each incoming connect request needs to be queued until the listening process is able to accept the connection. If the process that is being connected to has not done a **listen**, then the queue is zero length and any attempted connect from other processes will be rejected.

The **accept** call is a blocking read on the socket, waiting for an incoming **connect** message.

```
SOCKET accept(
     SOCKET s,
     struct sockaddr FAR* addr,
     int FAR* addrlen
);
```

A successful **accept** creates a new socket and returns it to the calling program. The ends of the virtual circuit will be the new socket on the end that executed the **accept** (the server) and the original socket on the end that executed the **connect** (the client). The process can then continue to **accept** connection requests on the original socket while a virtual circuit is established on the new socket.

The WinSock package requires that you call **WSAStartup** before you use any parts of the package and that you use **WSACleanup** after you have finished with them.

```
int WSAStartup(
     WORD wVersionRequested,
     LPWSADATA lpWSAData
);
```

The **wVersionRequested** parameter tells the startup package the latest version of the WinSock package that this code will use. The **lpWSAData** parameter is used to return a **WSAData** structure with the details of the version of WinSock you will be using. The **WSAData** has the following form.

```
typedef struct WSAData {
     WORD wVersion;
     WORD wHighVersion;
     Char szDescription[WSADESCRIPTION_LEN+1];
     Char szSystemStatus[WSASYS_STATUS_LEN+1];
     unsigned short iMaxSockets;
     unsigned short iMaxUdpDg;
```

```
            char FAR * lpVendorInfo;
} WSADATA, FAR * LPWSADATA;
```

See the MSDN documentation for the details of the field meanings.

The cleanup routine

int WSACleanup (void)

unregisters the process from making further use of the package (and frees resources allocated to support the process).

Here is a code skeleton for a client to use to initiate a connection.

```
#include   <winsock2.h>
client(){
      SOCKET skt;
      struct sockaddr_in *name;
      WORD versionRequested;
      WSADATA wsaData;

      versionRequested = MAKEWORD(..., ...);
      WSAStartup(versionRequested, &wsaData);
// Create the socket
      skt = socket(AF_UNIX, SOCK_STREAM, 0);
// Fill in the name data structure

// Connect to the server
      if (connect(skt, &name, sizeof(name))){
      // Failed connection
          fprintf(stderr, "...", WSAGetLastError());
          ExitThread(0);
      }
// Write a block to the slave
   ...
// Tear down the circuit
      closesocket(skt);
      WSACleanup();

}
```

Here is a code skeleton for a server to use to accept a connection.

```
#include <winsock2.h>
server() {
      SOCKET listenSkt, newSkt;
```

6

```
        sockaddr_in serverName, clientName;
        WORD versionRequested;
        WSADATA wsaData;

        WSAStartup(versionRequested, &wsaData);
    // Create the socket
        listenSkt = socket(AF_UNIX, SOCK_STREAM, 0);
    // Bind the socket to an external name
        bind(listenSkt, &serverName, sizeof(serverName));
    // Wait for the master to request a connection
        listen(listenSkt, 5);
    // The master is attempting to connect
        new_skt = accept(listenSkt,
                &clientName, sizeof(clientName));
        closesocket(listenSkt);      // No longer needed
    // Perform server tasks according to client requests
        ...
    // Close this end of the connection
        closesocket(newSkt);
        WSACleanup();
    }
```

PROBLEM STATEMENT

[*This assignment is the same as Exercise 15.9.1 for the Linux/BSD UNIX environment in Nutt (1997).*] You are to implement a skeletal "talk" facility between two threads in two different processes. The facility is assumed to be asymmetric in the sense that one of the processes acts as an initiator and the other as a receiver. The initiator begins the talk session by requesting a virtual circuit with the receiver (that is, the initiator takes the role of client and the receiver takes the role of server). Use the WinSock 2.0 socket communication mechanism with the internet address domain as the IPC mechanism. Each process should provide a single console window for both sending and receiving; precede outgoing messages with a > symbol and incoming messages with a < symbol.

Your system should be demonstrable on two processes on the same machine, for example between processes in two different windows or across machines without changing the code. Let the server's system choose a port number, and then specify the port number for the client at runtime.

When you use the WinSock package, you must be sure that the link editor uses the WinSock 2.0 library. To do this, add **wsock32.lib** to the list of libraries to be used. Also be sure that you are using **libc.lib**.

ATTACKING THE PROBLEM

You will be using facilities that allow you to place data on the internet. You should write and debug your software using only processes and threads on your local machine. Once it is working on the local machine (using IP addresses), you should only have to supply the names of other internets and hosts in order for the code to work over the network.

You can use the **hostname** command in **cmd.exe** to determine the name of the machine you are using. If you are working in a lab, the machine name is likely to change from one session to another, so you will probably find it simpler to include code that detects the host's name. Use the **gethostbyname** function call to determine the name of the machine you are using.

6

```
struct HOSTENT FAR * gethostbyname(
     const char FAR * name
);
```

This will fill the ASCII character string in the name parameter and will return a pointer to a **HOSTENT** description of the machine.

```
struct hostent {
     char FAR * h_name;
     char FAR * FAR * h_aliases;
     short h_addrtype;
     short h_length;
     char FAR * FAR * h_addr_list;
};
```

Take a look at the online documentation to interpret the fields in the HOSTENT data structure.

You will have to exercise a little care in filling in the fields of **sockadd_in**. You might find the following code segment helpful.

```
LPHOSTENT  host;
SOCKADDR_IN aServer;
```

```
...
host = gethostbyname(serverHostName);
ZeroMemory(&aServer, sizeof(SOCKADDR_IN));
aServer.sin_family = AF_INET;
aServer.sin_port = htons((u_short) port);
CopyMemory(&aServer.sin_addr,
        host->h_addr_list[0], host->h_length);
```

Multiple Inputs

One of the challenges of this assignment is writing your talk programs so that they react either to an incoming message from the network or to input from **stdin**, depending on which happens first. This will require that you be able to do nonblocking input operations on the socket and on **stdin**. And this will require some ingenuity on your part and some reading of the online documentation. (*Hint*: **CreateFile** can be used with the console. You might also find it helpful to see the routines in the console I/O package, under "Console and Port I/O," in the MSDN documentation.)

REFERENCES

Davis, Ralph, *Win32 Network Programming: Windows 95 and Windows NT Network Programming Using MFC*, Addison-Wesley, Reading, Mass., 1997.

Microsoft, *Win32 API Reference Manual*, MSDN online documentation.

Stevens, W. Richard, *UNIX Network Programming*, Prentice-Hall, Englewood Cliffs, N. J., 1990.

Stevens, W. Richard, *TCP/IP Illustrated*, Vol. I, Addison-Wesley, Reading, Mass., 1994.

Tanenbaum, Andrew S., *Computer Networks*, Second Edition, Prentice-Hall, Englewood Cliffs, N. J., 1989.

seven

Virtual Memory

In this exercise, you will experiment with various aspects of Windows NT's virtual memory mechanisms. Unlike most other operating systems, Windows NT provides an explicit API for manipulating certain aspects of the virtual memory (usually, virtual memory is completely transparent to the application programmer). In this exercise, you will learn about:

▶ The organization of Windows NT's virtual memory system

▶ How to control your virtual memory space

▶ How to write a monitoring and reporting tool

▶ The details of VirtualAlloc, VirtualFree, VirtualLock, VirtualUnlock, VirtualQuery, GetSystemInfo, and GlobalMemoryStatus

INTRODUCTION

Paging virtual memory is employed in most contemporary operating systems. In a paging system, each process has its own virtual address space that it uses to reference different objects—usually the contents of memory locations. Part of the virtual address space is defined by the link editor when it creates an execution image, the **EXE** file. The remainder of the address space can be dynamically defined at runtime by using techniques described in this exercise. After the static part of the virtual address space has been constructed, it is stored in the *secondary memory* (usually in a partition on a storage device called a *paging disk*). For most practical purposes, you can think of the paging disk as being a file.

In a conventional computer, the processor can only fetch instructions or load data that are located in the *primary* (or *executable*) *memory* (also called RAM, for random access memory). The primary memory is small and fast compared to the secondary memory. Primary memory is much more expensive than secondary memory, so it is usually orders of magnitude smaller than the secondary memory. Most computers do not have enough primary memory to store even one process's full virtual address space, but there is plenty of room on the secondary memory to store the virtual address spaces for several processes at a time. The primary memory is also much faster than the secondary memory. The processor can read or write a byte in the primary memory in a couple of processor cycles, but it requires thousands of processor cycles to read or write information in the secondary memory.

To conserve primary memory space, a paging virtual memory system loads at any given time only portions of the virtual address space of several different processes. As a thread executes in its process's address space, the part of the virtual address space that it is currently using is loaded into the primary memory, while other parts of the address space remain in the secondary memory. When the process no longer needs a portion of the virtual address space (at least for a while), that portion is copied back to the secondary memory. This allows the primary memory locations that were being used to store one portion of the virtual address space to be used to store a different part of the virtual address space at a later time.

In a virtual memory system, an efficiency in scale is achieved by copying a *block* of memory into the primary memory, or back to the secondary memory, whenever any movement between the two levels of the memory hierarchy is required. The efficiency comes from the fact that secondary storage I/O is block-oriented; that is, if a single word is needed from the secondary storage, a whole block must be read just to get the single word. So it makes sense to place the whole block into the primary memory, since it must be read to get the missing word.

There is another benefit in loading whole blocks rather than just words. When a thread references location i, there is a high probability that it will reference location $i + 1$ in the near future—this is called *locality* (you can read more about it in your textbook). A *paging* virtual memory loads and unloads fixed-sized blocks, called *pages,* whenever it moves information back and forth between the primary and secondary memories. The page boundaries are completely transparent to the programmer.[1]

---

[1] In a *segmented* virtual memory, the blocks are variably sized, with their sizes depending on directives from the programmer. The block boundaries are explicit in segmented virtual memory.

Figure 14 summarizes the operation of a generic paging virtual memory system. When a thread references a virtual address k (step 1 in the figure), the virtual memory first determines the number of the page containing the virtual address k (step 2 in the figure). If the page is currently loaded in the primary memory (step 3 in the figure), the virtual memory system transforms the virtual address into a physical address corresponding to the location in primary memory—the *page frame*—where the target page is located. If the page is not loaded at the time it is referenced, the normal thread execution is interrupted while the memory manager loads the target page into a page frame; once the page is loaded, the execution is resumed. In step 4, the reference to virtual address k is relocated to the physical address in primary memory, where virtual location k is currently loaded.

The positive aspect of a virtual memory system is that several processes can use the primary memory at the same time, even when the sum of their virtual address spaces is far larger than the amount of primary memory in the computer. The cost of supporting virtual memory is that an executing thread will encounter times when it must wait while part of its virtual address space is being

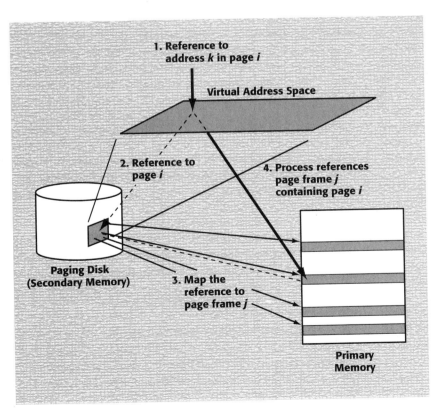

Figure 14

A Generic Paging System

1. Reference to address k in page i

Virtual Address Space

2. Reference to page i

4. Process references page frame j containing page i

Paging Disk (Secondary Memory)

3. Map the reference to page frame j

Primary Memory

loaded into the primary memory. Virtual memory is a good thing if the times a thread has to wait are infrequent—this is a classic *time versus space tradeoff*. Windows NT uses a paging virtual memory system. There are several unique features of Windows NT's virtual memory, so the remaining discussion will focus on the Windows NT design.

The Windows NT Virtual Memory Model

Every Windows NT process is given a fixed-size virtual address space—4GB—which, of course, is much larger than the amount of primary memory (RAM) in any contemporary PC. The process is not required to use all of the virtual address space, only as much as it needs. Ordinarily, the **EXE** file for a program is very much smaller than the address space. As illustrated in Figure 15, part of the virtual address space, usually 2GB, is used to allow a thread to reference user space memory objects and the remainder is used to reference addresses used by the OS (it is supervisor space).[2] Even though the supervisor space portion of the address space exists in a process's virtual address space, it can only be referenced by a thread if the thread is executing in supervisor mode.

In the normal configuration, the first 64K (addresses **0x00000000** through **0x0000FFFF**) of the virtual address space is not used. The rationale for this is that when programmers write code with pointer errors, the bad pointer is usually zero or a small number. In the Windows NT virtual memory system, if a program attempts to reference any address in the first 64K, the virtual memory system assumes that the reference is a programming error and a memory fault will occur. The first usable part of the address space begins at **0x0001000** and ends at **0x7FFEFFFF**—2GB less 128K; therefore the first location a program uses is generally **0x0001000**. Locations **0x7FFF0000** to **0x7FFFFFFF** are reserved as the first 64K for kernel-space programs, again as a safeguard for catching references to small addresses (Richter, 1997). **0x80000000** through **0xFFFFFFFF** is a full 2GB address partition in which the Executive, Kernel, and device drivers are located.

The OS needs some means of determining the amount of the address space that the process will actually use. As mentioned in the discussion of generic paging systems, the link editor builds the static execution image in an **EXE** file that will generally define the portion of the address space that will be used for

---

[2] The relative sizes of the application's portion of the process address space and the kernel portion of the space is different in Windows NT Server than it is in Windows NT Workstation. This is one of the configuration differences between the two OS versions. Windows NT Server has a larger part of the address space for the user space, thereby allowing applications to have large amounts of information in virtual memory.

Figure 15

*Windows NT
Paging System*

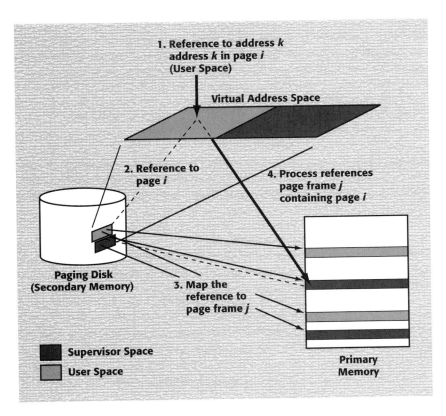

the compiled code. DLLs and other dynamically allocated portions of the address space can be added to the virtual address space at runtime.

There are two phases to dynamically add addresses to the address space:

1. Reserve a portion of the address space called a *region.*
2. Commit a *block* of pages in a region in the address space.[3]

In the first step, a thread in a process dynamically *reserves* a region of virtual addresses without actually causing anything to be written to the secondary storage *page file* (also sometimes called the *paging file*). A thread in the process may also subsequently *release* a region of addresses it previously reserved.

In the second phase, the processor *commits* addresses that were previously reserved (the committed block is frequently a proper subset of the reserved

---

[3] Just to make things complicated, the Windows NT documentation refers to a block of pages and an allocation region as "regions." The nomenclature here is taken from Richter (1997).

region). Once a portion of the address space has been committed, space is allocated in the page file. If a thread in the process then references committed memory, the page containing the referenced address will be loaded from the page file into the primary memory. (Of course, the part of the address space that has been reserved and committed will not have had anything written to it when it is first referenced, so a zero-filled page will be loaded on the first reference.)

Each processor supports a particular *allocation granularity* to determine the minimum size of a block of addresses that can be reserved. On all current implementations, the allocation granularity is 64K. (However, you can use **GetSystemInfo** to determine any processor's allocation granularity; see further details in this exercise.) Before a reservation is made, the address is automatically rounded down to the next lower allocation granularity boundary.

Each processor also supports its own page size, usually 4K or 8K (you can determine the processor's page size by using **GetSystemInfo**). Memory is committed in units of pages, so the actual commitment of addresses can be on a much smaller grain than reservation. Once virtual addresses have been committed, the thread can use the memory just like any statically allocated part of the address space.

Paging System Internals

Address translation refers to the task of translating a virtual address reference into a physical primary memory reference (Steps 1–3 in Figure 15). Address translation depends on the presence of certain elements in the hardware (see your textbook for more details) to detect missing pages and to rapidly map a page into a page frame. A virtual address is a 32-bit quantity generated by the processor. In contrast to conventional paging mechanisms, Windows NT uses a two-level address translation facility (see Figure 16). The page *byte index* is the K_1 least significant bits in the address; K_1 is 12 for Intel *x*86 processors with 4K pages and 13 for Digital Alpha processors with 8K pages. Conventional single-level paging mechanisms use the remainder of the address as a page number. In Windows NT, the remainder is called the *virtual page number*. It is separated into two parts called the *page table index* (K_2 bits) and the *page directory index* (the K_3 most significant bits in the address). In *x*86 processors, K_2 and K_3 are 10, and in the Alpha processor, K_2 is 11 and K_3 is 8.

Address translation uses these three fields in the address as follows.

1. The process descriptor (in the **KPROCESS** part of the process object) contains a pointer, *A*, to the (beginning of the) *page directory* for the given process.

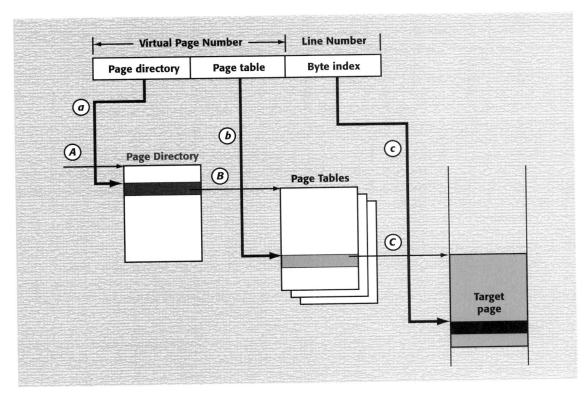

Figure 16

Address Translation

2. The page directory index, *a*, is an offset into the page directory where a *page descriptor entry* (PDE) for the specified page is located.

3. Each process can have several different *page tables*. The PDE references the particular page table to be used for this memory reference (pointer *B* in the figure).

4. The *page table entry* (PTE) is found by using the page table index, *b*, from the address as an index into the page table.

5. If the target page is currently loaded in primary memory at page frame *j*, then the PTE points to the page frame, *C*. If it is not loaded, the Virtual Memory Manager must locate the page in the page file, find a page frame, allocate it to the process, and then load the page into the page frame.

6. Finally, the byte index, *c*, is added to the page frame base address to obtain the location of the target byte in the primary memory.

While the page directory could be mapped to any location (pointer *A* in Figure 16), in practice it is located at a fixed point in the address space—0xC0300000 on *x*86 systems and 0xC018000 on Alpha processors. Both of these processors use a dedicated processor register to reference the page directory. The register is saved as part of the thread context whenever a new thread is dispatched to the processor.

Windows NT uses multiple page tables to distinguish among different uses of the address space. The most obvious difference among pages is that some are user-space pages and others are kernel-space pages; they are mapped in different page tables. Notice that because kernel-space pages are put in a separate page table, different processes have the PDEs for kernel space pointing to the same page tables. Further, the page tables can then make other distinctions about the physical memory used for the particular part of the address space. For example, in kernel space some parts of the kernel memory are paged in and out just like in user-space pages, but others are not allowed to be paged out. Rather, they are allocated from a special pool of nonpaged memory blocks.[4]

Each PTE references a page frame number when the corresponding page is loaded. There is also a collection of flags to describe how the page can be referenced, including whether the PTE is valid and whether the page is reserved, is dirty (it has had new values written into it since it was last loaded into primary memory), or has been accessed since the last epoch (see your textbook), and so on.

A memory reference requires that the PDE be found in the page directory and that the PTE be found in the page table. This means that an ordinary memory reference could result in several additional memory references if there was no special hardware provided in the processor. Contemporary computers, such as the Intel *x*86 and Digital Alpha processors, use an associative memory called a *translation look-aside buffer* (TLB) (you can find out more about the principles of these mapping memories in your textbook). Briefly, the TLB is a cache memory for recently translated PDEs and PTEs. The first reference to such an entry causes extra memory references to access the entries, but once a page has been mapped, its entries are copied into the TLB. Subsequent references are looked up associatively in the TLB, where they can be found in a single TLB associative memory cycle.

---

[4] Nonpaged memory blocks contain information or code that needs to be in the memory because it is currently being used (such as a buffer) or it is code that must be readily available (such as the Virtual Memory Manager or scheduling code).

Windows NT uses *demand paging*, meaning that pages are not loaded into the primary memory until they are referenced.[5] Further, PTEs are not even created until the corresponding page is loaded. The rationale for this approach is that a process might reserve memory addresses without ever using them; in fact, the process might even commit memory pages and then never reference them during execution. Since the address space is so large, if PTEs were made as soon as the information was known, many PTEs likely might be created and then never used, thereby resulting in considerable wasted memory for PTEs.

Because PTEs are not created until they are first used, the OS must keep other data structures to hold reservation and commitment operations. A *virtual address descriptor* (VAD) is created whenever a process reserves or commits virtual addresses. When a thread first references the addresses within a VAD, the PTE is then created so that address translation can proceed normally.

The last aspect of paging internals considered here is primary memory allocation. Windows NT uses working sets with a clock algorithm (see your textbook). It distinguishes between the *process* working set and the *system* working set used by a process. The process working set grows and shrinks like a classic working set; it starts with a default minimum size—20 to 50 pages—and is not allowed to grow larger than a default maximum size—45 to 345 pages. However, the maximum working set size can be changed by the system administrator.

7

There are many details to Windows NT's virtual memory system, and the details can change depending on the type of the underlying processor. This subsection provides you with an introduction to the virtual memory manager operation. See Chapter 5 of Solomon (1998) for a more complete discussion of the Windows NT paging mechanism.

Virtual Memory Functions

The Win32 API provides several functions for inspecting the virtual memory configuration and dynamically controlling the way the address space is used. **GetSystemInfo**, **GlobalMemoryStatus**, and **VirtualQuery** can be used to

---

[5] Windows NT also uses copy-on-write, which can defer PTE creation until a shared page is actually written by one of the processes using the page (see your textbook for a discussion of the copy-on-write semantics).

inspect the status of a process's virtual memory. The most basic information comes from the following.

```
VOID GetSystemInfo(
     LPSYSTEM_INFO lpSystemInfo
);
```

Here, the SYSTEM_INFO data structure is defined by the following.

```
typedef struct _SYSTEM_INFO {
     DWORD dwOemId;
     DWORD dwPageSize;
     LPVOID lpMinimumApplicationAddress;
     LPVOID lpMaximumApplicationAddress;
     DWORD dwActiveProcessorMask;
     DWORD dwNumberOfProcessors;
     DWORD dwProcessorType;
     DWORD dwAllocationGranularity;
     DWORD dwReserved;
} SYSTEM_INFO, *LPSYSTEM_INFO;
```

This function fills in the **lpSystemInfo** to inform you of various settings in the virtual memory for the host processor on which it is called. Specifically, the **dwPageSize** field is the page size used on the host processor. The **lpMinimumApplicationAddress** field provides the lowest address that can be used without incurring memory faults. The **lpMaximumApplication-Address** field is the highest address an application can use. The **dwAllocationGranularity** field is the allocation granularity used on the host processor.

The VOID GlobalMemoryStatus(LPMEMORYSTATUS lpBuffer) function returns more-detailed information on the virtual memory in a **MEMORYSTATUS** data structure

```
typedef struct _MEMORYSTATUS {
     DWORD dwLength;
     DWORD dwMemoryLoad;
     DWORD dwTotalPhys;
     DWORD dwAvailPhys;
     DWORD dwTotalPageFile;
     DWORD dwAvailPageFile;
     DWORD dwTotalVirtual;
     DWORD dwAvailVirtual;
} MEMORYSTATUS, *LPMEMORYSTATUS;
```

The **dwMemoryLoad** parameter is a value between 0 and 100 that reflects the relative current physical memory utilization. This number is useful only if you use it often so that you get an intuitive feel for different values versus observed performance. The physical memory measures, **dwTotalPhys** and **dwAvailPhys**, describe, respectively, the total amount of physical memory configured in the machine and the amount that is currently unallocated to any working set. The page file measures, **dwTotalPageFile** and **dwAvailPageFile**, report the total number of bytes that can be stored in this process's page file and the number of bytes currently available in the page file, respectively. The **dwTotalVirtual** and **dwAvailVirtual** fields are, respectively, the size of the user-space portion of the total address space and the number of byte addresses currently available.

The last function for observing the virtual memory state is **VirtualQuery**. This function focuses on a block of pages in a memory region.

```
DWORD VirtualQuery(
    LPCVOID lpAddress,
    PMEMORY_BASIC_INFORMATION lpBuffer,
    DWORD dwLength
};
```

The **lpAddress** parameter is an arbitrary address in the address space; before it is used, it is rounded down to the next lower page boundary. The corresponding page belongs to some contiguous set of pages in a block; that is, all of the pages in the block have the same properties, since they were committed using the same function call. A call on **VirtualQuery** to any address in a block will return the same information in the MEMORY_BASIC_INFORMATION structure for every address in the block.

```
typedef struct _MEMORY_BASIC_INFORMATION {
    PVOID BaseAddress;
    PVOID AllocationBase;
    DWORD AllocationProtect;
    DWORD RegionSize;
    DWORD State;
    DWORD Protect;
    DWORD Type;
} MEMORY_BASIC_INFORMATION;
typedef MEMORY_BASIC_INFORMATION
        *PMEMORY_BASIC_INFORMATION;
```

The **BaseAddress** is the address of the first page in the block, and the **AllocationBase** is the address where the region begins. The **AllocationProtect**

7

field indicates whether the pages in the block are read-only, read-write, execute-only, and so on (see the MSDN documentation). The **RegionSize** field is the number of bytes in the block (here is a case in which "region" means block of pages within an allocation unit region). The **State** field can have the value **MEM_COMMIT**, **MEM_RESERVE**, or **MEM_FREE** to reflect whether the pages in the block are, respectively, committed, reserved, or unreserved/uncommitted ("free"). The **Protect** field is the protection type for the pages in the block, and the **Type** field indicates the type of the pages that will be saved in the region (**MEM_IMAGE**, **MEM_MAPPED**, or **MEM_PRIVATE** – see the MSDN documentation).

The following extended version of **VirtualQuery** allows a thread to query a virtual memory block in another process.

```
DWORD VirtualQueryEx(
        HANDLE hProcess,
        LPCVOID lpAddress,
        PMEMORY_BASIC_INFORMATION lpBuffer,
        DWORD dwLength
};
```

The **hProcess HANDLE** specifies the target process for the query. The calling thread's handle must have **PROCESS_QUERY_INFORMATION** access to the remote process.

The **VirtualAlloc** and **VirtualFree** functions are used to dynamically reserve, commit, release, and decommit memory.

```
LPVOID VirtualAlloc(
        LPVOID lpAddress,
        DWORD dwSize,
        DWORD flAllocationType,
        DWORD flProtect
};
```

The **VirtualAlloc** function is used both for reservation and commitment. The **lpAddress** is intended to be the base address of the region (for reserve) or block (for commit) operations. (Remember that a region boundary is determined by the system's allocation granularity, but a block boundary is determined by page boundaries.) The **dwSize** parameter specifies the length of the region or block in bytes.

The **flAllocationType** parameter distinguishes among different forms of the allocation operation. If the value is **MEM_COMMIT**, this is a block commit operation; if the value is **MEM_RESERVE**, this is a region reserve operation. You can combine the **MEM_COMMIT** and **MEM_RESERVE** flags on one call, thereby causing a region of the address space to be reserved and every page in the region to be committed as the result of a single call.

The **MEM_RESET** flag specifies that a block of pages should not be saved on the page file when it is overwritten. The **flProtect** parameter specifies the access protection for the unit of memory. The **VirtualAllocEx** version of the function allows one process to reserve and commit addresses in another process's address space (on behalf of the other process).

The **VirtualFree** and **VirtualFreeEx** functions are used to decommit or release portions of the address space; see the MSDN documentation for details. Consider the following.

```
LPVOID VirtualFree(
    LPVOID lpAddress,
    DWORD dwSize,
    DWORD dwFreeType
};
```

Here, the **lpAddress** and **dwSize** parameters have the same meaning as in VirtualAlloc. The **dwFreeType** parameter uses a value of **MEM_DECOMMIT** to decommit reserved regions and **MEM_RELEASE** to release blocks of virtual memory.

There are five functions used to "lock" pages into the primary memory. A *locked page* cannot be paged out to the secondary storage by the virtual memory system. The five functions allow you to use different strategies for locking and unlocking a page. A process can use

```
BOOL VirtualLock(
    LPVOID lpAddress,
    DWORD dwSize
};
```

to lock a block of previously committed, consecutive pages in the primary memory. Every page that contains an address in the range

[lpAddress, lpAddress+dwSize]

up to a maximum of 30 pages will be locked in the primary memory.

If there is a shortage of physical memory in the computer, locking pages is likely to aggravate that shortage because it prevents the working set mechanism from using the locked pages. Further, the pages will be locked even when the owning process is dormant (but the lock will be released when the process terminates). If a process has the **SE_INC_BASE_PRIORITY_NAME** privilege, it is allowed to increase its working set maximum using the **SetProcessWorkingSetSize** function. Of course this, too, could have a significant impact on overall system performance, since it places more demand on the physical memory.

Locked pages are unlocked with the following. All pages containing addresses in the specified range become unlocked.

```
BOOL VirtualUnlock(
      LPVOID lpAddress,
      DWORD dwSize
};
```

Many threads can call **VirtualLock**, but any single call to **VirtualUnlock** will unlock the block of pages. If your intent is to match every lock operation with a corresponding unlock before a locked page becomes unlocked, then you should use either **GlobalLock** and **GlobalUnlock** or **LocalLock** and **LocalUnlock** functions to control global and local memory objects, respectively.

Finally, **ReadProcessMemory** and **WriteProcessMemory** can be used by one process to read and write another process's memory, provided the handle to the other process has the proper privilege. This is a very powerful mechanism for sharing memory, though it depends on the proper administration of handles. You can study the MSDN documentation to see how to use these functions.

Heaps

The heap is another form of virtual memory. A Windows NT heap is a generalization of the C runtime heap (**malloc** and **free** use the runtime heap). There is a set of Win32 API functions for creating and managing your own heap in the virtual address space. Once the heap has been created, you use another set of operations to allocate and release memory units from/to the heap. See Chapter 9 in Richter (1997) or the MSDN documentation for more about heaps.

In this exercise, you will use the Win32 API to experiment with the virtual memory functions. You will observe the effects of your experimentation by monitoring and reporting your observations. You will write a single process with one thread to simulate memory activity and a second thread to monitor the memory behavior of the first thread. Your simulation thread will read a trace file that contains one record for each virtual memory operation it is to perform. Each record has the form

Time, Region/Block number, Operation, Size, Access

The **Time** field is the time in milliseconds (from the time the process started) at which this record is to be processed. The **Region/Block number** is the region number for an operation based on the allocation granularity (such as a reserve operation) or a block number for an operation that uses a page granularity (such as a commit operation). The **Operation** field is the operation itself, indicated by one of the following values.

Reserve a region	1
Commit a block	2
Reset a block	3
Release a region	4
Decommit a block	5
Lock a block	6
Unlock a block	7

7

The **Size** field specifies the length of the region/block in bytes. The **Access** parameter sets the access for the operation according to the following table (from **windows.h**).

PAGE_READONLY	1
PAGE_READWRITE	2
PAGE_EXECUTE	3
PAGE_EXECUTE_READ	4
PAGE_EXECUTE_READWRITE	5

When the simulation reads a record, it calls an appropriate virtual memory function (described in the "Introduction"), using parameters it determines from the trace record operation.

Your monitor thread should be a *sampling monitor*, meaning that it sleeps for a period of time (experiment with different strategies for selecting the period) and then wakes up and checks the status of the virtual memory. It must record the memory status each time it checks it. When the test has completed, the monitor should print its report with at least the following information.

Page size: XXX
Lowest useable address: 0x XXX
Highest useable address: 0x XXX
Allocation granularity: XXX
Total physical memory: XXX
Total virtual memory: XXX
        Total page file memory: XXX

Physical Memory
     [0, YYY]: XXX
     [YYY, YYY]: XXX
     [YYY, YYY]: XXX

Virtual Memory
     [0, YYY]: XXX
     [YYY, YYY]: XXX
     [YYY, YYY]: XXX

Page File Memory
     [0, YYY]: XXX
     [YYY, YYY]: XXX
     [YYY, YYY]: XXX

Here, the last three parts of the report are *histograms* with N different bins. A histogram is a discrete distribution of observed values. For example, if there were 1,000 bytes of physical memory, then the first bin might represent the number of times that there were between 0 to 99 physical memory locations allocated on different samples, the second 100 to 199, and so on. When you sample the state of the memory, if there are 573 bytes of physical memory, then you add a count of 1 to the bin with a range between 500 and 599. You will need to experiment with your system to determine reasonable values for the number and size of bins to use in your histograms; obviously, the numbers will be much larger than 1,000 bytes. Each histogram will give you an idea of the distribution of physical, virtual, and page file memory sizes over the run of the program. Begin your experimentation using 20 bins.

Your instructor will supply an input script, though you can debug with a simple one such as the following.

1000	1	1	300000	4
1000	1	2	100000	4
1000	1	3	100000	4
1500	2	1	1000000	3
1750	2	2	500000	3
2500	3	1	3000000	5
2600	3	2	2000000	5
2605	3	6	1000000	5
2700	4	1	8000000	2
2800	4	2	6000000	2
3000	5	1	C000000	2
3100	5	2	800000	2
3200	1	5	100000	4
3300	6	1	4000000	2
3400	6	2	4000000	2
3450	1	4	300000	4
3475	3	7	1000000	5
3500	7	1	5000000	2
3600	7	2	4000000	2

There are many variables in this exercise: the configuration of the computer you are using, the size of other processes that are executing at the time you run your program, and so on. You will have to experiment with the machine to determine appropriate sampling intervals and histogram parameters. You might wish to use the Task Manager and/or Process Viewer to inspect the memory usage on your machine to help you determine some of these parameters.

LAB ENVIRONMENT

Tools: Task Manager and Process Viewer.

ATTACKING THE PROBLEM

Your solution will be a single-process program with two threads. The first thread reads the script file and performs the virtual memory actions, while the second one monitors the behavior of the first. The following skeleton will help you get started on writing the simulation thread.

```
int main (int argc, char *argv[]) {
// Initialization
        theClock = 0;
// Get parameters from the command line
// Open the script and report files
        scriptFID = fopen(argv[1], "r");      // script file
        reportFID = fopen(REPORT_FILE, "w");   // report file

// Get static information
// Create the measurement thread
// Processing loop
        while(fscanf(...) != EOF) {
            if(time >= theClock) {
                if(time > theClock)
                    simActivity(time-theClock, NULL, 0);
                theClock = time;
            }
// Parse the command and execute it
                switch (vmOp) {
                case 1:     // Reserve a region
                    break;
                case 2:     // Commit a block
                    break;
                case 3:     // Reset a block
                    break;
                case 4:     // Release a region
                    break;
                case 5:     // Decommit a block
                    break;
                case 6:     // Lock a block
                    break;
                case 7:     // Unlock a block
                    break;
                }
        }
// Terminate
}
```

```
void simActivity(int period,
        LPVOID lpAddress, DWORD dwSize) {
#ifdef REALTIME
    Sleep(period);
#else
    Sleep(100);
#endif
    if(lpAddress != NULL)
        ZeroMemory(lpAddress, dwSize);
}
```

Here is a skeleton for the monitor thread.

```
DWORD WINAPI monitorThread(LPVOID fid) {
// Report statistics that do not change
// Initialize histograms
// Start sampling the instrumentation
    while(...) {
    // Gather statistics and log them
        Sleep(INTERSAMPLE_TIME);
    }
// Report histograms
}
```

Monitoring and Reporting Behavior

This exercise requires that you manipulate the virtual address space and then observe the result of your manipulations. You might find it useful to review the Process Viewer and Task Manager that you first used in Exercise 1.

The "Processes" tab of the Task Manager provides a good high-level view of the memory performance. On the tab, select the "View" menu and then the "Select Columns ..." option. You will see several options you can display for each "Image Name," including "Memory Usage" (the process working set size) and "Virtual Memory Size" (the number of bytes used in the page file). On the "Performance" tab is a time plot of the physical memory usage, with sampled figures for the available memory and the amount of allocated memory being used for caching files. (See Exercise 9 for more information on file caching.) The kernel memory statistics show you the ratio of page space and nonpaged space.

The Process Viewer main display focuses on processes and threads. The "Memory Detail ..." option produces a detailed memory display for the selected process. With this tool you can inspect the user address space details (total; inaccessible; read only; write only, writeable, but not written; and executable). Also shown is the effect of commit operations—mapped space is potentially sharable, but the private space is not. Finally, the display shows summary information on the virtual memory performance for this process's address space: the current working set size, peak size, number of private pages, the number of page faults this process has incurred, and so on.

REFERENCES

Microsoft, *Win32 API Reference Manual*, MSDN online documentation.

Richter, Jeffrey, *Advanced Windows*, Third Edition, Microsoft Press, Redmond, Wash., 1997.

Solomon, David A., *Inside Windows NT*, Second Edition, Microsoft Press, Redmond, Wash., 1998.

eight

Memory-Mapped Files

Memory-mapped files are the primary internal OS mechanism used to implement sharing across address spaces (Richter, 1997). This exercise introduces you to the memory-mapped files. You will learn about:

▶ How to construct an application using memory-mapped files for IPC

▶ Memory-mapped file design

▶ The details of CreateFileMapping and MapViewOfFile

INTRODUCTION

Since threads within a process share the underlying process's address space, all threads implicitly share all of their information with their siblings. Windows NT, like all modern OSs, provides protection barriers between the address spaces for each process. This means that a thread running in one address space is ordinarily prevented from sharing information with a thread in a different process, since neither can ordinarily read or write the other's address space. Providing a mechanism to allow sharing across process address spaces is a classic problem for the OS. The IPC mechanisms introduced in Exercises 5 and 6 show some ways to accomplish the task, and the **ReadProcessMemory** and **WriteProcessMemory** functions mentioned in Exercise 7 can be used to accomplish sharing among address spaces. However, memory-mapped files are the preferred mechanism for sharing information among address spaces for processes on a single machine. Windows NT has been designed so that memory-mapped files are implemented at a low layer of the operating system—in the Virtual Memory Manager—and they are made to be very efficient.

Overview

Conceptually, a memory-mapped file is a disk-based file that is loaded into the primary memory. There is a strong similarity between the ways that memory-mapped files and virtual memory are designed in Windows NT. In the virtual memory case, a 4GB address space (much larger than almost any file) is defined in a page file. The Virtual Memory Manager loads selected pages from the page file into the primary memory on demand. Suppose the same mechanism is used with an arbitrary file rather than a page file, that is, the file defines an address space—a byte stream—that can be associated with a portion of a process's virtual address space. Then the process can read and write the file simply by reading and writing the virtual addresses to which the bytes in the file are mapped. As a bonus, the memory-mapped file can be paged from secondary storage without the knowledge of the application process. For example, if process A opens a 64K file and maps it into virtual addresses **0x20000000** to **0x2000FFFF**, then it can read or write the first byte in the file by reading or writing memory address **0x20000000** or it can reference the sixteenth byte by referencing **0x2000000F**.

The memory-mapped file mechanism, with the virtual memory mechanism, provides a simple loader for **EXE** and **DLL** files. After the process is created with its 4GB virtual address space, the system checks the size of the **EXE** file and then reserves that amount of space in the virtual address space (starting at location **0x00400000**). Finally, the system notes that the secondary storage that backs up the virtual address space is the **EXE** file rather than in a page file. The loading process continues by then determining the **DLL**s that are known at load time, reserving virtual addresses for each **DLL**, and noting that the backing store for the **DLL** is the **DLL** file rather than the page file.

Sharing a Memory-Mapped File

There is another aspect of memory-mapped files that makes them even more useful (see Figure 17). Since the information is logically referenced as a filename, more than one process can map the same file into its own virtual address space at the same time. Now suppose process A maps a 64K file into its locations **0x2000000** to **0x2000FFFF** and process B opens the same file and maps it to its virtual addresses **0x30000000** to **0x3000FFFF**. Then process B could "transmit" information to process A by writing information at, say, location **0x30001234** and then having process A read the information from its virtual address **0x20001234**. Windows NT assures that both processes can see memory write operations when they occur.

Figure 17

*Memory-Mapped
Files*

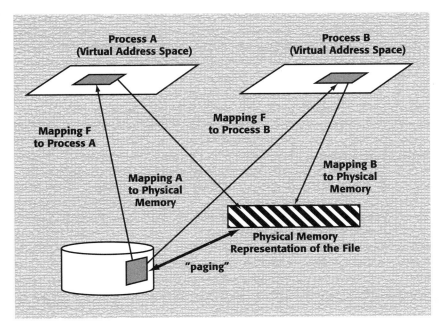

Shared memory-mapped files make no special provision for managing critical sections (see Exercise 4). If a memory-mapped file is being shared by a set of threads and any of the threads is updating the file, then all of the threads will have to use one of the normal Windows NT mechanisms—events, mutexes, semaphores, and so on—to ensure that critical sections are not violated. (Even though these mechanisms were used within a single process's address space in Exercise 4, they can be shared using inheritance, duplication, and so on.)

Memory-Mapped File Functions

To use a memory-mapped file, you must

- obtain a handle to the file by creating or opening it,
- reserve virtual addresses for the file, and
- establish a mapping between the file and your virtual address space.

A file handle is obtained using **CreateFile** or **OpenFile**. The **CreateFile** function is described in Exercise 5. When it is used with memory-mapped files, the normal parameters are used to create/open the file.

After a file has been opened, a file-mapping object (sometimes called a *section object* in the documentation) stores the mapping information. It is created with CreateFileMapping, as follows.

```
HANDLE CreateFileMapping(
      HANDLE hfile,
      LPSECURITY_ATTRIBUTE
      lpFileMappingAttributes,
      DWORD flProtect,
      DWORD dwMaximumSizeHigh,
      DWORD dwMaximumSizeLow,
      LPCTSTR lpName
);
```

The **hfile** parameter is the handle returned by **CreateFile** (or **OpenFile**). The **lpFileMappingAttributes** parameter is the usual pointer to a **SECURITY_ATTRIBUTE** data structure, which is used if the handle is to be inherited.

The **flProtect** parameter is one of **PAGE_READONLY**, **PAGE_READWRITE**, or **PAGE_WRITECOPY**. The value of this parameter must be compatible with the privileges in the hfile handle. For example, read-only access means that the calling process is requesting only read access to the region that holds the pages for the file. Another flag can be ORed with the basic protection parameter to cause virtual addresses for the mapping to be reserved or committed. The maximum size of the space to be mapped is a 64-bit value, so its two halves are passed using the next two parameters, **dwMaximumSizeHigh** and **dwMaximum-SizeLow**.

Finally, the mapping object may use a name, **lpName**, or use **NULL**. If **lpName** is NULL, the mapping object is created without a name and cannot normally be shared. If **lpName** is defined and already exists, this request is to use the existing named mapping object. If **lpName** is defined but does not exist, it is created.

The handle returned by the call to **CreateFileMapping** can be used like any other handle: It can be inherited by child processes or replicated in another address space using **DuplicateHandle**. The **OpenFileMapping** function can also be used with mapping objects that have a name, as follows.

```
HANDLE OpenFileMapping(
      DWORD dwDesiredAccess,
      BOOL bInheritHandle,
      LPCTSTR lpName
);
```

Once the mapping object has been created, the address space will have been established, though the file contents will not have actually been mapped to the process's address space. This is accomplished using the following.

```
LPVOID MapViewOfFile(
      HANDLE hFileMappingObject,
      DWORD dwDesiredAccess,
      DWORD dwFileOffsetHigh,
      DWORD dwFileOffsetLow,
      DWORD dwNumberOfBytesToMap
};
```

The **hFileMappingObject** parameter is the handle of the file-mapping object returned by the **CreateFileMapping** call. The **dwDesired-Access** parameter specifies the way the mapping object can be used to access data, provided it is compatible with the **flProtect** parameter used with **CreateFileMapping**.

- **FILE_MAP_WRITE**. Reading and writing via the mapping object is acceptable.
- **FILE_MAP_READ**. Threads will only read the memory-mapped file using the mapping object.
- **FILE_MAP_ALL_ACCESS**. Same as **FILE_MAP_WRITE**.
- **FILE_MAP_COPY**. This value uses the copy-on-write feature of the virtual memory. If the mapping object is created with **PAGE_WRITECOPY** and the view with **FILE_MAP_COPY**, the process will have a view to the file, but a write to the file will not go to the original data file.

8

You can map either the whole file into the address space or only a subset of it—called a *view* of the file. The 64-bit file offset (the two **DWORD** parameters) specifies the file pointer where the mapping should begin when a view is mapped, and **dwNumberOfBytesToMap** specifies the number of bytes in the view. The file pointer must be a multiple of the allocation granularity. The function chooses an acceptable place in the address space to which it will map the file and then returns that value. If you want to manually choose the location, use **MapViewOfFileEx**, which has a sixth parameter, **LPVOID lpBaseAddress**. This parameter can be set to be the virtual address at which the file mapping starts. **lpBaseAddress** must be a multiple of the allocation granularity.

File *coherence* refers to the situation in which every process that has the file open sees the same information in the file. The difficulty in ensuring coherence arises when there are copies of the information allocated in different parts of the system.

If one copy is changed, there is a lag time until the other copies can be updated. If two processes use the same mapping object—or use mapping objects where one is derived from the other—Windows NT assures that both processes always see the same file content. This is because the kernel does not make copies of the pages that are holding part of the file that is loaded in the primary memory. Instead, the two processes map to a single page that contains the target data.

However, if a memory-mapped file is being used as described earlier, then a third process opens the file as an ordinary file; the **ReadFile** and **WriteFile** operations performed by the third process will not necessarily be coherent with the memory-mapped view of the file. This situation arises because the unmapped file operations use conventional file caching and disk I/O, thereby potentially introducing two copies of the information that should be in the file. Windows NT does not assure that these two copies will be the same at all times.

Finally, you must unmap the view of a file when you have finished using it, as follows.

BOOL UnmapViewOfFile(
    LPCVOID lpBaseAddress
);

The **lpBaseAddress** parameter is the virtual address where the view begins—the value returned by the **MapViewOfFile** function.

Named Pipes

A short discussion of named pipes is included here because it is an option to use them in solving this exercise. A *named pipe* is an IPC mechanism that can be used between address spaces. It is specifically designed to be used by a server that intends to interact with multiple clients that are using named pipes over a network. Named pipes differ from ordinary pipes (see Exercise 5) in a few important ways.

- A named pipe can have several *instances*. All instances have the same parameters, since they are intended to be copies of the same pipe. However, each instance can be used by a different pair of processes. For example, a server might use a named pipe to establish the *class* of named pipes, while each client that connects to the server might use a new *instance* of the named pipe.
- Named pipes are bi-directional, meaning a process can read and write each end of the named pipe.
- Named pipes can extend over a network.

Since the motivation for multiple instances is a client-server scenario, one process (the server) creates the named pipe. Then clients open the named pipe using CreateFile with the pipe name.

```
HANDLE CreateNamedPipe(
    LPCTSTR lpName,              // pointer to pipe name
    DWORD dwOpenMode,           // pipe open mode
    DWORD dwPipeMode,           // pipe-specific modes
    DWORD nMaxInstances,        // maximum number of instances
    DWORD nOutBufferSize,       // output buffer size, in bytes
    DWORD nInBufferSize,        // input buffer size, in bytes
    DWORD nDefaultTimeOut,      // time-out time, in millisecs
    LPSECURITY_ATTRIBUTES lpSecurityAttributes
                    // pointer to security attributes structure
);
```

The **lpName** parameter is the name of the pipe; it must have the form \\.\pipe\pipename. The **dwOpenMode** parameter specifies several aspects of the way the pipe is to behave, including the access to the pipe, the overlapped mode, the write-through mode, and the security access mode of the pipe handle. Pipe access can be any of the following.

- PIPE_ACCESS_DUPLEX. Information can be transmitted in both directions on the pipe.
- PIPE_ACCESS_INBOUND. The data are allowed to flow only from the client to the server over the named pipe.
- PIPE_ACCESS_OUTBOUND. The data are allowed to flow only from the server to the client over the named pipe.

8

If the **FILE_FLAG_WRITE_THROUGH** flag is set, then a write to a named pipe—even over a network—does not return until the information is placed in the buffer at the receiving machine. The **FILE_FLAG_OVERLAPPED** flag sets the I/O to be overlapped (see Exercise 9). The security flags are used to specify how protection settings can be changed. The **dwPipeMode** parameter specifies the type, read, and wait modes for the operation. If the pipe is to be used for byte stream transmission, the type value is **PIPE_TYPE_BYTE**; if it will be used with messages, the **PIPE_TYPE_MESSAGE** value is passed. The read mode can be set to accept streams or messages by using **PIPE_READMODE_BYTE** or **PIPE_READMODE_MESSAGE**. The mode flag controls whether reads are blocking (**PIPE_WAIT**) or nonblocking (**PIPE_NOWAIT**). The **nMaxInstances** parameter specifies the maximum number of pipe instances that can be opened for this pipe. The **nOutBufferSize** and **nInBufferSize** parameters specify the size of the pipe's output and input buffers, respectively. The **nDefaultTimeOut** parameter provides a default timeout that may be used by the **WaitNamedPipe** call.

PROBLEM STATEMENT

This problem is a more complex form of the pipeline problem in Exercise 5. There are **source** and **sink** processes that read and write conventional disk-based files. Also included are two new processes, **encrypt** and **decrypt**, that should be designed to filter the information transmitted by the **source** and received by the **sink**. Figure 18 shows the way the four processes should communicate with one another. The **sink** reads a byte stream from an ordinary file and writes the output to the first memory-mapped file. **Encrypt** reads the memory-mapped file, encrypts each byte in the byte stream, and writes the stream to the (named) pipe. **Decrypt** reads encrypted bytes from the pipe, decrypts them, and writes them to the second memory-mapped file. **Sink** reads the data from the second memory-mapped file and writes them to a second ordinary file.

Your encryption algorithm can be very simple, for example converting upper-case letters to lowercase, and vice versa. The decryption algorithm should be

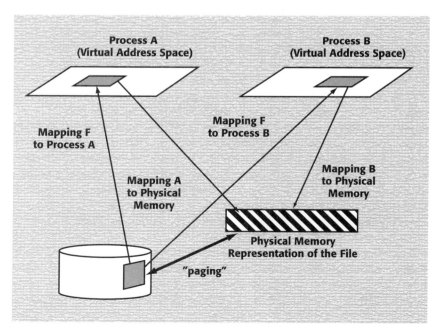

Figure 18

Process Configuration

the inverse of the encryption algorithm. There is no real need to use a named pipe between **encrypt** and **decrypt**, except to practice using another IPC mechanism.

To see the behavior of the configuration, you should once again use a delay in each of the modules (see Exercise 5).

LAB ENVIRONMENT

The lab environment for this exercise is the same as for the previous exercise. The use of tools to observe the performance is optional, but it is recommended because it will provide you with extra insight into memory-mapped file performance.

ATTACKING THE PROBLEM

This exercise involves a relatively large amount of code, so you are likely to find some challenge in getting all of the code written and working together. The solution uses a fifth process to launch the four processes specified in the assignment. The skeleton for this fifth program is shown next.

```
// The main program establishes the shared information used
// by the source, encrypt, decrypt, and sink processes
int main(int argc, char *argv[]) {
// Create the pipe from encrypt to decrypt
// Create producer process
    if (!CreateProcess(...)) {
        fprintf(stderr, "...", GetLastError())
        getc(stdin);
        ExitProcess(1);
    }
    Sleep(500);  // Give producer a chance to run

// Create encryption process
    if (!CreateProcess(...)) {
        fprintf(stderr, "...", GetLastError())
        getc(stdin);
        ExitProcess(1);
    }
    Sleep(500);  // Give Encrypt a chance to run
```

8

```
        // Create decryption process
            if (!CreateProcess(...)) {
                    fprintf(stderr, "...", GetLastError())
                    getc(stdin);
                    ExitProcess(1);
            }
            Sleep(500);   // Give Decrypt a chance to run
        // Create consumer process
            if (!CreateProcess(...)) {
                    fprintf(stderr, "...", GetLastError())
                    getc(stdin);
                    ExitProcess(1);
            }
            Sleep(500);   // Give consumer a chance to run
        // Wait for producer, encrypt, decrypt & consumer to die
        }
```

The **source** program has a relatively straightforward organization, as do the remaining three programs. The following code skeleton should get you started on a full solution.

```
/* The source process reads information from the source
 * file then uses a memory-mapped file to transfer
 * the information to the encrypt process.
 */
int main (int argc, char *argv[]) {
// Open the source file
        sourceFile = CreateFile (...)
        if(sourceFile == INVALID_HANDLE_VALUE) {
                fprintf(stderr, GetLastError());
                getc(stdin);
                ExitProcess(1);
        }

// Open the memory-mapped file and map it
        peMMFFile = CreateFile (...);
        if(peMMFFile == INVALID_HANDLE_VALUE) {
                fprintf(stderr, "...", GetLastError()
                getc(stdin);
                ExitProcess(1);
        }
```

```
// Create the mapping object
    peMMFMap = CreateFileMapping(...);
    if(peMMFMap == NULL) {
        fprintf(stderr, "...", GetLastError());
        getc(stdin);
        ExitProcess(1);
    }
// Create the view
    baseAddr = (PBYTE) MapViewOfFile(...);
    if(baseAddr == NULL) {
        fprintf(stderr, "...", GetLastError()
        getc(stdin);
        ExitProcess(1);
    }

    srand(P_RAND_SEED);      // Set random# seed
// Main loop to process the source file
    while(...) {
    // To exercise synch mechanisms
        Sleep(rand()%timeToProduce);
    // Write information to memory-mapped file
    // by writing to the baseAddr
    }
// Terminate
}
```

Notice that you will be sharing both memory-mapped files and that one of the threads is writing each file. This means that a correct solution must incorporate a synchronization mechanism to prevent critical section violations.

REFERENCES

Hart, Johnson M., Win32 *System Programming,* Addison-Wesley, Reading, Mass., 1997.

Microsoft, *Win32 API Reference Manual*, MSDN online documentation.

Richter, Jeffrey, *Advanced Windows*, Third Edition, Microsoft Press, Redmond, Wash., 1997.

nine

Fast File I/O

File I/O operations are a performance bottleneck for a significant fraction of all real programs. When the software is intended to process large amounts of information, it must read the information from one or more files, perform some operations on the data, and write processed information into other files. Windows NT has two specific mechanisms, in addition to the normal approach, for increasing file I/O performance: file caching and asynchronous I/O. In this exercise, you will experiment with both mechanisms. You will learn about:

▶ The organization of the Cache Manager
▶ The details of using CreateFile flags to pass directives to the Cache Manager
▶ The details of using asynchronous file I/O

INTRODUCTION

Memory-mapped files are a convenient way to read and write information that is stored in a file. They are especially useful for sharing file-based information across address spaces. However, they ultimately depend on demand paging, so there is no special attention paid to make the I/O be fast. The Cache Manager is an integral component of the Executive that is designed to work with the Virtual Memory Manager and the file I/O system to exploit opportunities to overlap I/O operation with the processor operation. Processes will not only make better use of the system's resources, but also take less time to execute if their I/O operations are overlapped with processing time (because two parts of the hardware are performing useful work simultaneously). Asynchronous I/O is an extension to the classic procedure-based I/O model. Programming languages have established procedure semantics so that a procedure is viewed as an abstract machine language statement that will be executed as part of a sequence of abstract machine instructions. That is, every instruction executes sequentially. This means that instruction $i + 1$ does not begin until after instruction i has completed. Asynchronous I/O abstract machine instructions can be made to execute *in parallel*. That is, if abstract machine instruction i is an I/O procedure call, then instruction $i + 1$ can be executed "soon after" instruction i has been started (and explicitly before instruction i has completed). You have seen several instances of asynchronous behavior in the previous exercises. Asynchronous I/O gives the programmer considerable control in achieving high overlap between I/O device and processor operations. Hence, it is a powerful tool for reducing a process's execution time.

File Caching

Storage devices and the processor operate at grossly disparate speeds. When software needs to read or write information from/to a storage device, then it must wait for a relatively long time from the point at which it requests the I/O operation to the time the operation has completed. OS designers use a number of techniques to reduce this waiting time, the most time-honored being *file buffering* (or *file caching*, as it is called in Windows NT). The basic idea is that if a thread opens a file for reading, then the OS can infer that the thread will read the first byte in the file, then the second, and so on throughout the file. As soon as the file has been opened, the File Manager can read the first block of information in the file from the storage device in anticipation of the read operation that will request the first set of bytes from the file. Similarly, the File Manager always attempts to read blocks prior to the time that the software actually asks for them. If it is successful, then whenever the thread requests a byte, the manager will have already read it from the device (into a buffer), so it simply copies the target byte from its buffer into the address space used by the thread.

With file caching, processor-I/O overlap is achieved by having the File Manager "read ahead" on an input file so that its buffers always contain the next bytes to be read by the application. Output file caching is achieved by having the File Manager "write behind" the application. When the application logically writes a byte to a file, the system stores the byte in a buffer. Then, when the buffer is full and the output device is idle, the system writes the buffer to the device. There is another opportunity for fast file I/O when output is buffered. Suppose that one process is writing to a file and another is concurrently reading from the file. If the data consumer is reading the file at about the same place in the file as the producer is writing data, then the consumer's read operation will just read the output buffer before it is ever written to the device. The read operation does not incur any I/O operation, since the desired data is still in the system buffer.

The Cache Manager is responsible for managing the file caching strategy. Because of the work that the Cache Manager must perform, it must interact heavily with the I/O Manager to coordinate buffer management. It also must deal with multiple address spaces and buffers. This means it can be more efficient if it is well-coordinated with the Virtual Memory Manager.

When Windows NT is booted, the Cache Manager reserves a region of the system virtual address space. Since this space is part of every process's address space, the Cache Manager's reserved memory is accessible (with appropriate privilege) to every process in the system. Like all virtual memory, even after the Cache Manager's space has been committed, it is not loaded until the Virtual Memory Manager allocates pages in the primary memory. If the system is lightly loaded, the Cache Manager will increase the size of its working set—and will tend to be allocated more primary memory pages. Conversely, heavily loaded systems will cause the Cache Manager's working set to shrink so that the memory can be used by other processes.

File caching is built on top of the kernel memory-mapped file mechanism. A file system driver makes a function call on the Cache Manager when it begins to operate on a file byte stream. The Cache Manager responds to the call by creating a section object to map the file to its virtual address space and hence to pages in the primary memory. The Cache Manager then performs buffering by dynamically mapping views of the file into its address space.

Nagar (1997) (Chapter 6) provides a detailed description of the steps involved in cached read and write operations. Nagar's description of the read operation is summarized here (and in Figure 19).

1. The user-space thread calls the I/O Manager with a read request, passing a buffer address for the result. The I/O Manager has different options as to how it will handle the user-space buffer. For example, it may map the user buffer into system space or pass the address on to the file system driver.
2. The I/O Manager then invokes the file system driver with an IRP (see Part 1 of this manual). The file system driver detects that the read operation is for a file that was opened with a buffering option enabled. The first read operation causes the file system driver to start the Cache Manager, which then creates a section object to map the cached information.
3. The file system driver calls the Cache Manager with a **CcCopyRead** request. The Cache Manager creates a mapped view of the file if none exists and then starts a memory copy from the mapped view to the user buffer.
4. If the information to be read is still on the disk, then the attempt to reference it using a virtual address will cause a page fault. The Virtual Memory

9

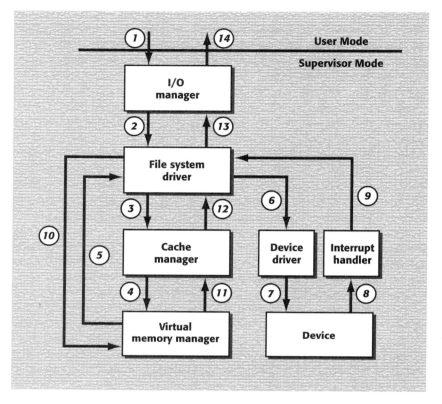

Figure 19

A Cached Read Operation

Manager will allocate physical pages to hold the information and issue a noncached paging read to the file system driver.

5. The file system driver initiates a read operation on the device driver for the device that contains the file.

6. The device driver issues a read operation on the physical disk driver.

7. The device performs the physical page read operation.

8. The device completes and raises an interrupt that will be fielded by the interrupt handler for the device.

9. The interrupt handler returns from the page read operation to the file system driver.

10. The file system driver notifies the Virtual Memory Manager that the page is now loaded into the primary memory.

11. The instruction causing the page fault is re-executed, thereby allowing the Cache Manager to move data from the mapped view of the file into the user buffer.

12. The Cache Manager returns the data in the user buffer to the file system driver.

13. The file system driver returns from the IRP to the I/O Manager.

14. The I/O Manager returns from the user read operation.

The fundamental assumptions made by the Cache Manager are that a file is a byte stream and that the application will reference the bytes in the stream sequentially. The **CreateFile** function has flag values that can assure the Cache Manager whether these assumptions are true and should be exploited. Recall that **CreateFile** has a file attributes parameter, **dwFlagsAndAttributes**.

HANDLE CreateFile(

    ...

    DWORD dwFlagsAndAttributes,

    ...

);

dwFlagsAndAttributes can take the values given in the following list. As usual, flags can be combined by ORing them together, unless they enable incompatible options. For example, it would not make sense to pass two flags, one saying "cache the file" and the other "do not cache the file." Whenever you specify any flag, that flag overrides the **FILE_ATTRIBUTE_NORMAL** flag.

- **FILE_FLAG_NO_BUFFERING**. This flag causes the file to be opened without using buffers. (You may do your own buffering, as in Exercise 12.) When this flag is combined with **FILE_FLAG_OVERLAPPED**, the system provides the best asynchronous performance possible. However, with this flag the usual synchronous operations on a sequential file will take more time, since no data will be cached. If a file is opened with this attribute, the following holds.

  - File access must begin at file pointer values that are on disk sector boundaries.

  - The number of bytes read or written must be a multiple of the disk sector size. For example, if the sector size is 512 bytes, an application can request reads and writes of 512, 1,024, or 2,048 bytes.

  - Buffer addresses for read and write operations must be aligned on addresses in memory that are integer multiples of the volume's sector size (see the **GetSystemInfo** function described in Exercise 7).

    You can use **VirtualAlloc** to allocate buffers so that they are aligned on integer multiples of the disk sector size. You can determine a volume's sector size by calling the **GetDiskFreeSpace** function.

- **FILE_FLAG_SEQUENTIAL_SCAN.** This flag tells the Cache Manager that the file will be accessed only sequentially, that is, byte $i + 1$ after byte i. The system can use this as a hint to optimize file caching. If you move the file pointer, optimum caching is not guaranteed to occur (even though the I/O will still be performed correctly). The documentation notes that "Specifying this flag can increase performance for applications that read large files using sequential access. Performance gains can be even more noticeable for applications that read large files mostly sequentially, but occasionally skip over small ranges of bytes." (MSDN, 1998).

- **FILE_FLAG_RANDOM_ACCESS.** This flag means that you will manually move the file pointer at various times while the file is open. Buffering will not take place.

- **FILE_FLAG_WRITE_THROUGH.** In OS terminology, "write through" means that when a thread writes to a copy of information in one level of the memory hierarchy, the write also is performed on lower layers of the hierarchy that contain the original version of the data. In file caching, this flag causes file writes to "write through" intermediate caches directly to the secondary storage.

Here is a quick summary of several other flags. (The descriptions are quoted from the reference manual; see MSDN (1998) for more flags and details.)

- **FILE_FLAG_DELETE_ON_CLOSE.** The operating system is to delete the file immediately after all of its handles have been closed, not just the handle for which you specified **FILE_FLAG_DELETE_ON_CLOSE**. Subsequent open requests for the file will fail, unless **FILE_SHARE_DELETE** is used.

- **FILE_ATTRIBUTE_ARCHIVE.** The file should be archived. Applications use this attribute to mark files for backup or removal.

- **FILE_ATTRIBUTE_HIDDEN.** The file is hidden. It is not to be included in an ordinary directory listing.

- **FILE_ATTRIBUTE_READONLY.** The file is read only. Applications can read the file but cannot write to it or delete it.

- **FILE_ATTRIBUTE_TEMPORARY.** The file is used for temporary storage. File systems attempt to keep all of the data in memory for quicker access rather than flushing the data back to mass storage. A temporary file should be deleted by the application as soon as it is no longer needed.

Asynchronous I/O

Whenever **CreateFile** is used to obtain a handle to a file or device (see Exercise 10 for more about device I/O), it has the option of specifying that operations performed on the handle be asynchronous. This means that the thread can initiate an I/O operation on the handle and then continue with other processing concurrently.

Asynchronous I/O is specified with the following.

HANDLE CreateFile(

    ...

    DWORD dwFlagsAndAttributes,// file attributes

    ...

);

The **FILE_FLAG_OVERLAPPED** flag for **dwFlagsAndAttributes** causes a read/write call to return after a short amount of time, with **GetLastError** returning a value of **ERROR_IO_PENDING**. When the read/write operation has completed, an event (specified in the read/write operation) will change to the signaled state. Since the file will be read or written asynchronously, there is the possibility that two or more I/O operations could be started on the same file. Of course, such a situation is inherently dangerous on write operations since the system would be trying to perform two writes to different parts of a file at the same time (implying that the file pointer would be inaccurate for one of the writes). Because of this possibility, the system does not maintain the file pointer. As a result, if you are using a file that was opened with the overlapped flag, then you will need to explicitly pass the file pointer for the operation with the I/O call. (What do you suppose that does to the Cache Manager if it is attempting to buffer the file?)

Recall that the function prototype for **ReadFile** and **WriteFile** (see Exercise 5) included a parameter of type **LPOVERLAPPED** that was set to **NULL** for synchronous I/O. If the file was opened as an **OVERLAPPED** file, then the read and write routines must provide a pointer to an **OVERLAPPED** data structure as the **LPOVERLAPPED** parameter to provide the extra parameters needed to control the function. The data structure must be valid for the duration of the I/O operation. (For example, it cannot be an automatic variable on a stack that might go out of scope and become deallocated while the I/O operation is in progress.)

typedef struct _OVERLAPPED {
    DWORD Internal;

9

```
        DWORD  InternalHigh;
        DWORD  Offset;
        DWORD  OffsetHigh;
        HANDLE hEvent;
    } OVERLAPPED;
```

The 64-bit **Internal** and **InternalHigh** fields are reserved for OS use; you should set them to zero. The **Offset** and **OffsetHigh DWORD** parameters define the 64-bit file pointer value for the position of the first byte where the operation will begin (notice that the number of bytes in the operation is specified in the read or write parameters). You can use asynchronous I/O with named pipes (and several devices; see Exercise 10). In this case, the offset is not meaningful and should be set to zero.

The challenge in asynchronous I/O is to know *when* the operation has completed. Windows NT allows you to use **event** objects (see Exercise 4) to provide notification that the operation has completed. The **hEvent** field is a handle to an event that will be set to the signaled state when the operation is completed. The application code must then explicitly make one function call to initiate an asynchronous I/O operation and another to detect that it has completed. Figure 20 shows the code skeleton to do asynchronous I/O.

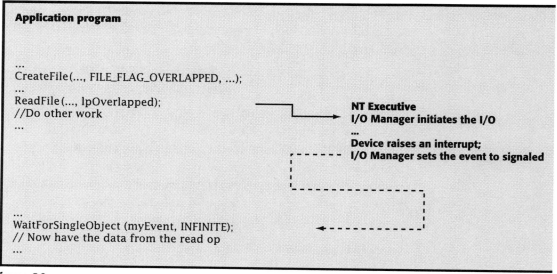

Figure 20

Asynchronous I/O

The traditional C file read operation is a synchronous read; that is, when a thread calls read, it blocks until the read has completed.[1] In this exercise, you are to design and implement programs to use asynchronous input and output commands with the underlying Windows NT facilities for asynchronous operation.

Write a main program that creates N (N ≤ 6) file filter processes organized as shown in Figure 21:

int filter(char source, char * sink, int f, char *fArg)

where **source** and **sink** are filenames and **f** is a filter function to be applied to the byte stream from **source** with the result written to **sink**. Of course, the function prototype will be for a main program rather than a function named "filter," so you will have to devise some mechanism to provide these parameters to the filter when it starts.

Part I

Build the set of filter programs so that information is read from a source file ("File 0") and then transformed by each filter and written to a sink file ("File N"). You will have to put a synchronization mechanism between the filters, since they will be sharing access to a file. Your source file should be at least 512K; your instructor will supply a test file, but you can easily generate your own file with the notepad application. Determine the total amount of real time for each filter to process its entire file, from the time the first process opens the source file until the last filter closes the sink file. This observed time depends on various factors, so the number will vary from one run of the code to the next.

Run the suite at least ten times, and find the average total time. Report the average total execution time along with the speed and the characteristics of the machine you are using (the type and speed of the processor and the amount of the machine's physical memory).

Part II

Use the FILE_FLAG_SEQUENTIAL_SCAN flag in the **CreateFile** call. This will add caching to each of your filter programs. Measure the average execution time, and compare it to the time for the execution in Part I.

---

[1] However, in the C runtime routines it is a simple matter to change a file descriptor so that it supports nonblocking read operations using an **ioctl** command. This option is not supported in the NT C runtime library because of the more general asynchronous facility described in this exercise.

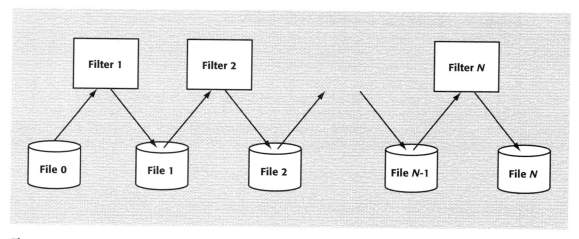

Figure 21

The Filter and File Relationships

Part III

Modify the process in Part I so that it uses the FILE_FLAG_OVERLAPPED file attribute. Use **ReadFile** and **WriteFile** in conjunction with wait functions on the file
handle to determine when an I/O operation has completed. You might need to
change the order of some of your code, since you will be using asynchronous I/O
in this case. Determine the average execution time and compare it to the average
execution times for the execution in Parts I and II.

LAB ENVIRONMENT

This exercise uses the standard VC++ environment.

ATTACKING THE PROBLEM

This exercise does not require you to write much software, but getting all of the
components working together properly will be tedious. Here is general plan of
attack you might find helpful.

1. Write a main program to create the *N* filter processes.
2. Write filter programs that use the simplest form of **CreateFile**, **ReadFile**,
   and **WriteFile** function calls; start out with one or two filters, and then
   generalize to *N*.

3. Finish Part I by modifying your code so that it eliminates oversimplifications. Take your measurements on Part I.

4. When you prepare your solution to Part II, use the #ifdef preprocessor feature to derive your solution from Part I. This will save you a lot of time in generating Parts II and III (and ensure that you have the same general structure in all solutions so that measurements will be easy to compare). Be sure that your code can then be used with all versions, depending on the #define statements you include with each compilation.

5. Continue in this manner for Part III.

REFERENCES

Microsoft, *Win32 API Reference Manual,* MSDN online documentation.

Nagar, Rajeev, *Windows NT File System Internals: A Developer's Guide*, O'Reilly & Associates, Sebastapol, Calif., 1997.

9

ten

Floppy Disk I/O

This is the first of three exercises to build a simple, user-space file manager for a floppy disk.[1] It focuses on the low-level I/O for the floppy disk. You will learn about:

▶ How to interact directly with the floppy disk

▶ The organization of a MS-DOS floppy disk

▶ The background for managing the MS-DOS file allocation table

INTRODUCTION

The floppy disk is a widely used secondary storage device that has been configured into PCs from the earliest days of MS-DOS to present Windows NT systems. The earliest PCs used a 5.25 inch, 360K floppy disk, though in the 1980s systems commonly switched to the 3.5 inch, 1.44M floppy disk. Even though software distributions increasingly use CD-ROMs (because of their larger capacity), the floppy disk drive is still used in most PCs. It is an inexpensive, removable, universal medium for saving modest-sized files.

The NT File Manager is built to accommodate many different kinds of disk devices, with several different file system organizations and disk formats. While it defines its own file system organization for hard disks (the Windows NT File System, or NTFS), it will also operate correctly on disks that are organized around MS-DOS file system formats. For floppy disks, Windows NT just uses the

---

[1] This exercise is derived from one that Norman Ramsey used in his OS class at Purdue University in 1996.

MS-DOS format. This exercise concentrates on the physical organization of a disk and on how to read and write information directly from/to a disk (with a user-mode program).

Physical Disk Organization

Disk are rotating magnetic media. Information is stored on a disk surface using a polar coordinate system. Any piece of information is located by specifying its location on the disk surface with a radius, R, and angle of rotation, θ. Because of the nature of the mechanism for magnetizing and reading an area at (R, θ) on the disk, there are constraints on R and θ. First, the read/write head for the disk operates on a logical concentric circle that has a radius of R_i and a width of W. The concentric circle, called a *track*, is an area on the disk surface whose inner edge is R_i from the center of the disk and whose outer edge is at $R_i + W$. Floppy disk are inexpensive mechanisms, so W is relatively large, meaning that floppy disk have only 40 to 80 tracks.[2] More expensive, higher-capacity disks have smaller W values and thus many more tracks.

Disk devices are block-oriented. This means that when you read or write a disk, you read or write a block of bytes, called a *sector*, in a single I/O operation. Each track on a disk is capable of storing some integral number of sectors, from 8 to 18 sectors. So θ is also discretized so that it can be used to position the read/write head at the beginning of a sector on a track. Because of these factors related to physical disk technology, the polar coordinate (R, θ) with discrete values for R and θ is more commonly described as (track, sector).

The last aspect of the disk polar coordinate system to understand is how the disk drive recognizes the origin for θ. There must be some point on the disk surface for which $\theta = 0$. The method for determining this is disk technology-dependent. Some drives use a hole or notch in the physical disk surface, while others use a magnetic pattern on the recording surface (hard disks almost always use magnetic patterns). When the disk drive detects the index point, it can then determine where each sector begins by measuring the angular rotation of the media.

Hard disks use the same polar coordinate system as floppy disks, though there are more tracks on a disk surface and more sectors on each track. A hard disk also commonly has multiple disk surfaces that can be used for recording information. Think of a hard disk as being a stack of M different disks, each organized as described for the floppy disk. A hard disk read/write head is actually a

---

[2] According to Messmer (1995), a 5.25 in., 360MB diskette has 40 tracks with $W = 0.33$ mm. A 3.5 in., 1.44MB diskette has 80 tracks with $W = 0.115$ mm.

ganged head with one read/write mechanism for every recording surface on the disk drive. (Both sides of a disk in the stack can be used, though the top surface of the top disk and the bottom surface of the bottom disk may not be used.) This means that whenever the ganged read/write head is positioned over track k on one surface, the read/write heads for the other surfaces are also positioned over the same track. As a result, in hard disks a track is sometimes called a *cylinder* to emphasize this characteristic of multiple surfaces with a ganged read/write head.

Every OS can use these logical aspects to define a disk format. This means that formatting can define the number of tracks and sectors on a diskette; this is called *hard formatting*. More commonly, you will soft format a floppy disk by simply causing a formatting program to write particular kinds of information into particular sectors on the floppy disk.

MS-DOS defined a particular soft format for disks, so Windows NT simply uses that format. The MS-DOS Basic I/O System (BIOS) provides a set of programs that can read and write disk sectors. BIOS also provides an additional abstraction on the polar coordinate addresses called *logical sector* addresses (that is also used in Windows NT). Logical sector 0 corresponds to the sector at surface 0 (on a hard disk), track 0, sector 1 of the disk. (While surfaces and tracks are numbered from zero, sectors are numbered from 1. The reasons for this have long been lost in obscurity.) Logical sector 1 is at surface 0, track 0, sector 2, and so on.

MS-DOS Disk Format

Before a disk can be used for normal I/O operations, it must be soft formatted to have essential information in prespecified locations on the disk. Specifically, logical sector 0 contains a *reserved area* (also called the *boot sector* or *boot record*). The MS-DOS boot sequence relies on the boot sector's being located at logical sector 0 and being organized as shown in Figure 22 (Messmer, 1995). Several of the fields will not make sense until you have had a chance to see all of the pieces of the file system and how they fit together.

10

The first location in the boot sector contains a machine instruction to jump to location 0x1e. The rationale for this is that on booting up the system, the processor will go to logical sector 0 of the boot disk, load it into memory, and begin executing the program loaded at the first location in the boot sector. Since there are several basic parameters that need to be known at boot time, their values are placed at locations 0x03 to 0x1d. Thus, when the processor begins to execute the boot sector, it will immediately encounter the jump instruction to bypass the boot information.

Figure 22

Boot Sector

0x00	0x02	**<A jump instruction to 0x1e>**
0x03	0x0a	**Computer manufacturer name**
0x0b	0x0c	**Sectors per cluster (discussed in Exercise 11)**
0x0d	0x0f	**Reserved sectors for the boot record**
0x10	0x10	**Number of FATs**
0x11	0x12	**Number of root directory entries**
0x13	0x14	**Number of logical sectors**
0x15	0x15	**Medium descriptor byte (used only on old versions of MS-DOS)**
0x16	0x17	**Sectors per FAT**
0x18	0x19	**Sectors per track**
0x1a	0x1b	**Number of surfaces (heads)**
0x1c	0x1d	**Number of hidden sectors**
0x1e	. . .	**Bootstrap program**

Hard disks can have an additional level of abstraction on them, called *disk partitions*. If a hard disk is partitioned, each resulting partition is treated like a physical disk above the abstract machine that accesses the physical disk (BIOS, in MS-DOS). In Microsoft systems, a hard disk can be partitioned to have up to four different logical disks, each with its own set of logical sectors. If a disk partition is a *bootable disk partition*, then its logical sector number zero will be a boot sector. In a partitioned disk the physical head 0, track 0, sector 1 will contain a *partition sector* rather than a boot sector. The partition sector provides information to describe how the hard disk is partitioned into logical disks. Roughly speaking, the partition sector starts off with a 446-byte program. When the hardware is powered up, it will go to head 0, track 0, sector 1 (as if the disk were not partitioned) and begin executing code. If the disk is partitioned, there will be a 446-byte bootstrap program at the first byte in the sector. If the disk is not partitioned, there will be a jump instruction to start the execution on the boot program stored at location **0x1e** in the sector. For partitioned disks, there is a 64-byte partition table for the disk immediately following the bootstrap program. It contains space for the four partition entries, each of which describes the portion of the physical disk that is used for its partition (the starting sector of the partition, ending sector, number of sectors in the partition, and so on). The last 2 bytes of the partition sector contain a "magic number," **0xaa55**, to identify the partition sector.

Figure 23 shows the organization of a floppy disk. When the floppy disk is formatted, this structure is set up on the disk. There are some variables in the table. The disk block management data structure—the file allocation table, or FAT, introduced shortly and explained more in Exercise 11—is generally replicated on the disk. Thus location **0x10** in the boot sector tells the system how many copies of the FAT are formatted onto this disk (this number is usually 2). The FAT is replicated so that if the first copy is accidentally destroyed, the disk

Figure 23

*Floppy Disk
Organization*

Logical Sector	Content
0	**Boot sector**
1	**First sector in the (first) FAT**
. . .	
10	**First sector in the second FAT (if there is a second one; see** $0x10$ **in the boot sector)**
19	**First sector in the diskette's root directory**
xx	**Last sector in the root directory (see** $0x11$ **in the boot sector)**
xx + 1	**Beginning of data area for the diskette**

can be recovered by copying the second copy over the first. Each root directory entry (again, see Exercise 11) uses 32 bytes. Location $0x11$ in the boot sector indicates how many entries are in the disk (1.44MB floppy disks have space for 224 directory entries, using 14 sectors).

Organization of the Windows NT File System Disk

The most serious limitation to the FAT organization is that it is cumbersome to extend the technique so that it can be used with large disks. The original design of the FAT would accommodate a 32MB disk. Today, hard disk drives can be 10GB or more. The NTFS is a new file system, better suited for large disks.

The NTFS on-disk structure is created by formatting a disk or disk partition (called a *volume* in Windows NT) as an NTFS logical disk. While the physical sector size on a disk might be 512 bytes (typical for PC disks), an NTFS logical disk is made up of *clusters* of 2^n (1, 2, 4, 8, and so on) contiguous sectors. Only the lowest levels of the software reference the disk with a sector number; the rest of the NTFS references the disk using *a logical cluster number* (LCN), meaning it reads and writes a cluster of sectors as if they were one big sector. Since clusters are contiguous groups of sectors, one can always determine the physical sector address of the beginning of a cluster by multiplying the LCN by the number of sectors per cluster.

10

Files are implemented at a very low level in the NTFS; the bootstrap information and structures used to access a file on a volume are kept in files. The analog of the MS-DOS FAT is the Master File Table (MFT), an array of fixed size (1K) file records. Every file on the disk, including the MFT, has an entry in the MFT. The other specialized information on the disk is stored in *metafiles*, such as $Boot (the boot file), $Bitmap (a cluster allocation bitmap), $Logfile (the system log of important events), and so on. The metafiles are kept as the first few files in the MFT; the MFT itself (named $MFT) is the first entry in the MFT.

Windows NT Device Drivers

A device driver is a set of procedures that provide a fixed abstract interface to device controller hardware. Device controllers differ in the way that software manages their activity—positioning media, moving read/write heads, passing a command to them, posting error conditions, and so on. The purpose of a device driver is to encapsulate device dependencies, thereby providing the standard interface to the rest of the software. An obvious difficulty of this is making the hardware look like the standard programming interface. However, another is that it must be possible to add drivers to an existing operating system (to accommodate the case in which the user buys a disk and adds it to the existing system). The Windows NT I/O system is explicitly designed with the idea that people other than the Windows NT developers will be adding kernel-mode driver software. Microsoft provides a Device Driver Kit (DDK) to assist programmers in designing and developing device drivers. Unfortunately, the effort to develop a kernel-mode driver surpasses the threshold for exercises in this lab manual. This subsection provides some insight into how drivers are organized, but the exercise itself is a user-mode program that invokes built-in drivers to read/write floppy disk drives.

Ultimately, the abstract interface to the device driver should be the (by now) familiar file interface (**CreateFile**, **ReadFile**, **WriteFile**, and so on). However, since these are Win32 API interface functions, the driver really implements Native API functions such as **NtCreateFile**, **NtReadFile**, **NtWriteFile**, and so on. Several of the Native API functions are remarkably similar to their Win32 API counterparts (Microsoft DDK, 1997; Nagar, 1997). The driver will be called by the I/O Manager whenever an application programmer calls the Native API for the specified device. This means that the driver has a predefined interface on which the I/O Manager is depending; the device driver must export/implement these functions. The interface that the driver uses is the device controller interface, which is fixed by the device manufacturer. Thus the interface that the device driver provides and the one that it uses are both well-defined (see Figure 24).

There are three categories of Windows NT device drivers (Solomon, 1998): user-mode, kernel-mode, and virtual. There can also be software in the subsystem layer to provide various I/O services that look much like driver functions.

- **User-mode drivers**

  This type of software runs in user mode and uses the Win32 API: **CreateFile**, **ReadFile**, **WriteFile**, and so on. These drivers are not subject to the same design and interface constraints as kernel-mode drivers. The following exercise is to construct a user-mode driver.

Figure 24

Device Driver
Interfaces

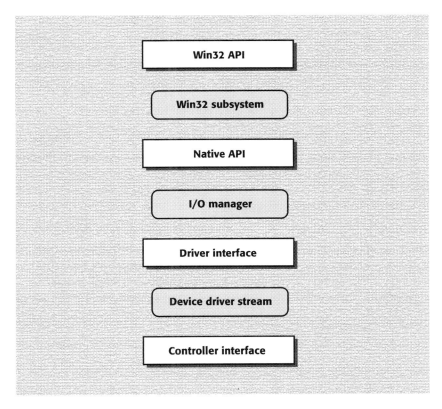

Win32 API

Win32 subsystem

Native API

I/O manager

Driver interface

Device driver stream

Controller interface

- **Kernel-mode drivers**

  These are the device drivers shown in Figure 24. As discussed in Part 1 of this manual, the functionality can be decomposed into a layered, or stream, model. The function call to the I/O Manager is packaged into IRPs and distributed to the elements in the stream; see Figure 7 in Part 1. The interface that the device driver exports is actually a set of IRPs that it recognizes. In some cases, a kernel-mode driver is implemented as a *class driver* that captures the behavior of a general class of devices such as SCSI disks. Whenever a device driver is needed for a specific device that has a class driver, a *miniport* driver is added to the class driver to implement device-dependent parts of the class driver functionality. Complicated classes of devices such as disk and network controllers have class drivers, so a specific device can be added to the system by writing only the miniport driver.

- **Virtual device drivers**

  A virtual device driver (VDD) is a user-mode device driver for virtualized hardware devices (Solomon, 1998). If a VDD is used to interact with a device, then an application's references to the device are intercepted by the

10

VDD to allow user-mode device manipulation to be handled by supervisor-mode Windows NT drivers. Application software written to interact directly with devices can be routed to a VDD without changing the software and without allowing the user-mode software to directly manipulate devices. This idea was exploited in the Windows extension to MS-DOS and Windows 95 and is part of the device driver repertoire for Windows NT.

Asche (1994) describes a checklist of items that you must address to write a driver.

- "Process input to the hardware as well as output to the hardware."
  This means that the driver is the only software that interacts directly with the hardware, so any aspects of its control that are provided by the hardware designers can be used only by the driver. Specifically, the driver must be prepared to handle interrupts from the device (as an ISR as described in Part 1). It also must supply the commands in the form expected by the device; this usually means that it writes device-dependent bit patterns to command registers. And it must take advantage of direct memory access (see your textbook).

- "Serialize the hardware with the I/O stream."
  This refers to the operation of the processor and the device. If the processor supplies information for the device, the driver must buffer the information until the device is ready to accept it. Conversely, on input, if the device supplies information, the driver must buffer it until it can be accepted by the processor (or written to the system memory). Windows NT provides deferred procedure calls (DPCs) explicitly to assist in this task. A DPC is a procedure call that is queued at the time the call is made, then dequeued and accepted when the called entity is ready to process the call (compare with the APCs described in Exercise 12). A DPC has the normal programming semantics of a procedure call, but it does not actually call the procedure until the processor is available to execute the DPC from the queue.

- "Process requests from the operating system."
  The driver must register a series of callback procedures with the OS so that it has entry points to invoke various driver services (driver callbacks use IRPs).

- "Trap error conditions, and provide error strategies."
  The Windows NT philosophy on errors is that their occurrence should be noticeable by many elements in the system. The driver must "announce" certain detected errors to the rest of the system.

- "Provide a means to install and recover the driver."

  This aspect of the design refers to associating drivers with the names (for example IRQs and ports) by which the services should be invoked.

Writing a Windows NT device driver is a nontrivial procedure that requires you learn the details of each of these aspects of the environment. There are various tools and documentation to assist you in writing a kernel-mode driver, but that information, itself, requires substantially more space than can be supplied in this laboratory manual.

User-Mode Device Management

Windows NT provides a means by which you can write a user-mode program to interact with many devices, almost as if you were manipulating them directly. The basic approach is that the device is manipulated through the normal virtual file abstraction using the normal file functions. The problem in this exercise is how to create a user-mode driver that looks very much like a supervisor-mode driver, using the virtual file interface.

CreateFile can be used to open a device, such as a floppy disk, so that it is treated as a virtual file. For example, if you wanted to open the floppy disk in drive A and read its contents as a linear byte stream, you could call the following.

```
CreateFile(
        "\\\\.\\A:",
        GENERIC_READ,
        FILE_SHARE_READ,
        NULL,
        OPEN_ALWAYS,
        0,
        NULL
);
```

If there is a floppy disk in drive A, CreateFile will return a handle that can be used by ReadFile and WriteFile to read the entire disk contents as a byte stream. To perform efficient reads and writes, you should read and write data on sector boundaries. For example, with a 1.44MB floppy disk, you should read 512 bytes only at byte addresses of 0, 512, 1,024, and so on.

Even though the floppy disk is opened as a file, you can still perform device-specific operations on it (and some of the normal I/O operations have a device-specific interpretation). Specifically, before reading or writing a floppy

10

diskette directly, you must know the disk geometry, that is, the information stored in the boot sector. This can be obtained using the following.

```
BOOL DeviceIoControl(
    HANDLE hDevice, // handle to device of interest
    DWORD dwIoControlCode,
        // control code of operation to perform
    LPVOID lpInBuffer, // pointer to buffer to supply input data
    DWORD nInBufferSize, // size of input buffer
    LPVOID lpOutBuffer,
        // pointer to buffer to receive output data
    DWORD nOutBufferSize, // size of output buffer
    LPDWORD lpBytesReturned,
        // pointer to variable to receive output byte count
    LPOVERLAPPED lpOverlapped
// ptr to overlapped structure for asynchronous operation
);
```

The **hDevice** handle is the result of the **CreateFile** call. The **dwIoControlCode** parameter should be set to a value of **IOCTL_DISK_GET_DRIVE_GEOMETRY**. Of course, you will also have to allocate space for the result in **nOutBufferSize** and provide for the length of the result to be returned in **lpBytesReturned**. For the 1.44MB floppy format, the values returned by **DeviceIoControl** are as follows.

- 512 bytes per sector
- 18 sectors per track
- Two heads (double-sided)
- 80 cylinders

Since you will want to read different parts of the virtual file—different sectors on the disk—you will need to use the **SetFilePointer** function to position the disk read/write head prior to issuing a read operation.

PROBLEM STATEMENT

In this exercise, you are to write a function to determine the basic information about a diskette in logical drive A, a function to read disk sectors, and a function to dump the information you find in the floppy disk to the standard output stream. You will also need a driver program to call these functions to demonstrate that they are operating properly.

Here are the function prototypes for this exercise.

```
Disk physicalDisk(char driveLetter);
void sectorDump(Disk theDisk, int logicalSectorNumber);
BOOL sectorRead
    Disk theDisk,
    unsigned logicalSectorNumber,
    char *buffer
);
```

The **physicalDisk** function is called to initialize the disk for subsequent operations. The **driveLetter** parameter identifies the disk drive. The code should then use **CreateFile** to open the device and obtain the disk geometry.

The **sectorRead** function reads a given **logicalSectorNumber** from the designated disk (handle) into the specified buffer. The read operation should return **TRUE** if it is able to read the designated sector into the buffer.

The **sectorDump** function calls **sectorRead** and then prints the results of the call onto **stdout**. You might find it useful, though it is not required, for this routine to recognize certain sector numbers (such as logical sector 0, 1, 10, and 19, where the boot sector, FAT copies, and root directory are stored) and to provide an option for formatting the output to reflect the format of these special sectors.

LAB ENVIRONMENT

This exercise uses the standard VC++ environment.

ATTACKING THE PROBLEM

Before you can perform disk I/O, you must create an abstraction of the details of the disk. The **physicalDisk** function must detect format information about the disk and then make it available in a data structure accessible by **sectorDump**. Each disk drive has a fixed geometry.

10

```
struct geometry {
    unsigned bytesPerSector;
    unsigned sectorsPerTrack;
    unsigned heads;  /* tracks per cylinder */
    unsigned cylinders;
};
```

A disk is formatted with the geometry in its boot sector (see the discussion in the "Introduction" of this exercise). Primarily, you will use the **bytesPerSector** value from the **struct**, but you are also free to use the other fields as you like.

In designing your file system, use an abstraction of the physical disk to read and write logical sectors.

```
typedef struct disk *Disk;
struct disk {
struct geometry (*geometryFunction)(Disk);
        HANDLE floppyDisk;
        DISK_GEOMETRY theSupportedGeometry[20];
};
```

This defines a suggested **Disk** data structure. Logical sectors are numbered from zero, even though individual sectors on a track are typically numbered from 1. The logical sector L on track T, head H, sector S is located at

L = S - 1 + T * (heads * sectorsPerTrack) + H * sectorsPerTrack

You will not have to perform the translation from logical sectors to track/head/sector coordinates, as Windows NT will do that for you.

The first procedure to implement is the disk abstraction based on direct I/O to a physical disk:

Disk physicalDisk(char driveLetter);

To implement this function, you must use the **CreateFile** function on the floppy disk drive (as described in the "Introduction"). The **lpszName** parameter must be \\.\X:, where **X** could be any letter depending on the drive letter being used. Be sure also to do the following.

- Map the drive letter to an uppercase character.
- Escape all of the backslashes in C string literals.

You will need read access to the disk drive, which you can specify using **OPEN_EXISTING** for the **dwCreationDistribution** parameter in the **CreateFile** call. Use FILE_FLAG_NO_BUFFERING and FILE_FLAG_RANDOM_ACCESS for the **dwFlagsAndAttributes** parameter. In the **fdwShareMode** parameter, you must set the GENERIC_READ, GENERIC_WRITE, FILE_SHARE_READ, and FILE_SHARE_WRITE flags. Once you open the disk, you can get the geometry with the **DeviceIoControl** call (see the "Introduction").

The following shows the contents of the header file used for the solution.

```
/* This interface is derived from one designed
* by Norman Ramsey for CSci 413 at Purdue University, 1996
*/

#ifndef DISKMODULE_H
#define DISKMODULE_H

#define    BOOT                    -1
#define    FAT1                    -2
#define    FAT2                    -3
#define    BOOT_SECTOR             0
#define    FAT1_SECTOR             1
#define    FAT2_SECTOR             10
#define    ROOT_SECTOR             19

#include <windows.h>
#include <winioctl.h>              // DISK_GEOMETRY

struct geometry {
    unsigned bytesPerSector;     // bytes in each sector
    unsigned sectorsPerTrack;    // number of sectors in a track
    unsigned heads;              // number of tracks per cylinder
    unsigned cylinders;          // number of cylinders on the disk
};

typedef struct disk *Disk;
struct disk {
    struct geometry (*geometry)(Disk);
    HANDLE floppyDisk;
    DISK_GEOMETRY theSupportedGeometry[20];
};

/* Function prototypes on the Disk interface */

// Abstraction of the NT physical disk
    Disk physicalDisk(char driveLetter);
    void sectorDump(Disk theDisk, int logSectorNumber);
    BOOL sectorRead (Disk, unsigned, char *);
#endif DISKMODULE_H
```

The **sectorRead** function reads a single sector from the disk. It should be implemented using **SetFilePointer** (to position the read head at the correct point in the virtual file corresponding to the floppy disk) and **ReadFile** (to read a sector from the floppy disk). The **sectorRead** function performs the same function as a kernel-level floppy disk device driver.

The **sectorDump** function should be designed to know about the boot sector and a FAT sector (this optionally allows you to write special output formats for these sectors). Write the output from **sectorDump** to **stdout**.

Solution Plan

You might consider developing your solution in the following order.

1. Write an implementation of **physicalDisk**.
2. Write an implementation of **sectorRead** and **segmentDump** that you can use to produce a hexadecimal dump of arbitrary sectors.
3. Use your **segmentDump** routine to inspect a floppy diskette.
4. Develop a driver program to test your low-level disk procedures. Here is a skeleton for the driver.

```
#include  "..\exercise10.h"      // data structures
                                 // introduced above

int main(. . .){
    Disk theDisk;
    int firstSector, lastSector;
    firstSector = . . .;          // first sector you wish to dump
    lastSector = . . .;           // last sector you wish to dump

    theDisk = physicalDisk(. . .);

// Dump some sectors
    sectorDump(theDisk, BOOT);
    sectorDump(theDisk, FAT1);
    sectorDump(theDisk, FAT2);
    if(firstSector >= 0) {
        for(i = firstSector; i <= lastSector; i++) {
            sectorDump(theDisk, i);
            printf("\n");
        }
    }
}
```

You will need to derive your solution using a real diskette. Prepare a diskette with a dozen simple files using the normal Windows NT interface. Your code should be able to open this diskette and dump arbitrary sectors from it.

REFERENCES

Asche, Ruediger R, "The Little Device Driver," Microsoft Development Network article, February, 1994.

Messmer, Hans-Peter, *The Indispensable PC Hardware Book*, Second Edition, Addison-Wesley, Reading, Mass., 1995.

Microsoft, *Win32 API Reference Manual*, MSDN online documentation.

Microsoft, *Windows NT DDK (for Windows NT Workstation 4.0 – U.S.)*, CD-ROM, Microsoft Corporation, January, 1997.

Nagar, Rajeev, *Windows NT File System Internals: A Developer's Guide*, O'Reilly & Associates, Sebastapol, Calif., 1997.

Solomon, David A., *Inside Windows NT*, Second Edition, Microsoft Press, Redmond, Wash, 1998.

10

eleven

File Systems and Directories

This is the second of three exercises to build a simple, user-space file manager for a floppy disk.[1] This exercise focuses on directory operations, using the low-level floppy disk I/O routines from Exercise 10. You will learn about:

▶ The details of the FAT organization

▶ How to implement basic directory operations

INTRODUCTION

The file system on a Windows NT floppy disk is the same as the one used on an MS-DOS floppy disk. You can read and write an MS-DOS floppy disk using Windows NT. The floppy disk format is based on a FAT file system in which the media (the removable floppy disk) is divided into a reserved area (containing the boot program), the actual allocation tables, a root directory, and file space; see Figure 25. The second copy of the FAT is the same as the first; it is used to recover the disk if the first copy is accidentally destroyed. Space allocated for files is represented by values in the FAT, which effectively provides a linked list of all blocks in the file. Special values designate end-of-file (EOF), unallocated, and bad blocks. The original FAT had many limitations. It had no subdirectories and was limited to very small disks, while recovering the disk if the allocation tables were damaged was very difficult.

---

[1] This exercise is derived from one that Norman Ramsey used in his OS class at Purdue University in 1996.

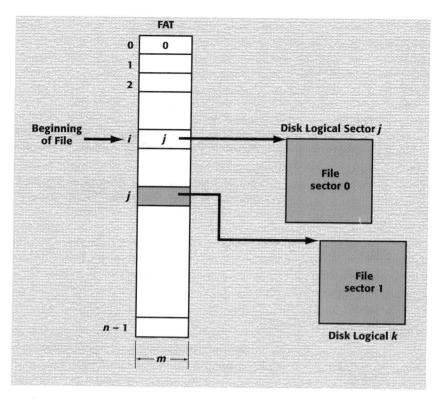

Figure 25

FAT Organization

During the time of the explosive growth of the PC, the capacities of disk drives also increased dramatically. At the same time, different variants of the FAT were derived to accommodate larger capacities. The basic FAT organization (see Figure 25) differs among disk types by

- the size of the entries (m in the figure can be 12 or 16 in Windows NT Version 4 and 12, 16 or 32 in Version 5),
- the number of actual tables, and
- the size of the logical sector addressed by a FAT entry.

In the simplest variant, there is one FAT entry corresponding to each sector on the disk. A file is a set of disk sectors, where the FAT entry corresponding to the first entry designates the logical sector number of the second block, the FAT entry of the second block specifies the logical sector number of the third block, and so on. The FAT entry for the last block contains an EOF designator. Thus the FAT is a linked list of disk sectors. If you know the address of the first sector, i — and therefore the index into the FAT— you can use the FAT to reference the next logical sector in the file (see the figure). The content, j, of FAT index i is a logical sector number. It is also an index to the second FAT entry for the file.

As disk capacities grew larger than 32MB, the FAT organization began to use the notion of a *cluster* of sectors. As in Windows NT, a cluster is a group of contiguous sectors that are treated as a virtual sector within the FAT. In contemporary implementations of the FAT file system, the FAT entry addresses a cluster rather than an individual disk sector. By using clusters, the FAT organization can address groups of, say, four sectors as if they were a single sector that has four times as many bytes as a single sector. This means that disk space is allocated to a file on a cluster-by-cluster basis. A 12-bit FAT is still limited to 128MB. Today, floppy disks use 12-bit FATs and hard disks use 16-bit or 32-bit FATs.

FAT-12 Implementation

The **Disk** abstraction you used in Exercise 10 allows you to treat a 1.44MB floppy disk (with 12-bit FAT entries) as a virtual file with an array of sectors organized according to Figure 25.

Directories and File Storage. Information about files is stored in a *directory*. You can look up information about a file (its size, where it is located on the disk, the time it was created, and so on) using the file's name. FAT-12 (the version of FAT with 12-bit FAT entries) uses a simple list of fixed-size *directory entries*. A directory entry can be found in a directory by searching linearly through the disk sectors that contain the directory list. That is, traversing the list of directory entries in a directory involves looking at multiple disk sectors and then at multiple entries within each sector.

A directory entry contains the file's name and a description of the location of its data. The entry also contains the file's size in bytes (in case the file size is not an exact multiple of the sector size). Directory entries use the same format whether they are in the root directory or in a subdirectory. Each entry is 32 bytes long, thereby allowing 16 entries per standard 512-byte sector. The root directory has a fixed maximum number of entries (the number is stored in the boot sector) and occupies a contiguous group of logical sectors, as determined by the format. By contrast, subdirectories are stored in a set of sectors that are managed in the same manner as files. Logically contiguous sectors are not necessarily physically contiguous on the disk and therefore must be accessed using the FAT.

The layout for a directory entry is shown in Figure 26. All multibyte integers are in *little-endian* order, meaning that the least significant byte is stored first.

The filename and extension are stored as uppercase ASCII characters.[2] Invalid entries have names beginning with **0x00** (the entry has not been used before) or **0xe5** (the entry was used before but has been released). The starting

---

[2] This discussion and exercise are for old-style MS-DOS names of 8 characters rather than the newer style, longer names.

Figure 26

Directory Entry

Offset	Length	Description
0x00	8	**Filename**
0x08	3	**Extension**
0x0B	1	**Bit field for attributes**
0x0C	10	**Reserved**
0x16	2	**Time (coded as Hour * 2048 + Min * 32 + Sec/2)**
0x18	2	**Date (coded as (Year − 1980) * 512 + Month * 32 + Day)**
0x1A	2	**Starting cluster number**
0x1C	4	**File size (in bytes)**

cluster number is slightly deceiving. While it does reference the starting cluster (sector) number, it cannot reference sectors used for the boot record, FAT copies, or root directory. A starting cluster number of k actually refers to logical sector number $31 + k$. See the further discussion on "Converting Clusters to Logical Sectors."

The attribute byte stores bits for attributes, similar to UNIX attributes. The bit fields are shown in Figure 27. Note that bit 0 is the least significant bit. A bit set to 1 means the file has that attribute and set to 0 means it does not. So, for example, a file with attributes **0x20 == 00100000b** has the archive bit set and all others cleared. A hidden, read-only subdirectory would be, for example, **00010011b == 0x13**.

Clusters and File Storage. Files on FAT disks are divided into clusters of N sectors. N ranges from 1 to 32, depending on the format (hard disks use large clusters so that their allocation tables do not get too big). To access a file, you need to determine the list of clusters it occupies. For example, a 2K file **FOO.TXT** might occupy clusters 34, 19, 81, and 47. There is no room to store an arbitrary list of clusters in the directory entry, since it has a fixed size. Instead, the system stores only the first cluster. Then the FAT is used to link the rest (refer to Figure 25). To find out what cluster follows cluster C, use the Cth entry in the FAT. So for **FOO.TXT**, the system would store 34 in the directory entry for the first cluster, as follows.

Figure 27

Directory Entry
Attributes

Bit	Mask	Attribute
0	0x01	**Read-only**
1	0x02	**Hidden**
2	0x04	**System**
3	0x08	**Volume label**
4	0x10	**Subdirectory**
5	0x20	**Archive**
6	0x40	**Unused**
7	0x80	**Unused**

Figure 28

*FAT Entry
Values*

Descriptor	Heads	Sectors/track	Cylinders	Capacity
0x0fe	1	8	40	160K
0x0ff	2	8	40	320K
0x0fc	1	9	40	180K
0x0fd	2	9	40	360K
0x0f9	2	9	80	720K
0x0f0	2	18	80	1.44MB

FAT[34] == 19
FAT[19] == 81
FAT[81] == 47
FAT[47] == 0xff8

The special value **0xff8** marks the last cluster in the file. Any value from **0xff8** through **0xfff** may be used for this purpose. Using this value is redundant because the file length tells how many clusters there are, but the redundant information helps in recovering damaged disks.

More on the FAT. The first two entries of the FAT (for clusters 0 and 1) are reserved. The first one holds the media descriptor, which, for floppy disks, takes on the values shown in Figure 28. The FAT space, for clusters with two or more sectors, can contain the values for an entry shown in Figure 29.

FAT Packing. Life would be simple if the cluster numbers in the FAT were just stored in the FAT sectors. But the early DOS machines were cramped for space, so the designers decided to pack two 12-bit FAT entries into 3 bytes. Here's how it works. Bytes $3k$ through $3k + 2$ contain elements $2k$ and $2k + 1$ of the FAT array. In particular:

- Byte $3k$ contains the least significant 8 bits of FAT[$2k$].
- The least significant 4 bits of byte $3k + 1$ contain the most significant 4 bits of FAT[$2k$].

Figure 29

*FAT Space
Values*

Value	Meaning
0x000	Unused
0xFF0–0xFF6	Reserved cluster
0xFF7	Bad cluster
0xFF8–0xFFF	Last cluster in a file
(anything else)	Number of the next cluster in the file

11

- The most significant 4 bits of byte $3k + 1$ contain the least significant 4 bits of FAT[$2k + 1$]].

- Byte $3k + 2$ contains the most significant 8 bits of FAT[$2k + 1$].

Consider this example. A short file has been written to a new 1.44MB floppy. This new file begins at the first part of the file space, which is cluster 2. The rest of its sectors follow contiguously (since the disk was not fragmented when it was written). The beginning of the FAT now appears as shown in the hexadecimal dump shown in Figure 30. The first 3 bytes (**F0 FF FF**) are the two reserved entries and can now be ignored. The first entry corresponding to the example file is that for cluster 2, its beginning block. Using the formulae for mapping cluster number to FAT entry number, the entry for cluster 2 is obtained by combining parts of bytes at offsets 3 and 4. This gives **0x003**, since the first byte is less significant. This means that the FAT entry for cluster 2 is a pointer to its next cluster, number 3. To fetch number 3 then, use the bytes at offsets 4 and 5. This gives **0x004**. So the FAT entry for cluster 3 points to the next cluster in the file, number 4. Similarly, cluster 4 has **0x005** for the next cluster, and so on. Finally, at cluster 9 (2 * 4 + 1), the entries at offsets 13 and 14 (3 * 4 + 1 and 3 * 4 + 2) are read. This gives **0xfff**, a reserved value, which indicates the last cluster in a file. So cluster 9 marks the end of the file, which began at cluster 2. The remaining clusters, from 10 on up, are still unallocated, so they have the reserved value 0.

Converting Clusters to Logical Sectors. If there is one logical sector per cluster, this means each logical sector has an entry. However, since the FAT area stores information only about file space and the first two entries are reserved, the first cluster in the file space is cluster 2. To convert from a cluster number to a logical sector number, do the following:

1. Subtract 2 from the cluster number.

2. Multiply the result by the number of sectors in a cluster. This is 1 for the disks used here. It is 2 for double-sided, 40-track, 5.25 in. floppies. It is 4 for DSDD 8 in. floppies. For hard disks, it varies.

3. Add the result to the logical sector number of the first sector in the data storage area.

Figure 30

Example FAT

F0	FF	FF	03	40	00	05	60	00	07	80	00	09	F0	FF	00
00	00	00	00	00	00	00	00	00	00	00	00	00	00	00	00

File Systems and Directories

Therefore, on media with 1 sector per cluster, with 1 sector of reserved area, 18 sectors for FAT, and 14 sectors for the root directory (exactly the description of a 1.44MB floppy), the logical sector number of the first sector of file space will be 0 + 1 + 18 + 14 = 33. This sector will correspond to FAT cluster 2, logical sector 34 will correspond to FAT cluster 3, and so on. You might wish to implement a function to perform this translation and read data by cluster (see the description of **readFat12Cluster** in the following "Attacking the Problem").

PROBLEM STATEMENT

In this exercise, you are to implement various features of a file manager using the floppy disk driver from Exercise 10. The part of the device interface you need is specified in the **exercise10.h** header file from that exercise. Following are the crucial functions.

```
Disk physicalDisk(char driveLetter);
BOOL sectorRead(
        Disk theDisk,
        unsigned sector,
        char *buffer

);
        BOOL sectorWrite(
        Disk theDisk,
        unsigned sector,
        char *buffer
);
```

Note that you will have to provide a new **sectorWrite** function.

This exercise is broken down into parts to reduce the overall complexity of the problem:

Part I: List directories.
Part II: Change directories.
Part III: Remove a file.
Part IV: Copy a file.

Part I

Design and implement a function to provide a directory listing (like the **dir cmd.exe** command or **ls** UNIX shell command). First, you need a function to make the physical disk ready for use (to call the disk driver initialization code to determine the disk geometry and any other initialization you choose).

```
int fdLoad(char driveLetter);
```

Your directory listing function need not be as complex as a production routine. It should be only the basic command, without support for options. Here is the function prototype for the directory listing function.

```
int fdListDir();
```

Notice that after you have completed Part I, you will be able only to list the files in the root directory.

Part II

Design and implement a function to change the current directory up one level or to a subdirectory in the current directory (you need not handle pathnames).

```
int fdChangeDir(char *directory);
```

Implicitly, this function assumes that you have implemented subdirectories (you can do Part I without implementing them). You will probably find it helpful to use a static variable in your file system implementation to represent the current directory (you could implement it as an environment variable, but that is not required for this exercise). This function manipulates that current directory variable.

Part III

Design and implement a function to delete a file. It should take as its argument the name of a file to delete (from the current directory).

```
int fdEraseFile(char *name);
```

The function will have to find the file, follow its links in the FAT, set each cluster's entry in the FAT to unused, and update the directory entry. In the case of deletion, pay attention to the hidden, read-only, and system attributes. Files with any of these set should not be deleted.

Part IV

Design and implement a function to copy an existing file to a new file.

```
int fdCopyFile(char *source, char *destination);
```

As a simplification, the names of the source and destination files are provided as arguments to the function—you need not do error checking on the names. Use the old-style 8-character names with 3-character extensions. This will require that you make a new directory entry in the current directory, allocate space using the FAT, and then copy the information from the file into the new sectors.

Part V

Design and implement a driver program to test each function.

LAB ENVIRONMENT

This exercise uses the standard VC++ environment.

ATTACKING THE PROBLEM

You will find it useful to write various supporting routines that will be used in writing solutions to the various parts of the exercise. You might wish to implement the following functions.

```
int scanFatDirectorySector(char *buf, char *name);
struct directoryEntry getEntryFromSector(
      char *buf,
      unsigned index
);
unsigned getFat12Entry(Disk d, unsigned index);
unsigned readFat12Cluster(
      Disk,
      unsigned cluster,
      char *buf
);
```

You might also find it useful to write functions to implement other routines, such as

```
int getBootInfo(Disk, BootDescriptor);
```

11

to extract critical information stored in the boot sector, returning the information in a **BootDescriptor** structure, for example of the following form.

```
typedef struct BootDescriptor_t *BootDescriptor;
typedef struct BootDescriptor_t {
        unsigned        sectorsPerCluster;
        unsigned        numberOfFATs;
        unsigned        numberOfRootDirEntries;
        unsigned        numberOfLogSectors;
        unsigned        sectorsPerFAT;
        unsigned        numberOfHiddenSectors;
};
```

The scanFatDirectorySector *Function*

The **scanFatDirectorySector** function should search part of a directory in a sector, looking for an entry with the given name. Do not forget that MS-DOS filenames are case-insensitive, so you will have to match names regardless of case. (Since filenames are stored on disk in uppercase characters, you can do this by applying toupper to the name for which you are searching.)

The function returns −1 if it fails to find a matching directory entry. Otherwise, it returns the index of the matching entry, which is guaranteed to be in the range 0 to 15.

The getEntryFromSector *Function*

The **getEntryFromSector** function uses the index returned by **scanFat-DirectorySector**. Invalid directory entries have filenames beginning with **0x00** (the entry has never been used) or **0xe5** (the entry was previously used but has been released). The directory entry can be represented by the following C structure (in **exercise11.h**).

```
struct directoryEntry {
        char fullname[13];  /*name & extension, null-terminated */
        unsigned short year, month, day, hour, min, sec;
        unsigned short firstCluster;
        unsigned long size;
        unsigned readonly:1;
        unsigned hidden:1;
        unsigned system:1;
```

```
        unsigned vlabel:1;
        unsigned subdir:1;
        unsigned archive:1;
};
```

You cannot simply do bitwise copies from the directory entry into this structure; you will have to unmarshal the directory entry and then fill in the fields as appropriate. Integers are little-endian on the disk. Also, the 2-byte field for the time is computed as

2048*hours + 32*minutes + seconds/2

Thus you will have to unpack it by building the 2-byte value and then performing an integer divide to determine the hour value, and so on. Similarly, the 2-byte date field is encoded as

512*(year–1980) + 32*month + day

The getFat12Entry *Function*

The **getFat12Entry** function takes an index (and **Disk** descriptor) and returns the unsigned index into a FAT. In the example FAT shown in Figure 30, **getFat12Entry(d, 9)** should return **0xfff**, which is the logical sector number in the ninth entry in the FAT.

The readFat12Cluster *Function*

The **readFat12Cluster** function should perform the translation of a cluster to a logical sector number described in the subsection "Converting Clusters to Logical Sectors" in the "Introduction." It should return zero on success and nonzero on failure.

Following is the header file used for the solution to this exercise.

```
/* This interface is derived from one designed
 * by Norman Ramsey for CSci 413 at Purdue University, 1996
 */

#ifndef FILESYS_H
#define FILESYS_H

#include   <windows.h>
#include   "..\exercise10.h"
```

11

```
#define DIR_ENTRY_SIZE   32

// typedef struct open_file *Open_File;
typedef struct file_system *FileSystem;

typedef struct BootDescriptor_t *BootDescriptor;
typedef struct BootDescriptor_t {
        unsigned      sectorsPerCluster;
        unsigned      numberOfFATs;
        unsigned      numberOfRootDirEntries;
        unsigned      numberOfLogSectors;
        unsigned      sectorsPerFAT;
        unsigned      numberOfHiddenSectors;
};

typedef struct directoryEntry {
        char fullname[13];  // filename and ext, null-terminated
        unsigned short year, month, day, hour, min, sec;
        unsigned short firstCluster;
        unsigned long size;
        unsigned readonly:1;
        unsigned hidden:1;
        unsigned system:1;
        unsigned vlabel:1;
        unsigned subdir:1;
        unsigned archive:1;
};

/* Function prototypes on the File System interface */
// File System Interface
        int fdLoad(char);
        int fdListDir();
        int fdChangeDir(char *directory);
        int fdCopyFile(char *source, char *destination);
        int fdEraseFile(char *name);

// Function prototypes used implement the file system
        unsigned fatOctet(Disk, unsigned);
        void findDate(
           unsigned short *year,
           unsigned short *month,
```

```
            unsigned short *day,
            unsigned char info[2]
      );

      void findTime(
            unsigned short* hour,
            unsigned short* min,
            unsigned short* sec,
            unsigned char info[2]
      );


      int allocSector(Disk, int);
      int getBootInfo(Disk, BootDescriptor);
      struct directoryEntry getEntryFromSector(char *buf,
            unsigned index);
      unsigned getFat12Entry(Disk d, unsigned index);
      unsigned getFATByte(Disk d, unsigned k);
      int getFreeDirectoryEntry(char *buf, char *name);
      int getRootDirSector();
      void intToExtName(char intName[], char extName[]);
      int markFATfree(Disk d, int);
      int nextRelSector(Disk d, int lastSector);
      int putEntryIntoSector(
            char *buf,
            struct directoryEntry dirEntry,
            unsigned index
      );
      unsigned putFat12Entry(Disk d, unsigned index,
            unsigned val);
      unsigned putFATByte(Disk d, unsigned k, unsigned val);
      unsigned readFat12Cluster(Disk, unsigned cluster,
            char *buf);
      int scanFatDirectorySector(char *buf, char *name);
      void toBin(unsigned char, int[8]);
```

11

```
// The following routine is implemented in disk.c
// It is an enhancement to the disk solution from Exercise 10
      BOOL sectorWrite (Disk, unsigned, char *);


#endif FILESYS_H
```

Notice that you will be reading and writing a single physical floppy disk with both your **sectorRead** and **sectorWrite** programs (in Part IV of this exercise). This is done using code that references the FAT (Parts III and IV). For this exercise, you should not attempt to copy the FAT into primary memory, though this will clearly have a performance impact when you implement Parts III and IV.

You need to derive your solution using a real floppy disk. Prepare a floppy disk with a dozen simple files using the normal Windows NT interface, and keep a copy of all of your files on the hard disk. Format a floppy disk to use while you debug, realizing that you will probably have to reformat it and restore its files during the debugging process. You might find it worthwhile to write a simulated floppy disk with an in-memory image (by writing alternative **physicalDisk**, **sectorRead**, and **sectorWrite** functions).

REFERENCES

Messmer, Hans-Peter, *The Indispensable PC Hardware Book,* Second Edition, Addison-Wesley, Reading, Mass., 1995.

twelve

File Operations

This is the last of three exercises to build a simple, user space file manager for a floppy disk. This exercise focuses on file I/O operations. You will learn about:

▶ The details of using the FAT for accessing a file

▶ How to implement buffered I/O

▶ How to pack and unpack sectors to implement a byte stream

▶ How to use APCs

INTRODUCTION

In this exercise, you will implement functions that allow a programmer to read and write byte stream files using a conventional API. You will implement a simplified version of an interface similar to the NT Executive File Manager interface (and the UNIX kernel byte stream file interface).

Your previous experience with byte stream files should tell you that you will need open and close functions to prepare descriptors that the read and write routines can use for manipulating the file. In Exercise 9, you exploited buffering (file caching). In this exercise, you will implement read-ahead and write-behind buffering on top of the logical disk system you developed in Exercises 10 and 11. You will use the Windows NT APC feature to overlap sector input and output buffering. That is, your code will start an asynchronous read to fill input buffers while the user program executes and an asynchronous write to run in parallel with the read and application processing.

The Byte Stream File API

When a file is opened for reading or writing, the file manager must determine where the sectors that contain information for the file are stored on the disk. It also must position the file pointer, add and delete sectors to/from the file on write operations, and so on. The *open-file table* is the data structure used to do this. It usually contains some information from the disk-resident file descriptor (the FAT directory entry), though other information kept in the open-file table describes the state of the I/O session.

The Open and Close Operations. An open operation takes a filename and the access mode as input parameters. It finds an unused entry in the open-file table, fills in information extracted from the file system, initializes other fields, and returns an open-file table handle (index) to the caller.

The open operation must resolve the filename (it may be a pathname) to get the directory entry for the file. Processing a pathname is laborious, but straight-forward.

1. Start at the root directory or current directory (depending on if the path-name is absolute or relative), and look up the subdirectory whose name appears first in the path. If the name cannot be found, then the open fails. Otherwise, go on to the next step.
2. The found subdirectory has a directory entry, so the corresponding file is then treated as a directory as in step 1. Continue this path traversal until the leaf name—the last name in the path—is encountered. If this name is found in the appropriate subdirectory, an open-file descriptor can be pre-pared.
3. Check the file access permissions.
4. Allocate space for an open-file descriptor, and copy the information from the directory entry that you will need, including the name, attributes, the start cluster address, and the file size (see Figure 26).
5. Set the file pointer to zero. Return the handle to the open-file descriptor to the calling process.

The close operation writes all relevant information, for example the size (if it has changed) from the open-file table entry, back to the directory entry. It also writes any write-behind buffer contents to the disk. Finally, it releases the entry in the open-file table.

Read and Write Operations. The first order of business for the read and write operations is to *serialize* the byte stream on read operations (also called *unmarshalling* the data) and to *pack* (or *marshal*) the byte stream into sectors for write operations (see Figure 31). If the file pointer is addressing byte number $j + 2$ and this byte is stored in the ith sector in the file, then the file system must determine where sector i is located on the disk. In the floppy disk file system, this means that the FAT is used to determine where sector $i + 1$ is located, given that it is using sector i. The file manager must then read the disk sector into memory so that the read routine can return byte $j + 2$ as the result of the function call.

The byte stream interface allows a process to read or write an arbitrary-sized block of bytes, from 1 byte long to a block that is larger than a sector (or cluster). The first read operation causes the read routine to read at least one sector from the disk. If the read operation requests less information than is in a sector, the entire sector is read and kept in memory. Subsequent reads (on a file being read sequentially) will reference the remaining bytes in the buffered sector. If a read operation requests more bytes than are currently in the buffer, the routine will read another sector (sector $i + 1$ in Figure 31) in order to satisfy the request. The new sector will then be buffered, and the old sector (sector i) will be released.

Figure 31

Serializing and Packing Byte Streams

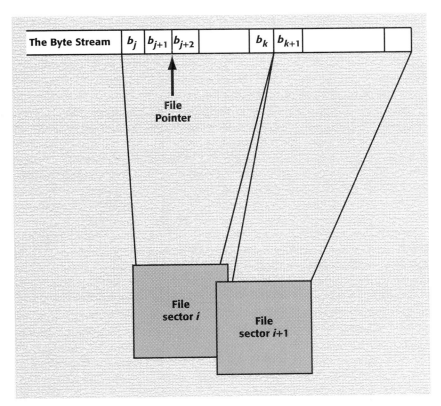

12

A write operation behaves similarly. In many byte stream file systems, if a thread writes to some point in the file, then the new information is appended to the file at the file pointer's location and all old information from the original file pointer to the end of the file is released. This means that the current sector is retained, but all later sectors in the file are deallocated from the file. In some cases, a file manager may allow the thread to simply overwrite bytes in the middle of a file.

Generalizing Buffering

Ordinary sector-based read and write operations implicitly cause the file manager to buffer at least one input and one output sector per open file as part of serializing and packing blocks. As you saw in Exercise 9, and as summarized in Figure 32, it is possible to exploit buffering by having a number of buffers used on input and output streams. The advantage is in performance. That is, the file manager can read ahead on the input stream to avoid making the application block on a sector read. Similarly, the file manager can write behind so that the thread does not have to block while waiting for a sector write operation to finish.

Buffering is ordinarily implemented in kernel space, though you can also implement the same mechanisms in user space; you will do this in this exercise. The idea is to design a user-space file manager that uses asynchronous I/O to start sector reads (to read ahead N sectors on the byte stream) and writes (that write behind the current file pointer up to N sectors). When a read operation requests information that has not yet been read, it must wait for the device read operation to complete before it can return a result to the application. As soon as it has determined that the read operation has completed on buffer i, it can

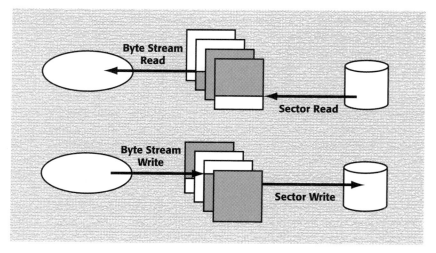

Figure 32

Buffering Sectors

immediately start an asynchronous read on sector $i + 1$. In the kernel-space implementation, an interrupt notifies the software when the device has completed its operation. In the user-space buffer manager, an APC can be used to notify the application that the sector read has completed. That is, an APC can be used in a user-mode manager much like an interrupt is used in a kernel-mode manager to implement buffering.

Asynchronous Procedure Calls

Asynchronous I/O techniques were introduced in Exercise 9. As a refinement to the basic strategy, a process can provide its own *callback* procedure. A callback procedure is registered with the called entity (the device in this case) so that it will be able to call the original calling thread when the (device) operation has been completed. This allows the caller to overlap processing with the device operation without having to periodically poll the device or manually catch an event with a wait function. As an introduction to callback procedures, recall that in Exercise 3, **SetWaitableTimer** was used to set a timer object so that it became signaled after a given amount of time.

```
BOOL SetWaitableTimer (
        HANDLE htimer,   // handle to a timer object
        Const LARGE_INTEGER *pDueTime,
                    // when timer will become signaled
        LONG lPeriod,   // periodic timer interval
        PTIMERAPCROUTINE pfnCompletionRoutine,
                    // pointer to the completion routine
        LPVOID lpArgToCompletionRoutine,
                    // data passed to completion routine
        BOOL fResume // flag for resume state
);
```

You did not use the **pfnCompletion** and **lpArgToCompletionRoutine** parameters at that time. They are used with the Windows NT APC facility. An APC is a procedure call to a procedure in the address space that will occur at some time after it was issued. The APC, when issued, is queued on the thread. If the Executive issued the APC, the procedure call will be made the next time the thread is scheduled. However, if another user-mode thread issues the APC, the procedure will not be invoked until the thread becomes alertable—this happens only when the thread calls **SleepEx**, **SignalObjectAndWait**, **MsgWaitForMultipleObjectsEx**, **WaitForMultipleObjectsEx**, or **WaitForSingleObjectEx**. When the APC

12

is to be processed, the thread interrupts its normal control flow and calls the procedure specified by the queued APC request.

For waitable timers, the **pfnCompletionRoutine** is the callback procedure that will be called with the argument **lpArgToCompletionRoutine**. The APC completion routine can do any processing you wish, though it must have a header for the prototype.

```
VOID(APIENTRY * pfnCompletionRoutine)(
    LPVOID lpArgToCompletionRoutine,
    DWORD dwTimerLowValue,
    DWORD dwTimerHighValue
);
```

When **pfnCompletionRoutine** is called, it will also be passed the time, in the **FILETIME** format, at which the APC was made (see Exercise 3 for more on the **FILETIME** data type).

As shown in Figure 33, APCs can also be used with file I/O operations, specifically with the **ReadFileEx** and **WriteFileEx** functions, for example:

```
BOOL ReadFileEx(
    HANDLE hFile,
    LPVOID lpBuffer,
    DWORD nNumberOfBytesToRead,
    LPOVERLAPPED lpOverlapped,
    LPOVERLAPPED_COMPLETION_ROUTINE lpCompletionRoutine
);
```

Notice that when you use **ReadFileEx**, you will have provided a handle to an event within the **OVERLAPPED** structure passed by using **lpOverlapped** and an **lpCompletionRoutine** with the last argument. Since the **lpCompletionRoutine** callback procedure will be called when the read operation completes, the event pointer is ignored with **ReadFileEx** and **WriteFileEx**. The **lpCompletionRoutine** pointer specifies the entry point of the callback routine that will be called when the read operation has completed. The application thread cannot use the buffer involved in the asynchronous I/O operation until it has completed. If you try to read or write the buffer, you might corrupt the data in the buffer.

ReadFileEx and **WriteFileEx** use a different function prototype for the callback routine than is used with waitable timers. The **lpCompletionRoutine** parameter must point to a function with a prototype of the following form.

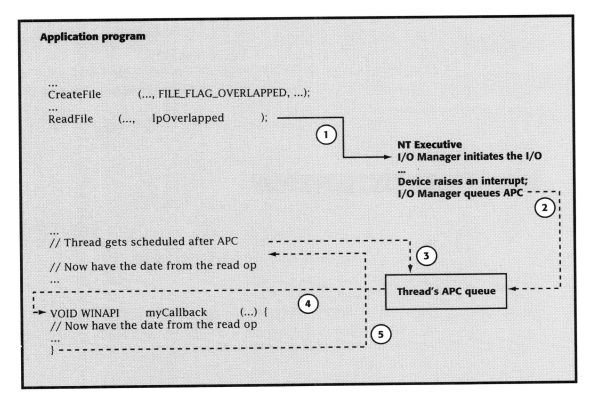

Figure 33

Asynchronous I/O with Callback

```
VOID WINAPI completionRoutine(
     DWORD dwErrorCode,
     DWORD dwNumberOfBytesTransfered,
     LPOVERLAPPED lpOverlapped
);
```

The **dwErrorCode** will be zero in the APC if the I/O operation was successful or have the value **ERROR_HANDLE_EOF** if an EOF file condition was detected. The **dwNumberOfBytesTransfered** value will be the number of bytes actually read/written on the operation. The **lpOverlapped** parameter is the pointer to the **OVERLAPPED** function passed to the I/O routine when it was called.

Obviously, **ReadFileEx** and **WriteFileEx** are more complex than the usual read and write operations. While they allow you to write callback proce-

12

dures to handle the I/O completion, they also introduce new failure modes. For example, there is a limit to the number of asynchronous I/O operations that you may have executing at any given moment. As usual, **GetLastError** will tell you the nature of an error if one occurs. This might require you to cancel pending operations using the **CancelIo** function (see the MSDN documentation).

PROBLEM STATEMENT

Part I

This exercise is to extend the file system software from Exercise 11 so that it provides a byte stream I/O API. It is to implement the following functions.

```
int fdFMInit(char driveLetter);
int fdChangeDir(char *directory);      // same as Exer. 11
FD_Handle fdOpenFile(char* name, int mode);
void fdCloseFile(FD_Handle fdHandle);
int fdReadFile(
        FD_Handle fdHandle,
        char* buffer,
        int length
);
int fdWriteFile(
        FD_Handle fdHandle,
        char* buffer,
        int length
);
```

The **fdFMInit** routine is an initialization routine that should call your **fdLoad** routine from Exercise 11 and/or **physicalDisk** from Exercise 10 and perform any other initialization you require. The **fdOpenFile** and **fdCloseFile** functions will perform tasks that you choose when you design your read/write functions (see the previous discussion of the open-file descriptor). The **fdReadFile** and **fdWriteFile** routines implement byte stream writes similar to the Windows NT **ReadFile** and **WriteFile** routines. They are to be implemented on top of the physical disk and FAT abstractions you constructed in Exercises 10 and 11. Your code should work with files on an ordinary Windows NT/MS-DOS floppy diskette. This means that the implementation should be able to traverse a file using the FAT, allocating and deallocating sectors as required.

You will have to design an open-file descriptor to keep the state of the open file, for example its file pointer value, whether it is open for read or write (you need not implement files that are open for read and write at the same time). Finally, you will have to design and implement a driver program to test each function.

Part II

Implement the **sectorAsynchRead** routine. Your read routine must implement read-ahead buffering for up to $N = 3$ buffers. You are to implement buffering using APCs with the **ReadFileEx** routine on the physical disk abstraction. That is, you will have to use the FAT to determine which sectors to read and then perform sector reads on the floppy disk handle. You will likely need to add a new **sectorRead** routine to your disk implementation from Exercise 10 and/or 11.

```
BOOL sectorAsynchRead(
    Disk d,
    unsigned sector,
    char *buf,
    LPOVERLAPPED lpOLap,
    LPOVERLAPPED_COMPLETION_ROUTINE apcFunc,
    FD_Handle h
);
```

Several simplifying assumptions apply to the buffer implementation.

- You do not need to worry about shared files (you will not have to worry about consistency).
- A file can be open only for reading or writing.
- Files will be accessed only sequentially.
- The read routine you provide is to be synchronous (even though you will be using asynchronous routines to implement buffering).
- Filenames should be the old-style MS-DOS names (up to eight characters in the name and up to three characters in the extension).
- You can ignore file protection.

Part III

Implement the **sectorAsynchWrite** routine. Your write routine must implement write-behind buffering for up to $N = 3$ buffers. You are to implement buffering using APCs with the **WriteFileEx** routine on the physical device abstraction. That is, you will have to use the FAT to determine which sectors to write

12

and then perform sector writes on the floppy disk handle. You will likely need to add a new **sectorWrite** routine to your disk implementation from Exercise 10 and/or 11.

```
BOOL sectorAsynchWrite (
    Disk theDisk,
    unsigned sector,
    char *buf,
    LPOVERLAPPED lpOLap,
    LPOVERLAPPED_COMPLETION_ROUTINE apcFunc,
    FD_Handle h
);
```

The simplifying assumptions identified in Part II also apply to Part III.

LAB ENVIRONMENT

This exercise uses the standard VC++ environment.

ATTACKING THE PROBLEM

Your software will have to deal with several different issues in order to use the disk abstraction and the FATs and to incorporate buffering. Figure 34 shows the organization of one solution to the problem; the numbers refer to the following steps in a read operation.

1. The application performs a read call on the File Manager.
2. The File Manager interrogates the open-file table to determine if the required information resides in a buffer or if it needs to be read from the disk.
3. If a disk read is required, the File Manager reads the FAT to determine which disk sector needs to be read next.
4. The File Manager then reads the required disk. If there are other input buffers available, the File Manager starts an asynchronous I/O operation that will call a read callback routine when the next sector has been read.
5. The kernel-level asynchronous I/O mechanism will issue an APC to the file manager's read callback routine (which will perform any housekeeping to finish the read and then initiate the next read operation).
6. The block of bytes is returned to the calling program.

The state you will want to store in an open-file descriptor should include the

- the disk on which the file is stored,
- the length of the file,

Figure 34

*Organization of
One Solution*

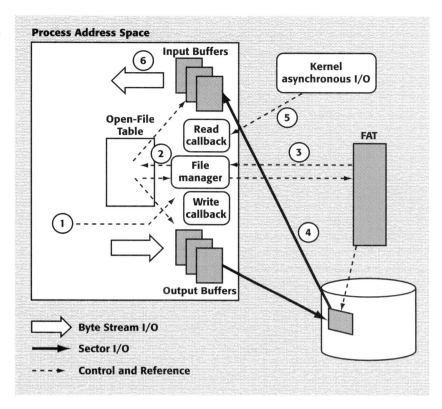

the file pointer to the next character to be read (equivalently, a count of the number of characters already read),

- a pointer to the *N* buffers, and
- the number of the buffer containing the next character to be read.

If there are characters remaining to be read, you should maintain the invariant that the buffer holds the next character to be read. You can guarantee that invariant at file-open time by reading in the first cluster. If a read request exhausts the cluster, you can maintain the invariant by reading in the next cluster.

Use the simulated time mechanism from Exercise 5 to introduce some sporadic processing time in your driver program (between reads and writes). Rather than just sleeping, you might consider performing some compute-intensive task in a loop, such as is done in the following code skeleton.

```
while(...) {
// Read a record
// CPU burst phase
        for(i = 0; i < busyTime; i++)
```

12

```
            y = pow(x, e);
        Sleep(napTime);
// Write a record
}
```

Here is a skeleton for the read routine for Part II.

```
int fdReadFile(
     FD_Handle fdHandle,
     char* buffer,
     int length)
{
     // If the buffer pool is empty, start a read, and
     // then wait for it
     if(...) {
     // First, determine which sector to read from FAT
     // Fill the first buffer
        SetFilePointer(...);
        ReadFile(...);

     // Start the disk reading the next sector
     // but continue
        SetFilePointer(...);
        ReadFileEx(..., callbackRoutine);
     }

     // Unmarshal bytes from the buffer and return them
}

VOID WINAPI callbackRoutine(LPVOID argPtr) {...}
```

Finally, your solution to this exercise should attempt to perform multiple operations on the floppy disk at one time. Besides the obvious read and write operations for the normal data I/O, if your FAT manipulation routines also read and write the FAT in place, the floppy disk will become the performance bottleneck. If you have a machine with two floppy disk drives, you should do reads on one drive and writes on the other. You might find it a very challenging exercise to support FAT I/O and data I/O on one diskette so that everything works correctly. If you decide to use a single floppy disk drive with two open files and to cache the FAT when you open the file, then you will have to be very careful to propagate FAT updates so that all file operations use the correct FAT values (rather than stale copies). This problem will become especially difficult in Part III.

As in Exercise 11, you will need to derive your solution using a real floppy disk. Prepare a diskette with a dozen simple files under the normal Windows NT interface, and keep a copy of all of your files on the hard disk. Format a floppy diskette to use while you debug, realizing that you will probably have to reformat it and restore its files during the debugging process. You might find it worthwhile to write a simulated floppy disk with an in-memory image (by writing alternative **physicalDisk**, **sectorRead**, and **sectorWrite** functions).

REFERENCES

Messmer, Hans-Peter, *The Indispensable PC Hardware Book*, Second Edition, Addison-Wesley, Reading, Mass., 1995.

12

Appendix:
The Visual C++ Programming Environment

If you have used a UNIX environment for your C and C++ programming, you will find the Visual C++ environment to be a much different environment. Visual C++ is a window-based, point-and-select, graphical, programming environment. However, the exercises in this manual can be solved using any C compiler and environment you like, provided they are compatible with the Win32 API.

EXECUTABLE FILES

An executable file, which has an **EXE** extension, is built as follows.

1. The programmer writes application programs.
2. The compiler translates each application program into an object file (which has an **OBJ** file extension). The compiler marks external references that appear in the code in each file so that the link editor can resolve them in the next step. This means that the compiler needs the correct header files (which have file extension **H**) that provide the function proto- types for each external reference.
3. The link editor reads all of the external references made by all of the code it is processing. If procedure X is called in any of the code, then the link editor must ensure that a copy of procedure X is incorporated into the **EXE** file and that the call references in the code will point at that copy. Some of these references to procedures defined elsewhere are to proce- dures that the programmer wrote but that are placed in a different file. Others are procedures that are provided as part of the runtime environ-

ment; they will be kept in a library. The C runtime library is a set of basic procedures that have evolved over the years with UNIX and C. There are also math libraries, the standard I/O library (**stdio**), the standard windows library (referenced by using **windows.h**), and many others.

4. After the **EXE** file has been prepared, it is written to a disk file, where it is available to be loaded and executed. All exercises in this manual should result in an **EXE** file that can be loaded and executed from the **cmd.exe** command shell by typing the pathname for the **EXE** file.

Following are the essential elements of a programming environment:

- An *editor* to allow you to enter a program into the computer and to modify it as you debug it
- A *compiler* to translate source code files into object code
- A *link editor* for combining **OBJ** and library procedures
- A set of *runtime library* routines that can be used to perform various generic operations
- A *loader* to place the **EXE** file contents into memory for execution

The link editor is usually packaged to run as a part of the compilation step. The loader is implicit in the command line interpreter (see Exercise 2). This means that the essential tools you need to write software are an ASCII text editor, a compiler (all compilers include a link editor), and a command line interpreter with an implicit loader (such as **cmd.exe**).

However, programming is a labor-intensive task, so if the environment provides additional facilities beyond the essential ones, you'll find it easier to prepare software. The Visual C++ environment included on the CD-ROMs with the bundled version of this laboratory manual provides many more tools than the essential ones. The heart of Visual C++ is a syntax-driven editor that "understands" C and C++ programs.[1] This is reflected in a number of ways, including the following.

- The editor attempts to automatically indent according to the block structure of the code.
- Normal program text appears in a black font. Keywords are recognized and appear as blue text. Comments appear as green text. This allows you to quickly recognize various kinds of typos and to avoid silly mistakes where you misuse a variable name.

---

[1] You can also use a different editor with VC++ if you like. The description in this appendix assumes the use of the built-in editor.

- All of the normal edit features are available in the editor: text cut, copy, and paste; text searching; and so on.
- You can have multiple files open in the editor at one time, thereby allowing you to edit parts of one file and then quickly switch to another. In addition, the editor provides alternative subwindows to describe the results of operations and to navigate through the different parts of your code.

There are several other major components of Visual C++. One is a set of tools to define and manage a full project—you will normally have a new project for each exercise. The editor interface also allows you to invoke the compiler, link editor, and loader (though you will not load and run any of your programs for this manual from Visual C++). A window-based debugger allows you to set breakpoints from the editor and then to correlate debugging with the source code in the editor window. Finally, the environment can have the MSDN documentation embedded in it.

There is considerable documentation and tutorial information about Visual C++ with the product, over the Web, and in various reference books. The intent of this appendix is to provide you with an overview of the facilities, especially the parts that are most critical for you to know to solve the exercises in this laboratory manual.

WORKSPACES AND PROJECTS

UNIX evolved from its initial stages, in which it had very few software development tools, to a comprehensive programming environment. Visual C++ has built on the logical model used in UNIX development environments, adding new abstractions to create the idea of a software project in a system workspace. Even if you do not have an extensive background in software development (no special background is presumed for someone using this manual), you are likely to have encountered some of the UNIX C tools.

In UNIX, users interact with the system using a command line shell program, similar to the **cmd.exe** command line shell program. When the shell prompts the user, the user can type a string of characters onto the command line and send it to the shell by pressing the "Enter" (or "Return") key. The compiler and link editor are invoked using the "**cc**" command for the default C compiler, though many UNIX/Linux installations now use the "**gcc**" command for the Gnu Foundation C compiler. The compiler has a number of options (the exact options depend on the compiler you are using). For example, one flag tells the compiler that the code it generates should accommodate a debugger and another controls the amount of time the compiler should spend optimizing the machine language that is generated from the source code. As a programming project grows, it is very easy to forget all of the arguments that should be used with the compiler in order to translate a particular file.

The **make** facility allows the programmer to create a file, called a makefile, to prepare a script for how to compile and combine files so as to build an executable (an **a.out** file in UNIX, but the same kind of file as an **EXE** file). The makefile provides a means by which the programmer can cause different parts of the code to be compiled depending on changes to files. For example, suppose you change a source code file. The makefile will include a dependency that indicates that if the source code is modified, it must be recompiled to "make" a new version of the overall program. In production UNIX environments, creating the makefile is an important step in creating production software from a collection of source files and libraries.

In Visual C++, it is also possible to generate a makefile. However, you can accomplish much the same effect by using workspaces and projects instead. A workspace defines a logical set of one or more projects. A project is represented by a set of C program files that are used to build an **EXE** file. When you open Visual C++, you will need to open a workspace and project. When you create a project in the workspace, a folder will be created that holds all of the project information, for example the names of the source programs in the files. Normally, you will place your source files in the project folder. A file is added to a project either by creating a new source file (using the "File" menu) or by explicitly adding the file to the project with the "Add to project" selection on the "Project" menu in Visual C++. You will probably want to keep only a single project in a workspace, so you will not need to focus too closely on the difference between a workspace and a project. (In Exercises 10–12, you might decide to keep multiple projects in a single workspace, but by the time you work on Exercise 10, you will have accumulated considerable experience with the simple configurations.)

When you are ready to create the project, close the current workspace (from the "File" menu) and select "File/New." You will be given a wide set of choices about what new file you wish to create, organized under four tabs: "Files," "Projects," "Workspaces," and "Other Documents." Select the "Projects" tab. Selections on this tab are related to using various options and packages for your project. Every exercise in this manual uses the "Win32 Console Application" choice from the menu. This tells Visual C++ that the project will be to generate an **EXE** that will be run from the **cmd.exe** command line. The display will also require that you provide a pathname for the project folder and a name for the project (which will also be the name of the project folder). The default is to create a new workspace, though you can override the default from this tab display.

Once you have created a project, the "Set Active Project" selection from the "Project" menu will allow you to select the project you want to work on (if you have multiple projects in a workspace).

After you have created a project, you begin adding source code files to the project by selecting "Files/New/C++ Source File." If you have prepared a file elsewhere (for example you copy a file from another project), you can just open the file in the editor and add it to the project using the "Add to Project" selection from the "Project" menu. Once you have built a project with one or more source files in it, you can compile and link files using the "Rebuild All" selection from the "Build" menu. This option recompiles all files in the project (unlike the dependency-driven compilation of a makefile). You can also selectively "Compile" and "Build" parts of the project if you like.

The "Build" option generates a default set of parameters to pass to the compiler and link editor. The default is to create a debug version of the code. (You can create and test all code in this manual using the debug version, though you might find it interesting to experiment with the "Build" option in Exercise 9.) The debug version creates a subdirectory inside the project directory and writes the **EXE** file in the debug directory.

To control other command line parameters for the compiler or link editor, you specify them using the "Settings ..." selection on the "Project" menu. There are nine different tab displays for choosing settings. Only the "C/C++" and "Link" tabs were used in preparing solutions to the exercises. The C/C++ tab provides several useful settings, as follows.

- **Warning level.** There are four different levels (the default is level 3) for reporting compilation warnings. Level 4 is the most comprehensive, and level 0 essentially disables warnings. All solutions to the exercises in this manual were prepared using level 3.
- **Preprocess definitions.** These are flags you can pass to the compiler preprocessor. If you were to run the compiler from **cmd.exe**, you would provide these flags as arguments to the compiler.
- **Project options.** These are flags for the compiler itself. You can edit this field directly in the dialog box from the "Settings ..." selection. You can experiment with the other fields from the C/C++ tab.

The "Link" tab controls the actions of the link editor.

- **Output filename.** This field allows you to change the name and location of the **EXE** file. The default is the project name with the **EXE** extension in the debug folder.

- **Object/library modules.** Here is where you can control the set of libraries that the link editor will search to resolve external references. If you are using a function from a library, the name of the library must appear in this field. In a few of the exercises in this manual, you will have to edit the default list, particularly if you are using multithreaded C code.
- **Project options.** This editable field changes when you edit the "Object/library modules field." You can also add or delete link editor arguments by editing the field directly.

Multithreaded C Programs

Exercise 2 includes an explanation of the incompatibilities between the standard C runtime library and thread operation. You must use **_beginthreadex** in place of **CreateThread** to create a copy of the process's runtime variables for each thread in the process. You must edit the C/C++ and link editor settings in the project for Visual C++ to compile your multithreaded code. As described in the exercise, there is a special C runtime library used with **_beginthreadex** (the default C runtime library will not work with multithreaded code). So you must direct the link editor to use the correct library, which means you have to edit fields in the C/C++ tab and the link tab in the "Settings ..." selection.

Under the "C/C++" tab, the default "Project options:" field contains a compiler flag value of **/MLd**. This value means that the compiler is to translate under the assumption that the code is single-threaded. The flag must be changed from **/MLd** to **/MTd** so that the compiler will generate code for multithreaded use.

The link editor must also be passed specialized flags, so you need to edit the "Link" tab. Change the "Object/library modules:" field to use the multithreaded C runtime library by adding "**/libcmt.lib**" to the field. Unfortunately, a different version of the library must be used if you are debugging; you must add "**/libcmtd.lib**" instead of the production library.

THE DEBUGGER

The visual debugger is also run from within the Visual C++ environment. The "Edit" menu includes the "Breakpoints ..." selection. This is another multitabbed set of selections. They cause the normal execution of the **EXE** to be interrupted when it encounters a source code line containing a breakpoint. The debugger will be started, thereby allowing you to inspect the state of the process and thread at the time of the interruption. The debugger is also invoked if Windows NT detects a runtime error.

MSDN ONLINE DOCUMENTATION

An extensive collection of online documentation for Windows NT and Visual C++ is available, distributed as part of the MSDN. You can get the current online documentation from the MSDN Web site (**www.microsoft.com/msdn**), though you will have to become a member[2] of MSDN before you can download the documentation. The MSDN documentation was not included as part of this manual for two reasons. First, the most recent version is always available on the Web. Second, including the documentation in this manual would have required at least two more CD-ROMs. Your instructor might have already downloaded a copy of the MSDN documentation and made it available as part of the course materials.

EXAMPLE

This example examines the steps to create a very simple C program to be executed in the **cmd.exe** shell.

1. Start Visual C++ from the menu "Start/Program/Microsoft Visual C++ 6.0/Microsoft Visual C++ 6.0."
2. If Visual C++ starts with an existing workspace opened, close it using the "CloseWorkspace" command from the "File" menu.
3. Select the "New" command from the "File" menu, and then select the "Projects" tab from the "New" dialog box.
4. Edit the "Location:" box on the right side of the dialog box so that it references the folder in which you wish to create your project. For example, you might type

C:\MyFolder\Exercise A

into the "Location:" box.

5. Type a project name, such as **Project_0**, into the "Project name:" box.
6. Be sure that "Win32" is checked in the "Platforms:" box.
7. Select "Win32 Console Application" from the "Projects" tab file type list.
8. Create the project by selecting the "OK" button at the bottom of the dialog box.
9. Use the Windows File Manager to browse through the file system to find the project folder you just created and to see the files that Visual C++ created inside the folder.

---

[2] Membership in MSDN is free, but registration is required. To get copies of Microsoft software, you have to be a paying subscriber.

Example   217

Now you are ready to create one or more files to make up your project.

1. From the "File" menu, select the "New" command.
2. Enter a filename, such as **main.c**, into the "File name:" box on the right side of the "New" dialog box.
3. Select the "C++ Source File" type from the list of types on the left side of the dialog box.
4. Create the C file by selecting the "OK" button at the bottom of the dialog box.
5. Use the mouse to place the editing cursor in the editing window for the new file, and then type a simple program (such as the following one) into the editor window.

```
#include   <windows.h>
#include   <stdio.h>
int main () {
      printf("This is my first Win32 Console Application\n");
      printf("prepared using the Visual C++ environment.\n");
      bad line       // intentionally incorrect statement
      return(0);
}
```

6. You can save the file (or all of the files in the project) at any time using the "Save" (or "Save All") command from the "File" menu. Save your file(s) now.
7. Select the "Rebuild All" command from the Visual C++ "Build" menu. If you included the intentionally erroneous statement (see bad line in the previous program) in your C program, the Visual C++ compiler will report a message something like the following in a small, scrollable window below the main editing window:

Project_0.exe - 4 error(s), 0 warning(s)

8. In the error-reporting window, scroll upward to see the nature of the four errors. You will see something like the following (the output is shown in a small font to represent the actual display in the error-reporting window).

Deleting intermediate files and output files for project 'Project_1 - Win32 Debug'.
----Configuration: Project_0 - Win32 Debug----
Compiling...
main.c
D:\Book\Exercise A1\Project_0\main.c(7) : error C2065: 'bad' : undeclared identifier
D:\Book\Exercise A1\Project_0\main.c(7) : error C2146: syntax error : missing ';' before identifier 'line'

```
D:\Book\Exercise A1\Project_0\main.c(8) : error C2065: 'line' : undeclared identifier
D:\Book\Exercise A1\Project_0\main.c(8) : error C2143: syntax error : missing ';' before 'return'
Error executing cl.exe.
Project_0.exe - 4 error(s), 0 warning(s)
```

9. Select the first error by double-clicking on the line. This will cause a line in the editing window to be selected by an arrow in the right border of the edit window. The selected line contains the code that the compiler has found to be in error.

10. Delete the line, save the file, and rebuild the project. After the project has been rebuilt, Visual C++ should report the following in the error-reporting window:

Project_0.exe - 0 error(s), 0 warning(s)

11. At this point, you will have created a debug version of the program. Using the File Manager again, notice that you now have a new "Debug" folder in your project folder. Inside the "Debug" folder is an executable file named **Project_1.exe** that can be run from **cmd.exe**.

Now you are ready to execute your example program from **cmd.exe**.

1. From the "Start/Programs" menu, select the "Command Prompt" command. Doing this will open a new window running **cmd.exe**; the window is a 25-line, character-oriented display.

2. Use the **cd** command to change the current directory in **cmd.exe** to the project folder you created. Use the **dir** command to list the folder (directory) contents. The contents should correspond to what you see in the Windows File Manager view of the folder (directory).

3. Use the **cd** command to change to the "Debug" directory. You might also want to invoke the **dir** command again to see the contents of this directory.

4. Run your program by entering **project_0** (cmd.exe does not distinguish between uppercase and lowercase characters). Your program will then be executed, with **stdin** as the keyboard and **stdout** as the **cmd.exe** window.

EXERCISES

1. Using the Visual C++ environment, create a Win32 console application to read an integer, N, from **stdin** (using the normal C runtime **stdio** package, **scanf**) and to print the first N Fibbonacci numbers. Recall that the

Fibbonacci numbers are the sequence of integers

$$0, 1, 1, 2, 3, 5, 8, 13, \ldots, i, ((i - 1) + i), (i + (i + 1)), \ldots$$

When you test your program, try various values up to 40.

2. Create a Win32 console application to read two filenames, **inFile** and **outFile**, from **stdin** (using the normal C runtime **stdio** package). Use the C runtime file open function (**fopen**) to open **inFile** for reading and **outFile** for writing. Copy all characters from **inFile** to **outFile**, and close both files.

Bibliography

Asche, Ruediger R., "The Little Device Driver," Microsoft Development Network article, February, 1994.

Davis, Ralph, *Win32 Network Programming: Windows 95 and Windows NT Network Programming Using MFC*, Addison-Wesley, Reading, Mass., 1997.

Deitel, Harvey M., *An Introduction to Operating Systems*, Second Edition, Addison-Wesley, Reading, Mass., 1990.

Hart, Johnson M., *Win32 System Programming*, Addison-Wesley, Reading, Mass., 1997.

Microsoft, *Win32 API Reference Manual*, MSDN online documentation.

Microsoft, *Windows NT DDK (for Windows NT Workstation 4.0 – U. S.)*, CD-ROM, Microsoft Corporation, January, 1997.

Messmer, Hans-Peter, *The Indispensable PC Hardware Book*, Second Edition, Addison-Wesley, Reading, Mass., 1995.

Nagar, Rajeev, *Windows NT File System Internals: A Developer's Guide*, O'Reilly & Associates, Sebastapol, Calif., 1997.

Nutt, Gary J., *Operating Systems: A Modern Perspective*, Addison-Wesley, Reading, Mass., 1997.

Pearce, Eric, *Windows NT in a Nutshell*, O'Reilly & Associates, Sebastapol, Calif., 1997.

Rector, Brent E., and Joseph M. Newcomer, *Win32 Programming*, Addison-Wesley, Reading, Mass., 1997.

Richter, Jeffrey, *Advanced Windows*, Third Edition, Microsoft Press, Redmond, Wash., 1997.

Ritchie, Dennis M., "A Stream Input-Output System," *AT&T Bell Laboratories Technical Journal, 63, 8* (October 1984), 1897–1910.

Russinovich, Mark, "Inside the Native API," technical report, March, 1998, available at www.sysinternals.com.

Silberschatz, Abraham and Galvin, Peter Baer, *Operating System Concepts*, Fifth Edition, Addison-Wesley, Reading, Mass., 1998.

Solomon, David A., *Inside Windows NT*, Second Edition, Microsoft Press, Redmond, Wash., 1998.

Stallings, William, *Operating Systems*, Second Edition, Prentice-Hall, Englewood Cliffs, N. J., 1995.

Stevens, W. Richard, *UNIX Network Programming*, Prentice-Hall, Englewood Cliffs, N. J., 1990.

Stevens, W. Richard, *TCP/IP Illustrated*, *Volume I*, Addison-Wesley, Reading, Mass., 1994.

Tanenbaum, Andrew S., *Computer Networks*, Second Edition, Prentice-Hall, Englewood Cliffs, N. J., 1989.

Tanenbaum, Andrew S., *Modern Operating Systems*, Prentice-Hall, Englewood Cliffs, N. J., 1992.

Index

What You Should Know Before Running Setup

Checklist to organize your information before running Setup:

1. Have you read the Windows NT workstation readme files? If possible, read the file Setup.txt on your compact disc for information pertaining to hardware and configuration. Also it is helpful to have a printed copy on hand for reference during the setup procedure.

2. Have you backed up all of the files currently on your computer to either a network share or a tape storage device?

3. Have you checked all your hardware (network adapter cards, video drivers, sound cards, CD-ROM drives, etc.) against the Windows NT Hardware Compatibility List? Up-to-date versions are available on the World Wide Web at http://www.microsoft.com/ntserver/hcl/hclintro.htm and/or Microsoft's ftp server at ftp://microsoft.com/bussys/winnt/winnt_docs/hcl

4. Do you have all the device driver disks and configuration settings for your third-party hardware? *Note:* If the setup process does not recognize the correct hardware, accept the defaults and change them after setup through the control panel.

5. Do you have ready a formatted disk for Emergency Repair Disk (ERD)?

6. Do you have your CD-Key number ready (see CD-ROM label)?

Previous Operating System (if any):

Windows 95 cannot be upgraded to Windows NT 4.0. If you are running Windows 95, you must install Windows NT 4.0 in a separate directory, and your computer will dual boot. If you have Windows 95 or Windows NT 3.51, run Winnt32.exe instead of Winnt.exe. Winnt32 is a more efficient setup process.

If you will be using this computer on a network, you will need to know the following:

- Computer Name
- Workgroup/domain name. If adding to a domain, verify from domain administrator that the computer has an account in the domain.
- IP address: (if your network does not have a DHCP server)
- Other information needed for protocols other than TCP/IP

Installing Windows NT:

Insert the CD-ROM into your computer's CD-ROM drive.

Start Setup according to the instructions for your computer. Then follow all instructions on your screen, typing in the necessary information as Setup asks you to do. During this phase, Setup restarts your computer as needed in order to copy and process the Setup files.

Finishing Setup and Starting Windows NT:

After you have given Setup all the information it needs, it fully installs your operating system and then restarts your computer. Windows NT Workstation is now ready to use.

Insert the CD-ROM into your computer's CD-ROM drive and the Visual C++ Installation Wizard starts automatically. You can use the Wizard for initial product install and for later additions or modifications. The Installation Wizard also enables you to install the documentation. If the Wizard does not open automatically, you can use the Setup.exe at the root of the CD-ROM.

Installing with Microsoft Windows NT® Workstation, Operating System Version 4.0

The Installation Wizard will upgrade Microsoft® Windows NT® with SP3 if it is not already installed.

Installing Microsoft Internet Explorer

The Installation Wizard will install the latest version of Microsoft ® Internet Explorer 4, which provides many essential components: the newest version of Microsoft® Virtual Machine for Java, the latest user interface and common control libraries, and upgrades to the HTML-based online Help system

Restarts During Installation

During installation, you will be required to restart your computer. The Wizard will automatically return you to the right step in the installation process.

Files for Programming Projects

The LAB_MAN directory at www.awl.com/cseng/titles/0-201-47707-6 contains additional files needed to complete some programming projects in this publication:

Exercise 1

Worksheet1.doc: This is a MS Word document with the worksheet for Exercise 1. To use it, copy it to a folder, then open it with MS Word. **cpuload.exe:** This is an executable program. Copy it to a folder. It can be executed like any other MS .exe file, i.e., by typing the file name. **diskload.exe:** This is an executable program. Copy it to a folder. It can be executed like any other MS .exe file, i.e., by typing the file name.

Exercise 3

skeleton.c: This is a code skeleton. Copy it to a folder, then open it with Visual C++.

Exercise 4

skeleton.c: This is a code skeleton. Copy it to a folder, then open it with Visual C++.

Exercise 10

exercise10.h: This is a C header file that defines data structures and the function prototypes for the functions to be written in the exercise. Copy it to a folder, then open it from your Visual C++ project.

Exercise 11

exercise11.h: This is a C header file that defines data structures and the function prototypes for the functions to be written in the exercise. Copy it to a folder, then open it from your Visual C++ project.

Exercise 12

exercise12.h: This is a C header file that defines data structures and the function prototypes for the functions to be written in the exercise. Copy it to a folder, then open it from your Visual C++ project.

Appendix

Main_0.c This is a code example from the Appendix. Copy it to a folder, then open it with Visual C++.

Instructions for Using the CD-ROM Set

The bundled version of this book includes two CD-ROMs with the following Microsoft software for Windows NT-compatible systems: 486, Pentium, MIPS, R4x00, Alpha, PowerPC, and Pentium PRO:

An object version of Windows NT (Version 4.0, Service pack 3) and Visual C++ (Version 6.0). To run the software you need the following:

- PC with a 486/66 Mhz or higher processor, Pentium 90 or higher processor recommended
- 24 MB of RAM (32 MB recommended)
- Microsoft Internet Explorer 4.01 Service pack 1 (included on the CD-ROM)
- Hard-disk space required: Typical installation: 225 MB, Maximum installation: 305 MB
- Additional hard-disk space required for the following products:
- Internet Explorer: 43 MB typical, 59 MB maximum
- MSDN: 57 MB typical, 493 MB maximum
- CD-ROM drive
- VGA or higher-resolution monitor, Super VGA recommended
- Microsoft Mouse or compatible pointing device.

For installation instructions see pages 234 and 235

CDROM Included
With Book